NAVY

PAGE 1: During World War II in the Pacific, as the invasion of Okinawa begins and amtracs advance toward the beach, the battleship USS Tennessee (BB-43) opens with her 16-inch guns on enemy positions spotted by observation aircraft.

THIS PAGE: During ground operations along the DMZ in Korea in mid-1952, the battleship USS Iowa (BB-61) provides heavy fire support to U.N. troops.

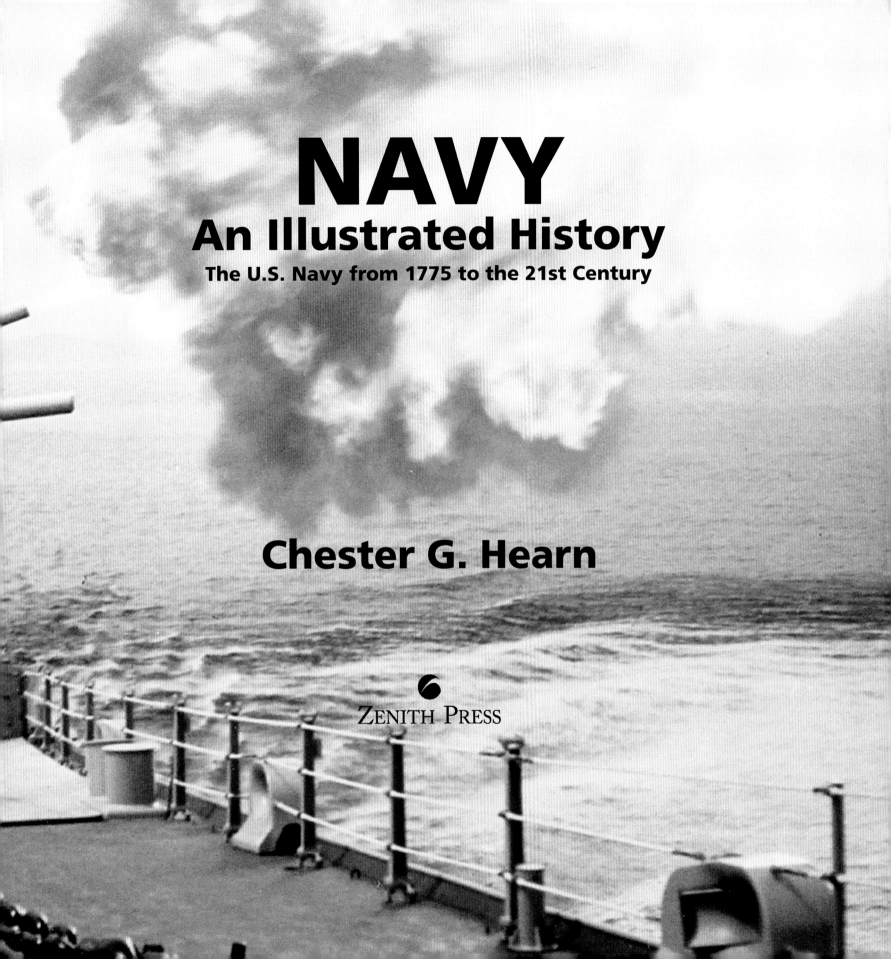

NAVY
An Illustrated History
The U.S. Navy from 1775 to the 21st Century

Chester G. Hearn

ZENITH PRESS

Project manager: Ray Bonds
Design: Mark Tennent/Compendium Design
Maps: Mike Marino
Diagrams: Mark Franklin
Photo research: Anne and Rolf Lang

ISBN-13: 978-0-7603-2972-6
ISBN-10: 0-7603-2972-9

Printed in China

CONTENTS

On February 20, 1998, during Operation Southern Watch, an F-14B Tomcat from Fighter Squadron 102 takes off from the USS George Washington (CVN-73) in the Persian Gulf. Two F/A-18C Hornets are parked in the foreground.

INTRODUCTION

ABOVE: Reacting with sadness and determination, sailors on the USS Harry S. Truman (CVN-75) interrupt training exercises to pledge allegiance to the National Emblem and recite the Sailor Creed during a memorial service for victims of the September 11, 2001, terrorist attack.

The Sailor's Creed

"I am a United States Sailor. I will support and defend the Constitution of the United States of America and I will obey the orders of those appointed over me. I represent the fighting spirit of the Navy and those who have gone before me to defend freedom and democracy around the world. I proudly serve my country's Navy combat team with honor, courage, and commitment. I am committed to excellence and the fair treatment of all."

—*All Hands*, Magazine of the U.S. Navy.

Today, nearly 500,000 men and women now serving in the navy and the ready reserves have taken that oath shown in these pages ("The Sailor's Creed"), and more than 350,000 of them are on active duty. They have a tradition that dates back to October 13, 1775, when the Continental Congress, after weeks of quarrelsome debates, created the Continental Navy. During those discussions, Samuel Chase of Maryland made his most remembered rebuttal, calling the creation of a Continental Navy "the maddest idea in the world." Our forefathers, who wisely ignored Chase's advice, never envisioned that two centuries later the United States Navy would become the largest and most powerful in the world.

Because of a lack of experience and the absence of funds, the Continental Navy never amounted to much, but it sailed to sea and began a tradition that has suffered ups and downs through war and peace yet has stubbornly strengthened and flourished through the centuries. No armed service in America has gone through more convolutions than the United States Navy. Abolished after the Revolution, it revived again in the early 1800s to protect American commerce. After the War of 1812, the navy trod water until the Civil War, when once again it made a quantum leap and produced iron warships and naval guns that rendered every other navy in the world obsolete. Once again a parsimonious Congress decided that a powerful navy was simply too expensive to maintain during peacetime. In the late 19th century when European nations and Japan began building armored

battlecruisers and the first great dreadnoughts, America began replacing its antiquated fleet with ships that for more than twenty years became obsolete the moment they rolled down launching ramps and splashed into the water.

Every war has made the navy stronger and more capable of dealing with threats. With training, technology, and professionalism within the ratings and ranks has come a legacy of pride among its members. Today the navy stands a half a million strong as the only totally integrated armed service in the world with its own fleet, its own air force, and its own ground force of readily deployable marine responders. Aside from combat ships, it is the most complex of all the armed services in weaponry, technology, training, and readiness.

ABOVE: During World War II, aircraft carriers became the greatest projector of seapower and swiftly grew in number. In 1975 the 97,000-ton Nimitz-class nuclear-powered USS Carl Vinson (CVN-70) became the third in a new class of ten massive supercarriers, the most recent being the George H. W. Bush (CVN-77).

Part of understanding the navy of today is to understand the navy during the days of its origin. George Washington, an army man, created the first fleet out of lightly armed fishing schooners because there was no organized navy. In a sense, Washington could take credit for establishing the first American navy, though the credit traditionally goes to John Adams, who steered the legislation through the Continental Congress. Over a period of more than two centuries, Wash-ington's schooners evolved into supercarriers, nuclear submarines, Mach-2 jet-powered aircraft, guided missiles, satellites, and mariners in space.

The navy has a history longer than the United States has had a Constitution. How the navy grew through the years to become the superb organization it is today and will continue to be in the coming years is the subject of this book. The United States could not have survived, expanded, and prospered without a navy. Nor can America remain strong and prosperous without its navy. The story is vastly rich in the officers and men who fought the battles and created the strategies that have taken the navy into the first decade of the 21st century. It is a history that traces the progress and expansion of technology and tactics from the early colonial days of privateering to shielding the nation today from a multitude of threats, including ballistic missiles armed with lethal chemical, biological, and nuclear warheads.

Most Americans today accept the navy as a fact without fully understanding what it is or how it came to be. Even many of today's sailors are not fully aware of the fascinating story behind the origins and development of the service, or the role the navy must play in our national security both today and in the decades to come. Much history has been lost or forgotten since the days when a ship's lookout gathered intelligence from a crow's nest in a sailing ship's masthead. Today, technicians keep navy command centers informed through aircraft, submarines, satellites, networked computers, and integrated electronic systems. There are tremendous career opportunities in the navy today. One does not have "to go down to the sea in ships" to join the navy, though the journey might be surprisingly rewarding.

This book is about the evolution of American sea power. Its pages are full of information, intrigue, and excitement, written for landlubbers and sailors alike.

RIGHT: Nuclear-powered submarines, such as the USS Tennessee (SSBN-734) firing Trident D-5 missiles, perform a dual capability by providing a first line of defense against nuclear attack and an aggressive response with sophisticated weapons against enemy targets.

THE FORMATIVE YEARS 1775–1815

CHAPTER 1

ABOVE: The 14-gun brig Andrew Doria *went to sea on February 17, 1776, under the command of Captain Nicholas Biddle, and during a four-month summer cruise between Maine and the Delaware Capes captured ten prizes.*

RIGHT: General George Washington created a navy months before the Continental Congress authorized one. The fishing schooner Hannah *became Washington's first ship. His eight schooners captured 55 British transports, demonstrating that, to survive, America must have a navy.*

Long before the Continental Navy there were American privateers, ships whose captains obtained letters of marque and reprisal to prey upon the commerce of France when at war with Great Britain. The ships were not frigates or double-deckers, but lightly armed fishing schooners and sloops, and an occasional brig or a bark. After the outbreak of the American Revolution in April 1775, the colonies issued more than two thousand commissions to shipmasters willing to risk their vessels for a share of plunder, and though this action fell far short of creating an official navy, men went to sea as privateers and during the course of the war captured 2,208 British prizes worth about $66 million in 1780 dollars, a figure far beyond the damage inflicted on the enemy by the Continental Navy.

George Washington's Schooners

When General Washington became commander-in-chief of the Continental Army, he lacked everything

"… for building at the Continental expense, a fleet of sufficient force, for the protection of these colonies, and for employing them in such a manner and places as will most effectively annoy our enemies …."
—Resolution by the State Assembly of Rhode Island, August 26, 1775.

from lead and gunpowder to muskets and cannon. Because the Continental Congress dragged its feet on forming a Continental Navy, Washington commissioned his own fleet of eight armed fishing schooners as a branch of the army. He manned the ships with fishermen-turned-soldiers, armed them with 4-pounders and swivels, and sent them to sea out of Marblehead and Beverly, Massachusetts. He put Captain John Manley, a rough-and-ready Boston shipmaster who had served in the Royal Navy, in charge of the schooners. Over a period of two years, Manley's rag-tag fleet captured fifty-five British ships laden with tons of military provisions, clothing, muskets, shot, gunpowder, and cannon.

Despite the eventual formation of the Continental Navy, Washington's schooners continued in business until 1777, when the last of the men transferred to the navy.

Creation of the Continental Navy

The Continental Congress debated for six months over the matter of creating a national navy. In fact, Congress did not know until October 5, 1775, that Washington

LEFT: When the 14-gun brig Andrew Doria sailed into the Dutch Port of St. Eustatius on November 16, 1776, Captain Isaiah Robinson experienced the first opportunity to exchange and receive a salute to the American flag.

The opposition…was very loud and Vehement," John Adams recalled. "It [the navy] was represented as the most wild, visionary, mad project that had ever been imaged.
Nathan Miller, Sea of Glory.

had already created his own fleet. The reaction to Washington's seaborne activities drew a riotous response.

John Adams of Massachusetts, Silas Deane of Connecticut, and John Langdon of New Hampshire agreed to investigate the matter. On October 13, 1775, the date the U.S. Navy regards as its official birthday, the three men returned to Congress with a plan to purchase, fit out, and arm two ships to pursue a pair of British transports en route to Canada. The first Continental vessels became the *Andrew Doria* and *Cabot*, and having cleared the initial hurdle, Congress authorized two larger ships on October 30, the *Alfred* and *Columbus*, "to be employed…for the protection and defense of the united Colonies."

Organization of the Continental Navy

In conjunction with the act, Congress also formed a seven-member Naval Committee as the cornerstone for expanding the Continental fleet. The committee held evening meetings in a waterside tavern and began purchasing and converting merchant vessels into men-of-war. John Adams drafted navy regulations, based upon British naval statutes, but with differences. He called for more humane treatment of sailors, limiting flog-

ABOVE: At the outbreak of the Revolution, every state developed its own colonial flag. The Continental Navy participated in the process and on December 3, 1775, adopted a fancy design for the first Navy Jack inscribed "DON'T TREAD ON ME."

Monthly Navy Pay 1776

Captain/Commander	$32.00
Chaplain	$26.67
Captain's clerk	$20.00
Lieutenant	$20.00
Master	$20.00
Master's mate	$15.00
Surgeon	$21.33
Surgeon's mate	$13.33
Boatswain	$15.00
Boatswain's mate	$ 9.33
Carpenter	$15.00
Ordinary seaman	$ 8.00
Steward	$ 6.67
Captain of marines	$ 8.00
Marine	$ 6.67

ABOVE: At Philadelphia on December 3, 1775, Lieutenant John Paul Jones raises the Grand Union flag—having thirteen stripes with the British jack in the field— aboard the Alfred, marking the first American flag unfurled on a Continental ship.

ging, for example, to a dozen lashes. On November 28, 1775, Congress adopted the regulations, which with minor changes were readopted in 1798 after Adams succeeded Washington as president.

Next came the selection of officers, which unfortunately mimicked the same nepotism rampant in the Royal Navy. Congress named Rhode Islander Esek Hopkins, brother of Naval Committee member Stephen Hopkins, commodore of the fleet with the 30-

gun *Alfred* as his flagship. Dudley Saltonstall of Connecticut, brother-in-law of committee member Deane, became senior captain. Abraham Whipple, who had married into the Hopkins' clan, became captain of the 28-gun *Columbus*. Nicolas Biddle, whose brother represented Pennsylvania in Congress, drew command of the 16-gun *Andrew Doria*. Esek Hopkins' son John commanded the 14-gun brig *Cabot*. Even John Paul Jones, whose somewhat mysterious past was the subject of rumor, became a first lieutenant on the 12-gun *Providence* because of the influence of committee member Joseph Hewes. None of the ships carried a gun larger than a 9-pounder. Congress then authorized the building of thirteen frigates—one for each state—during the next three months: an impossible task demonstrating the ineptness of Congress to understand naval matters.

A Bankrupt Organization

In November 1775 Congress disbanded the Naval Committee and established the Marine Committee, consisting of one member from each of the thirteen

Comparative list of American-armed vessels (1776–1782)

Class	1776	1777	1778	1779	1780	1781	1782
Continental	31	34	21	20	13	9	7
Privateers	136	73	115	167	228	449	323

Comparative number of guns carried on the above vessels

Class	1776	1777	1778	1779	1780	1781	1782
Continental	586	412	680	462	266	164	198
Privateers	1,360	730	1,150	2,505	3,420	6,735	4,845

colonies. They met in the same tavern as the former Naval Committee, during which meetings the Continental Navy rose and declined because of a combination of incompetent commanders and a lack of funds. By 1781, nobody wanted to be associated with the committee, so on February 18, 1781, Congress transferred the responsibility to Robert Morris, the secretary of finance, and named him Agent of Marine. Morris happened to be an excellent administrator, but the fleet had always been small, never containing more than thirty-four ships at one time, and by 1781 virtually ceased to exist.

Morris held the job until 1784. By then there were only two Continental ships in commission. Throughout the war Morris faced unsolvable shortages in men and material. At times the navy was so short of funds that its administrators had to pledge their own credit to get ships to sea. With few exceptions, nothing caused England more grief and greater loss than the 1,697 American privateers preying on British commerce.

The Continental Frigates
The thirteen frigates authorized on December 13,

Daily Ration
Sunday: 1lb bread, 1lb beef,
1lb potatoes or turnips
Monday: 1lb bread, 1lb pork, half pint
peas, 4oz cheese
Tuesday: Same as Sunday with
pudding
Wednesday: 1lb bread, 2oz butter, 4oz
cheese, half pint rice
Thursday: As Monday, without cheese
Friday: Same as Tuesday
Saturday: Same as Monday
Every day: A half pint of rum per man

Commodore Esek Hopkins (1718–1802)

Born in Rhode Island on April 26, 1718, Esek Hopkins went to sea at the age of twenty, spending most of his life then as a merchant sailor and a captain. During the Seven Years' War (1756–1763) he served as a successful privateer for the British. When war began in April 1775, he became a battery commander and a brigadier general. Hopkins appeared to be amply qualified to lead the Continental fleet.

In January 1776 Hopkins took command of an eight-ship squadron at Philadelphia. Using the converted merchantman *Alfred* as his flagship, he ignored orders to clear the enemy out of Chesapeake Bay and led the squadron on an assault of New Providence in the Bahamas. After a poorly directed effort to surprise the city's British garrison, Hopkins sailed around the island and attacked the forts from the rear. By then, the British had removed most of the ammunition and stores from the city, and Hopkins had to be content with what was left.

During the voyage home, the Continental squadron crossed paths with the 20-gun British frigate *Glasgow*. Hopkins seemed unable to corral *Glasgow*. He maneuvered ineptly, suffered considerable damage among his ships, and to the extreme annoyance of Lieutenant John Paul Jones let the frigate get away.

The episode took the fight out of Hopkins. In June 1776, after failing to break the British blockade off Narragansett Bay, he was censured for inaction and insubordination and on March 1777 suspended from command. Finding politics safer than sea duty, he joined the Rhode Island legislature, where he served until 1786.

ABOVE: The 8-gun sloop of war Wasp, one of the first of eight ships authorized by the Continental Congress, became part of Commodore Esek Hopkins's squadron that assaulted New Providence Island in the British colony of the Bahamas.

BELOW: Commodore Esek Hopkins, commanding the first Continental Fleet of eight ships, receives a dispatch from Captain Samuel Nicholas of the Continental Marines reporting the successful assault of New Providence Island in the Bahamas.

Bushnell's *American Turtle*

ABOVE: David Bushnell's manually propelled Turtle, the first American submarine, crawls slowly across the harbor at Staten Island in an unsuccessful effort to sink the anchored HMS Eagle, British Admiral Sir Richard Howe's flagship.

David Bushnell grew up on a farm at Saybrook, close to where the mouth of Connecticut River looked out across Long Island Sound. He entered Yale at the age of thirty-one, and while there experimented with underwater explosive devices. Among his inventions, he perfected a clockwork trigger system that enabled an operator to escape from the area before the explosion occurred. During his final year at college, and having grown annoyed with the presence of British frigates in the harbor, he drew his brother Ezra into a project to build a one-man submarine capable of attaching a 250-pound mine to a British ship.

After Bushnell's graduation in 1775, he and Ezra began constructing an underwater craft that resembled two tortoise shells bolted together. The elliptical hull measured 7½ feet by 6 feet and was made of oak staves reinforced with iron bands. The contraption had ventilating tubes that closed automatically while submerging and allowed the occupant to remain beneath the surface for thirty minutes. The operator supplied the motive power

by cranking a network of vertical and horizontal propellers, a rudder, and a ballast tank. Bushnell named the submarine the *American Turtle*, but he never had the strength to operate it and left the muscular work to Ezra.

On September 6, 1776, the Bushnells set out to destroy Admiral Richard "Black Dick" Howe's flagship, the HMS *Eagle*, which was conspicuously anchored in the harbor. When Bushnell's brother unexpectedly fell ill, the mission went to Ezra Lee, an inadequately trained soldier. Lee positioned the *Turtle* incorrectly under *Eagle* and failed to attach the mine. In the *Turtle* he bobbed to the surface and was pursued by a boatload of British sailors. Lee released the 250-pound mine, which soon exploded, and the British retreated back to the *Eagle*.

The Bushnells made two more attempts to sink a British ship, but both failed. When the British captured Manhattan, Bushnell probably destroyed the *Turtle* to keep it out of enemy hands. His creation disappeared, with all its plans, but introduced submarine warfare to the American navy.

1775, to be built within three months consisted of five ships of thirty-two guns, five of twenty-eight guns, and three of twenty-four guns. The Marine Committee spread the contracts around the colonies without regard for the capabilities of the shipbuilders. As a consequence, the first of the 32-gun frigates did not get to sea until June 1777, and they all suffered checkered careers. The seven frigates that reached sea were either captured or sunk. The other six were destroyed to keep them from falling into enemy hands.

One of the typical episodes involved Captain John Manley, who had previously commanded Washington's schooners, and his flagship, the 32-gun frigate *Hancock*. On June 7, 1777, in company with the 24-gun frigate *Boston*, Manley captured the British frigate *Fox*. After a month of successful prize taking, he encountered the 44-gun HMS *Rainbow* and the armed brig *Victor* off Nova Scotia. Expecting help from the *Boston*, Manley planned to capture the British double-decker, but the captain of the *Boston* fled. Instead, the *Rainbow* captured Manley and the *Hancock* and recaptured the HMS *Fox*. Manley's bad luck was no worse than what befell every other frigate.

The Continental Navy in Europe

Towards the end of 1776, seventy-year-old Benjamin Franklin went to France in an effort to draw Louis XVI into war with Great Britain. The king rebuffed Franklin's efforts but he agreed to lend America money and opened the ports of France to Continental warships and privateers. Though Franklin had never taken much interest in naval matters, the king's offer was all the inducement he needed to create a second Continental navy in Europe. He immediately commissioned three privateers, *Black Prince*, *Black Princess*, and *Fearnot*, which in 1779-1780 captured 114 prizes, scuttled 11, and ransomed 76.

Meanwhile, in late 1777 John Paul Jones arrived in France in the 18-gun sloop *Ranger* to bring the war to

The Continental Frigates

Name	Guns	Career
Hancock	32	Captured 1777
Raleigh	32	Captured 1778
Randolph	32	Lost in action 1778
Warren	32	Destroyed 1779
Washington	32	Destroyed 1777
Congress	28	Destroyed 1777
Effingham	28	Destroyed 1777
Providence	28	Captured 1780
Trumbull	28	Captured 1781
Virginia	28	Captured 1778
Boston	24	Captured 1780
Delaware	24	Destroyed 1777
Montgomery	24	Destroyed 1777

ABOVE: In a running battle on October 11-13, 1776, Brigadier General Benedict Arnold's flimsy freshwater squadron on Lake Champlain lost the Battle of Valcour Island but delayed Major General John Burgoyne's New York campaign until spring 1777.

LEFT: On February 14, 1778, Captain John Paul Jones guided the Continental sloop-of-war Ranger into Quiberon Bay, on the coast of France. Jones became the first American to exchange salutes with a French man-of-war, Admiral Lamotte-Picquet's flagship Robuste.

John Paul Jones (1747–1792)

John Paul Jones, born John Paul, Jr., grew up on Solway Firth, Scotland, the son of a gardener. Apprenticed to a merchantman, he made his first voyage to Virginia, where he renewed ties with his elder brother, a tailor who lived in Fredericksburg. In 1766, when his employer went bankrupt, Jones joined a Jamaican slaver as first mate. After flogging a sailor who later died, and in 1773 unintentionally killing a mutinous sailor, he was put on trial for murder by the British. Rather than wait for the inevitable, he changed his name to Jones and fled to Fredericksburg, arriving in time to settle his recently deceased brother's estate.

In 1775 the Marine committee hired Jones to fit out the 20-gun *Alfred*, the first ship purchased by Congress. He commissioned the ship December 3, 1775, earning the rank of senior lieutenant. He sailed to the Bahamas as part of Commodore Hopkins's squadron and in March 1776 was instrumental in capturing New Providence. Promoted to captain on August 8, 1776, he commanded the 12-gun *Providence*, and during a seven-week cruise captured or destroyed sixteen British ships. In 1777, the Marine Committee gave him command of the 18-gun sloop-of-war *Ranger*, which he later sailed to France. Though Jones had already established a record for audacity, his tactical fight on September 23, 1779, in the

old *Bonhomme Richard* against the 44-gun British frigate *Serapis* off Flamborough Head wrote his name permanently into the annals of American naval history for remarkable single-ship actions. His ship was no match for the British frigate, and as the *Bonhomme Richard* began to sink, British Captain Richard Pearson called for Jones to strike her colors. Jones shouted back, "I have not yet begun to fight!" Instead, *Serapis*'s mainmast fell and an American grenade touched off an explosion that swept her deck, forcing Pearson to surrender. Jones transferred his men to the *Serapis*, and as *Bonhomme Richard* slowly sank, he sailed the British frigate into Texel, Netherlands.

ABOVE: John Paul Jones (1747–1792) became the most famous naval hero of the American Revolution and was undoubtedly the most successful, courageous, and determined of all the captains commissioned by the Continental Congress.

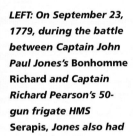

LEFT: On September 23, 1779, during the battle between Captain John Paul Jones's Bonhomme Richard and Captain Richard Pearson's 50-gun frigate HMS Serapis, Jones also had to fight the 20-gun British sloop-of-war Countess of Scarborough (right).

LEFT: Captain John Paul Jones, after defeating the HMS Serapis, takes possession of the British frigate and, with his officers nearby, salutes the valiant old Bonhomme Richard as she sinks off the east coast of England.

the doorstep of Great Britain. He sailed into Quiberon Bay and gave a thirteen-gun salute to the French flagship and received a nine-gun salute in return—the first salute to the Stars and Stripes by a foreign man-of-war. Finding himself on good terms with the French, Jones sailed on April 10, 1778, for the Irish Sea and invaded England. He set fire to ships docked at Whitehaven (near his place of birth), and crossed Solway Firth to St. Mary's Island in an effort to capture the Earl of Selkirk (who was not at home). It was the first purely foreign invasion of England since the Norman Conquest in 1066. On the way back to France, Jones fought and captured the 20-gun sloop-of-war *Drake*.

> The victory was wholly and solely due to the immovable courage of Paul Jones. The *Richard* was beaten more than once; but the spirit of Jones could not be overcome.
> *Captain Alexander Slidell Mackenzie,*
> The Life of Paul Jones.

Franklin was so pleased with Jones's escapades that eight months later he borrowed enough money from French supporters to buy an old 900-ton East Indiaman, the 42-gun *Duc de Duras*. The vessel did not impress Jones, but it was twice the size of *Ranger* and had good French guns. In deference to Franklin, Jones christened her *Bonhomme Richard*, after his benefactor's popular *Poor Richard's Almanac*.

The Final Curtain

On August 4, 1781, the southern British army in America under the command of General Lord Charles Cornwallis moved with seven thousand troops to Yorktown, Virginia, to link by sea with General Sir Henry Clinton's army in New York. The linkage never occurred. After the French fleet under Admiral François J. P. de

Grasse intervened on September 5-9 and severed Cornwalis's communications with the British fleet, the English general held out until October 19 and surrendered. In the final naval action of the American Revolution, there were no ships from the Continental Navy involved.

Twenty-three-year-old Captain John Barry, however, still commanded the 36-gun frigate *Alliance*, which had first made its appearance in a squadron under John Paul Jones. For Barry, the war was not over. In March 1783 he sailed into the Atlantic and captured the *Duc de Lauzun*, loaded with 100,000 Spanish dollars. On his way to port, Barry encountered three British men-of-war. He fought off the 28-gun *Sybil* and made it safely to port with his prize. On March 24, Congress recalled all privateers and ships of the Continental Navy. More than three hundred privateers ceased operations, but only one Continental frigate did so, Barry's *Alliance*, because there were no more. On August 1, 1785, Congress ordered the *Alliance* placed at auction, and the last vestige of the Continental Navy disappeared on the block, leaving the American merchant fleet everywhere vulnerable.

The Question of a Navy

In 1785, the same year that Congress abolished the navy, Algerian corsairs captured two Yankee merchantmen and held their crews for $59,496 ransom. Congress offered only $4,200. Having been charged with negotiating a solution, John Adams and Thomas Jefferson said it would be cheaper to build a navy to protect American shipping than to pay tribute. Congress had no money for ships and no money to pay tribute. Four years elapsed without anything done, and Barbary pirates continued to seize American vessels. When Jefferson returned to the United States from Europe in 1791 to become secretary of state, he again requested ships, but Congress tabled the matter.

On April 20, 1792, England and France declared war on each other, and before a lasting peace would be

As with most government appropriations, six states participated in the frigate-building program:

Chesapeake,	44 guns,	Baltimore, Maryland
Congress,	36 guns,	Portsmouth, New Hampshire
Constellation,	36 guns,	Norfolk, Virginia
Constitution,	44 guns,	Boston, Massachusetts
President,	44 guns,	New York City
United States,	44 guns,	Philadelphia, Pennsylvania

ABOVE: The first War of 1812 battle between frigates occurred on August 19 when Captain Isaac Hall's 44-gun Constitution dismasted the 38-gun HMS Guerrière and forced her surrender during a forty-minute action 700 miles east of Boston.

RIGHT: While cruising in the Caribbean in February 1799, Captain Thomas Truxton, commanding the 48-gun frigate Constellation, came under attack by two French warships. After damaging the smaller ship, Truxton crossed the bow of the French frigate L'Insurgente and forced her surrender.

concluded in 1815, the United States would be drawn into wars at different times with the Barbary pirates, France, and Great Britain.

In 1793, President George Washington became impatient with congressional procrastination and asked for six frigates. Another year passed before Congress, on March 27, 1794, authorized three frigates of forty-four guns and three of thirty-six, but the legislators added a caveat that the project would be canceled if peace with Algiers occurred before the ships were completed. Almost on cue, on September 5, 1795, the United States negotiated a treaty with the Dey of

Algiers, paid a ransom of $525,000, and agreed to pay an annual tribute of $21,000. On March 2, 1796, Congress ordered construction of the frigates to be ceased. The ransom almost equaled the $600,000 cost of building all six ships. During the summer and fall of 1796, however, French privateers seized more than three hundred American ships, and Congress allowed three of the frigates to be finished, the *Constitution*, *United States*, and *Constellation*. Washington disagreed with the decision. He recommended the strength of the navy be increased, but to no avail.

Benjamin Stoddert (1751–1813)

On April 30, 1798, Congress decided the time had come to create the office of secretary of the navy. President John Adams of Massachusetts nominated forty-seven-year-old Benjamin Stoddert of Maryland, who was not his first choice but probably his best choice. Upon hearing of his nomination, Stoddert quipped, "It was unfortunate that in conferring the appointment… upon me, the President could not also confer the knowledge necessary." Nonetheless, Stoddert was the right man for the job. He had served on the Board of War during the Revolution, understood finance, was a good judge of character, and he knew how to run a merchant fleet. Soon after taking office, he created a marine corps and obtained an appropriation for fitting out twenty-four more ships, in addition to completing the three frigates held up by Congress.

With six frigates under construction he now needed competent commanders. He declared, "We had better have no Navy than have it commanded by indifferent men…." As the first three frigates were readied for sea, he assigned John Barry to the *United States*, Thomas Truxtun to the *Constellation*, and Samuel Nicholson to the *Constitution*.

During the Quasi-War with France, Stoddert also placed capable naval agents in key American ports and made them accountable for obtaining ships, ordnance, supplies, and crews. During his thirty-three months in office, the navy grew to fifty-four ships. He raised a force of seven hundred and fifty officers and more than five thousand men for the navy and eleven hundred officers and men for the marine corps. He raised the pay of able-bodied seamen from $8 to $17 a month and thereafter encountered no trouble raising volunteers. When Congress refused to authorize money for building naval facilities, Stoddert raided another project and opened facilities at Portsmouth, Boston, New York, Philadelphia, and Norfolk, all of which became permanent naval bases. Stoddert gave the navy its very first example of true professionalism.

ABOVE: Benjamin Stoddert (1751–1813) became the nation's first secretary of the navy, serving from 1798 to 1801. He presided over the expansion of the new U.S. Navy, during his term authorizing the purchase of fifty warships and the construction of the first navy yards.

The Quasi-War With France

The navy that went to sea against the French in 1799 soon proved to be a much superior force when compared with the rag-tag group of ships commissioned during the Revolution. On February 9 Captain Thomas Truxtun, commanding the 48-gun frigate *Constellation*, overhauled the 40-gun French frigate *L'Insurgence*, crossed her bow, raked her twice, and forced her to strike her colors. Stoddert commissioned the prize frigate into the navy as the *Insurgent*.

On February 1, 1800, Truxtun struck again. After a full day's chase the *Constellation* overhauled the 56-gun

French frigate *Vengeance* southwest of Guadeloupe. In a five-hour action during the night, *Vengeance* struck her colors twice but continued to fight when her surrender went unobserved. After a lucky shot knocked down *Constellation's* main mast, *Vengeance* sheered away in the dark.

On September 30, preliminary peace talks began, during which Captain George Little, sailing the 28-gun *Boston*, captured the 24-gun French frigate *Le Berceau* in the West Indies. On February 3, 1801, when the Quasi-War officially ended, the French had lost eighty-five ships and two frigates, compared with the American loss of one warship, the 14-gun schooner *Retaliation*.

The Barbary War

The 1801-1805 Barbary War, also known as the Tripolitan-American War, occurred during the presidency of Thomas Jefferson, who had never been a strong advocate of a navy but now accepted having one as imperative. When on May 14, 1801 Tripoli's pasha declared war on the United States, Jefferson sent a punitive expedition to the Mediterranean; for two years it lackadaisically blockaded Tripoli. On October 31, 1803, the 36-gun frigate *Philadelphia*, commanded by Captain William Bain-

bridge, ran aground while chasing a frigate attempting to enter Tripoli's harbor. Surrounded by Tripolitan gunboats, Bainbridge surrendered. The pasha's sailors refloated the frigate and sailed her into the harbor, along with Bainbridge's crew of 307 officers and men.

On February 16, 1804, Lieutenant Stephen Decatur gathered seventy-three volunteer officers and men from the blockading squadron, sailed a small captured Tripolitan vessel into the harbor, burned the *Philadelphia* where she lay at anchor beneath the city fortress, and escaped.

TOP LEFT: During the night of February 16, 1804, Lieutenant Stephen Decatur and eighty volunteers slipped into Tripoli harbor and burned the USS Philadelphia. Decatur and his men safely escaped on a captured ketch the navy later named Intrepid.

ABOVE RIGHT: Captain S. P. Humphreys, commanding the 56-gun HMS Leopard, opened fire on the 36-gun frigate USS Chesapeake, killing and wounding 24 American sailors during a search for British deserters. The unprincipled act hastened the War of 1812.

ABOVE LEFT: Captain Thomas Truxton first went to sea as a privateersman during the American Revolution. Appointed captain in the U.S. Navy in 1794, he superintended the construction of the Constellation and, as her commanding officer, captured the L'Insurgente.

ABOVE: During the War of
1812, the first battle between
frigates resulted in an
American victory when
Captain Isaac Hall's 44-gun
Constitution *dismasted the*
38-gun HMS Guerrière *and*
forced British Captain James
R. Dacres to surrender.

Frigate's Provisions—Four-month Cruise

Bread	22,320 pounds
Beef	14,652 pounds
Pork	10,914 pounds
Flour	1,819 pounds
Raisins	910 pounds
Tea	400 pounds
Sugar	3,210 pounds
Rice	3,636 pounds
Beans	5,460 pounds
Pickles	1,819 pounds
Vinegar	228 gallons
Spirits	750 gallons

Later in the year, naval agent William Eaton
mounted the first American overseas land operation
with eight marines, a navy midshipman, and a hundred
mercenaries. After a six-hundred-mile march over the
Libyan desert, Eaton stormed Tripoli's outpost, the city
of Derna. Commodore Samuel Barron made peace
with the reigning Tripolitan pasha. In return for a
$60,000 cash bounty and an agreement that all ransom
payments would cease, Barron freed Bainbridge and his
crew. After the pasha yielded, Tunis fell in line, and in
1805 the Barbary War ended.

Friction with Great Britain

Had it not been for the expansion of the American fleet
during the Barbary conflict, and had Jefferson succeed-

ed in his plan to decommission all the ships and discharge most of the sailors, the navy would not have been prepared for the next great contest—the War of 1812. Relationships with Great Britain had been cordial, and Jefferson was again thinking about naval reductions when on June 22, 1807, the British 56-gun *Leopard* fired upon and boarded the 36-gun *Chesapeake* off Cape Henry, Virginia, killing and wounding several American sailors under the pretext of searching for four British deserters. Americans became instantly outraged at the insult. Instead of building more frigates or finishing the six new 74-gun ships under construction, Congress appropriated $250,000 to build 188 relatively useless gunboats for coastal defense.

On May 16, 1811, the 44-gun frigate USS *President* overhauled the HMS *Little Belt*, which had been impressing American sailors, and disabled her with gunfire. "War Hawks" called the attack retaliation for the *Leopard-Chesapeake* affair and urged the conquest of Canada while England was engaged in war with France. President James Madison, who in 1809 became the fourth president, knew nothing about preparedness but sided with the "War Hawks" and on June 19, 1812, declared war on England. Six months later his poorly planned three-prong invasion of Canada promptly collapsed.

The War of 1812—Naval Actions

During the war, operations on land took a back seat to battles at sea. On August 19, 1812, the same day that General William Hull ignominiously surrendered Detroit to the British, the 44-gun USS *Constitution*, commanded by Captain Isaac Hull, demolished the 38-gun HMS *Guerrière* off Nova Scotia. On October 18, five days after the British repulsed Major General Stephen Van Rensselaer at Queenstown, Ontario, the 18-gun sloop-of-war USS *Wasp* smashed the 18-gun sloop-of-war HMS *Frolic* in a forty-three-minute broadside-to-broadside hammering. One week later the 44-gun USS *United States*, commanded by Captain

LEFT: Commodore Stephen Decatur (1779-1820) served during the Quasi-War with France, commanded the Enterprise during the Barbary Wars, and after earning a reputation for bravery at Tripoli, commanded the frigate USS United States during the War of 1812.

LEFT: In 1796 Congress authorized the completion of three unfinished frigates, the Constitution, the United States, and the Constellation. On October 21, 1797, the 44-gun Constitution went to sea and during her career earned the nickname "Old Ironsides."

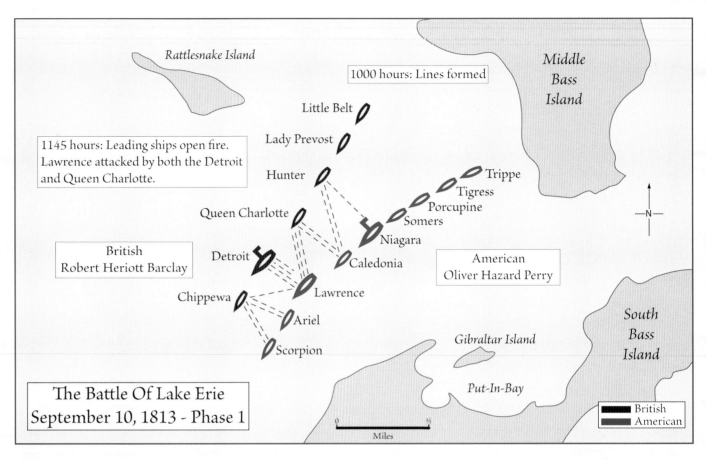

Rattlesnake Island

1000 hours: Lines formed

Middle Bass Island

Little Belt

1145 hours: Leading ships open fire. Lawrence attacked by both the Detroit and Queen Charlotte.

Lady Prevost

Hunter

Trippe
Tigress
Porcupine
Somers

Queen Charlotte

Niagara

British
Robert Heriott Barclay

Detroit

Caledonia

American
Oliver Hazard Perry

Chippewa

Lawrence

South Bass Island

Ariel

Scorpion

Gibraltar Island

Put-In-Bay

The Battle Of Lake Erie
September 10, 1813 - Phase 1

—N—

British
American

0   ½
Miles

The Battle of Lake Erie, September 10, 1813

When war erupted, England operated several warships on the Great Lakes. In particular, naval superiority on Lake Erie enabled the British to hold Detroit and frustrate President Madison's efforts to invade Canada. American Commodore Isaac Chauncey began building warships at Sackett's Harbor, New York, to serve on Lake Ontario, and he sent twenty-eight-year-old Captain Oliver Hazard Perry to Presque Isle (now Erie), Pennsylvania, to build a naval squadron for service on Lake Erie, some five hundred miles from the sea. When it came to ships, Perry knew his craft. He had joined the navy at the age of fourteen, became a lieutenant while fighting Tripolitans, constructed gunboats under Jefferson's naval program, and commanded the Newport, Rhode Island, gunboat flotilla at the outset of war.

By July 1813, Perry had miraculously fitted out two 20-gun brigs, the *Niagara* and the *Lawrence*, six schooners, and a sloop—fifty-five guns in all. Pitted against his squadron were British Commodore Robert H. Barclay's blockading fleet of six vessels mounting sixty-three guns. During the first week of August, while Barclay's fleet disappeared on other business, Perry nudged his squadron over Presque Isle's bar and into Lake Erie. Perry expected a fierce fight from Barclay, a tenacious one-armed veteran of the Battle of Trafalgar.

At noon September 10, Barclay's squadron approached the American anchorage at Put-in-Bay, Ohio. Perry sailed out to meet the enemy in his flagship, *Lawrence*, preceded by the 6-gun schooner *Ariel* and the single-gun schooner *Scorpion*. For two hours, and for inexplicable

reasons, the balance of Perry's squadron lagged behind. After the *Lawrence* became completely disabled, Perry transferred by rowboat to the approaching *Niagara*. Taking charge of the brig, he sheered to starboard and sailed straight through the British line, firing both broadsides and disabling three British ships, including the 19-gun *Detroit*, Barclay's flagship. By 3:00 P.M. Barclay's entire squadron had struck. Losses in men on both sides were about even.

Perry returned to Ohio with his prizes and notified General William Henry Harrison, who had assembled an army of seven thousand men to recapture Detroit, "We have met the enemy and they are ours...." Harrison promptly recaptured Detroit, and Perry's victory became the turning point of the war in the northwest.

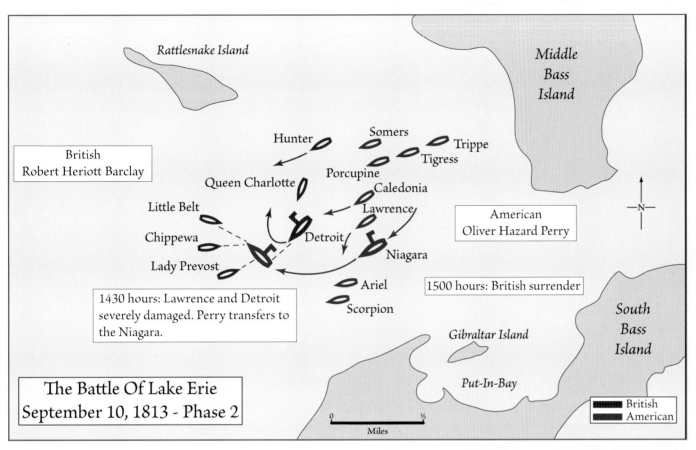

Rattlesnake Island

Middle Bass Island

British
Robert Heriott Barclay

Hunter
Somers
Trippe
Tigress

Porcupine
Queen Charlotte
Caledonia
Little Belt
Lawrence
—N—
American
Oliver Hazard Perry
Chippewa
Detroit
Lady Prevost
Niagara

Ariel
1500 hours: British surrender

Scorpion
South Bass Island

1430 hours: Lawrence and Detroit severely damaged. Perry transfers to the Niagara.

Gibraltar Island

The Battle Of Lake Erie
September 10, 1813 - Phase 2

Put-In-Bay

British
American

0   ½
Miles

LEFT AND FAR LEFT: *The Battle of Lake Erie took place in the western basin, off the present city of Sandusky. Winds on the lake blew from the southwest, which gave Perry an advantage when he swung the Niagara to the windward and raked the Detroit while forcing a path through the British column.*

ABOVE: *After building a freshwater squadron in Presque Isle Bay, Commodore Oliver Hazard Perry engaged the British blockading fleet on Lake Erie on September 10, 1813, and after a brutal battle announced: "We have met the enemy and they are ours."*

LEFT: *Commodore Oliver Hazard Perry (1785–1819) became one of the navy's distinguished heroes when his remarkable victory during the Battle of Lake Erie helped turned the tide in the War of 1812.*

Stephen Decatur, met the 38-gun HMS *Macedonian* off Madeira, forced her to strike, and hauled her back to Newport to be refitted as an American frigate. Finally, on December 29 the USS *Constitution*, now commanded by Captain William Bainbridge, encountered the 38-gun HMS *Java* off Bahia, Brazil, and in a two-hour battle completely wrecked the British ship. What appeared to be American superiority on the high seas soon ended when toward the end of 1812 Great Britain sent eleven ships-of-the-line, thirty-four frigates, and fifty-five smaller warships to blockade American ports.

During 1813, partly because of the sudden superiority of British naval strength on the high seas, hundreds of American privateers joined the fight and turned to commerce destruction. After that, the only strategically important naval engagements occurred on fresh water.

The Other Freshwater Navy

On August 14, 1814, Major General Sir George Prevost, with a fourteen-thousand-man army of the Duke of Wellington's veterans, advanced on Lake Champlain from Montreal. Prevost planned to assault the weak American garrison at Plattsburg, New York, while a British naval squadron defeated Master Commandant Thomas Macdonough's American freshwater squadron posted at the southern end of Champlain. Like Perry on Lake Erie, Macdonough had built a small squadron, consisting of the 24-gun corvette *Saratoga* (flagship), the 20-gun brig *Eagle*, the 17-gun schooner *Ticonderoga*, the 7-gun sloop *Polly*, and ten gunboats. British Captain George Downie had assembled a much stronger squadron, consisting of the 37-gun frigate *Confiance*, the 18-gun brig *Linnet*, the 11-gun sloops *Chub* and *Finch*, and thirteen gunboats.

On September 11 the two squadrons clashed in Plattsburg Bay. In an action of two hours and twenty minutes, Macdonough's squadron crippled Downie's three largest vessels and forced them to strike. The rest

LEFT: Captain Gustavus Connyngham purchased a brig at Dunkirk, fitted her with fourteen guns, named her USS Revenge, and in July 1777 sailed into British coastal waters. While capturing twenty prizes, he sometimes fought two ships at the same time.

FAR LEFT: Throughout the night of September 13-14, 1814, British warships pummeled Baltimore's Fort McHenry. At dawn, after Francis Scott Key observed the fort's flag still flying, he retired to his cabin and wrote "The Star Spangled Banner."

fled. General Prevost suspended his operations against Plattsburg and retreated to Canada. One British veteran who had fought at Trafalgar referred to it as "child's play" compared to the fight on Lake Champlain. The defeat, more than any other, convinced the British to seek peace, and on December 24, 1814, American and British commissioners agreed on the terms that became the Treaty of Ghent.

During the War of 1812, Americans suffered a number of humiliating defeats on land, such as the burning of Washington and raids on its defenseless coast, but they would always remember with pride the exploits of Truxtun, Decatur, Perry, Macdonough, and the many others who fought so gloriously on water. It was the navy that fostered the spirit of nationalism and preserved the national honor. For the first time, the navy gained acceptance for itself.

LEFT: Francis Scott Key's "The Star Spangled Banner" was written as a poem on the back of a letter, and the words were soon adapted to a popular drinking song, "To Anacreon in Heaven." In 1931 it became the national anthem.

FAR LEFT: Captain Thomas Macdonough won one of the most important victories during the War of 1812 when he scraped together a squadron of sloops and gunboats and in 1814, using masterful tactics, drove a superior British flotilla off Lake Champlain.

CHAPTER 2

A CENTURY OF DEVELOPMENT 1814–1898

On January 16, 1815, Benjamin Crowninshield of Salem, Massachusetts, became the fifth secretary of the navy. His experience in business, seamanship, and politics made him a particularly good choice. When still a lad, his father removed him from school and sent him to sea as a cabin boy to learn navigation. During the war of 1812, Crowninshield observed administrative weaknesses in the navy department, and soon after taking office he corrected the deficiency by asking Congress to create a Board of Navy Commissioners. The first members were commodores John Rodgers, David Porter, and Isaac Hull. Rodgers served as president of the board until 1837, taking only three years off to serve at sea. Asked twice to become secretary of the navy, Rodgers refused to give up his commission and was never appointed.

Had it not been for a resumption of war with the Dey of Algiers, Crowninshield may not have convinced the president and Congress of the importance of a long-range building program to steadily augment the navy's strength. Congress agreed to allocate $1 million a year for six years to build six 74-gun ships-of-war and twelve 44-gun frigates. Although the larger ships were called "74s," they carried anywhere from eighty-six to a hundred and two guns, while the USS *Pennsylvania*, which became the largest sailing ship to ever serve the navy, carried a hundred and twenty guns. When John Quincy Adams visited the *Pennsylvania*, he said she looked "like a city."

ABOVE: Commodore John Rodgers (1772–1838) served on the USS Constellation during the Quasi-War with France and commanded the 28-gun frigate John Adams during the Barbary Wars. In 1823, after a long naval career, he served as acting secretary of the navy.

"The importance of a permanent naval establishment appears to be sanctioned by the voice of the people, and…the means of its gradual increase are completely within the reach of our national resources."
Secretary of the Navy Benjamin Crowninshield.

The appropriation also called for three experimental steam batteries, though little was implemented. In 1814 Robert Fulton had created the steam-powered, paddlewheel-propelled *Demologos*, renamed *Fulton* in honor of her creator, but she had no steering mechanism other than her two side-wheels. Although the navy deemed her unsuitable for operations, the new technology interested Rodgers, who in 1834 at the age of sixty-three recommended twenty-five steamships for the future navy.

New Challenges

With the return of peace, America's idled merchant fleet rushed to sea. In the interlude between the War of 1812 and the Civil War (1861-1865), the navy's mission became the protection of an expanding maritime commerce. Yankee merchant vessels carried cotton, flour, tobacco, rice, and lumber around the world in exchange for silks, tea, porcelains, and pepper from East Asia, and sugar, rum, mahogany, coffee, and fruit from the Caribbean and Brazil. To protect the

Barbary Corsairs

During the War of 1812, the Dey of Algiers preyed on American commerce, enslaved merchant sailors, and in early 1815 expelled the United States consul and declared war because he wanted to be paid more tribute. Despite being at the height of its prestige and popularity in 1815, the navy might well have become victimized by an economically minded Congress had it not been for the dey. On May 20, 1815, the most powerful American squadron ever assembled put to sea under Commodore Stephen Decatur. His pennant flew from the graceful new 44-gun frigate *Guerrière,* which was accompanied by the frigates *Constellation* and *Macedonian,* and seven other warships. Decatur departed from Sandy Hook, New Jersey, and sailed straight to the Mediterranean to settle unfinished business that had been dangling since 1801.

Decatur pressed into the Mediterranean and on June 17, 1815, captured the 46-gun Algerian frigate *Mashouda* and the brig accompanying her. Word spread, and every Algerian corsair on the Mediterranean scattered into neutral ports. Decatur did not bother chasing any more ships. He sailed directly into the harbor at Algiers and at cannon-mouth demanded and received cancellation of all tribute, release of American prisoners without ransom, and the cessation of piracy. Decatur then sailed to Tripoli and Tunis, obtained the same terms, and received compensation for American vessels seized in those waters by the British during the War of 1812. Decatur's swift resolution of the Barbary problem merely proved to a parsimonious Congress that a nation without a navy is a nation without security, thereby reinforcing Crowninshield's program for a sustainable navy with better ships.

ABOVE: During the Barbary Wars, 25-year-old Lieutenant Stephen Decatur led a boarding party that captured two enemy gunboats by subduing the Tripolitans in hand-to-hand combat.

merchantmen, the navy needed to be handy wherever the traders went, but other problems surfaced. Between 1815 and 1822 as many as three thousand American ships were attacked between the passages of the West Indies and off the Mississippi delta.

> Wars often arise from the rivalry in trade, and from the conflicts and interests which belong to it. The presence of an adequate naval force to protect commerce…is one of the best means of preventing those disputes and collisions.
>
> *Secretary of the Navy Abel P. Upshur.*

Porter and the Pirates

By 1823, Boston-born Commodore David Porter (1780-1843) stood high among the most accomplished commanders in the navy. He had accumulated a distinguished record during the Quasi War with France (1798-1800); Tripolitan War (1801-1805); and the War of 1812, during which he rounded Cape Horn in the 32-gun frigate *Essex* and destroyed more than $2.5 million in British whaling operations. After serving on the Board of Navy Commissioners, he grew tired of Washington life and on February 23, 1823, accepted command of the pirate-chasing West Indies Squadron. Porter included a 100-ton Hudson River steamboat in his flotilla, the 3-gun paddle-wheeler *Sea Gull,* the first time in combat history that such a vessel had been used. Porter added her to his considerable fleet because

ABOVE: On October 29, 1814, New Yorkers watched as Robert Fulton launched the Demologos (Fulton I), the world's first steam-powered warship. Designed for harbor defense, the gunboat was propelled by a central paddle-wheel and carried thirty-two small cannon.

Essex, Phoebe, and Cherub

she could pursue pirates through shallows when even the lightest sailing craft lay becalmed.

For two years Porter pursued pirates among the islands and reefs of the Caribbean. His eight small schooners and five 20-oared barges did most of the work while his frigates escorted merchant ships through danger areas. Though Porter successfully suppressed the pirate trade, he proved to be an inept diplomat. In 1825 he created an international dispute by sending a force into Fajardo, Puerto Rico, after the local Spanish authority allegedly insulted one of his pirate-chasing officers. President James Monroe had on December 2, 1823, promulgated his famous doctrine promising to protect the Americas against foreign aggression, and Porter became the first aggressor. Recalled and court-martialed on charges of insubordination for violating Spanish sovereignty, Porter was suspended from active duty for

six months. Having a volatile nature, Porter resigned to become commander-in-chief of the newly organized Mexican Navy. Captain Lewis Warrington took over the West India Squadron and by mid-1826 reported the islands cleared of the scourge of piracy.

> I had always fancied that the stories of worm-eaten bread…were little more than apocryphal…[but] I have seen a biscuit literally crawl off the mess cloth….
> *Charles Nordhoff,* In Yankee Windjammers.

Curbing the Slave Trade

In 1808 Congress outlawed transatlantic slave trade with Africa and in 1820 made slaving punishable by death. In 1817 the American Colonization Society suggested repatriating slaves by returning them to Africa. Two naval officers, Robert Stockton and Matthew C.

ABOVE: When slaves took over the Amistad in 1839 and killed the ship's captain and the cook, the incident made headlines in the United States and intensified the navy's effort to curb the slave trade emanating out of Africa.

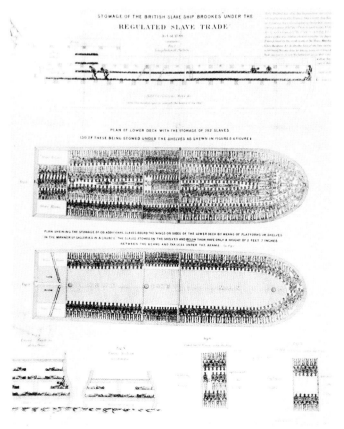

LEFT: Slave ships such as the Brookes became vessels of horror and death. Men and women filled every empty space. Unless they died en route to America, slaves remained chained together for weeks, with barely enough space to breathe.

ABOVE: Slaves during the middle passage to America on the ship Gloria suffered horrible treatment and unspeakable misery. They were abused, beaten, and poorly fed during a voyage that often lasted two months.

RIGHT: *The 3,241-ton sailing ship-of-the-line USS* Pennsylvania *went to sea in 1837 and soon became obsolete with the advent of side-wheel steamers. Sailors burned her on April 20, 1861, when the Union Navy abandoned the Norfolk Navy Yard.*

Perry, agreed with the proposal and promoted the idea of creating Liberia. In 1820 the navy department formed the African Squadron for the suppression of the slave trade and to aid in the settlement of Liberia. Two years later the navy withdrew the African Squadron because shallow-draft vessels were needed to combat piracy in the West Indies.

Not for twenty years did the United States make further efforts to suppress the slave trade. In 1843 Commodore Matthew C. Perry returned to the West Coast of Africa after several American merchant ships had been captured and their crews barbarously murdered. He anchored his squadron off the Guinea Coast and sent a force of marines and sailors ashore that destroyed four slaving towns and killed the gigantic native chief, King Crack O. On December 16 Perry brought the Africans to the table and consummated the treaty of Great Berribee, which officially but not entirely ended the slave trade.

The Seminole Wars

When the Second Seminole War erupted in 1835, Secretary of the Navy Mahlon Dickerson had allowed the navy to disintegrate to forty-one ships and six thousand men. Commodore Alexander Dallas, who had been patrolling the Gulf of Mexico to interdict the smuggling of slaves into Texas, found his ocean-going squadron called upon to assist in rooting out Seminoles who inhabited the inland swamps and waterways of Florida and who had refused to be relocated to the Indian Territory of Oklahoma. In 1836 the Creek Indians of Georgia and Alabama joined the opposition, and for ten years the navy became involved in sending small, light-draft steamers up rivers to keep soldiers and marines supplied. Sailors called it the brown water "mosquito fleet." Using flat-bottomed barges and dugouts, Lieutenants J. T. McLaughlin and John Rodgers penetrated hundreds of miles up rivers and

LEFT: On August 25, 1843, Captain John T. Newton's side-wheel frigate Missouri *became the first steam-powered U.S. naval vessel to cross the Atlantic. The following night, off Gibraltar, a fire broke out in one of her storerooms and destroyed the ship.*

into swamps to find and subdue the elusive Indians.

The skirmishes continued until 1845, when the navy put forces ashore in southern Florida. Marines captured Seminole chieftain Osceola and rounded up the rest of his band. By then, the naval force of the United States had withered away to a number of shallow-draft vessels and a few old frigates.

The Mexican War (1846-1847)

President Polk laid the foundation for the Mexican War when on March 1, 1845, he annexed Texas and in July sent General Taylor's army to the Rio Grande River to intimidate the Mexicans. What began on April 23, 1846, as the Mexican War became a struggle between land forces because Mexico had no navy. Commodore David Conner blockaded Mexican ports in the Gulf of Mexico, and Commodore Robert F. Stockton sailed around Cape Horn in the old frigate *Congress* and assimilated Sloat's

ABOVE: Captain Robert F. Stockton, commanding the navy's first screw steamer USS Princeton, *invited President John Tyler and other dignitaries for a demonstration of "the Peacemaker," a 12-inch gun he designed. But "Peacemaker" blew up and killed eight persons, including the navy secretary.*

mini-squadron in the Pacific. Landing parties from *Congress* and the 20-gun sloops-of-war *Cyane* and *Portsmouth* captured southern California and Los Angeles against light opposition. Mexican forces in California surrendered on August 14, 1846, and Stockton organized and headed a civil government.

In the Gulf of Mexico, Conner conducted a blockade but did little to help the war effort because of disease among his men and a paucity of steamers to bring in supplies. Bancroft sent the side-wheel steamer *Mississippi*, launched in 1841, into the gulf with a new commander, Commodore Matthew C. Perry. Secretary of the Navy John Young Mason immediately began

building and commissioning new steamers, among them the *Powhatan, Susquehanna, San Jacinto*, and *Saranac*. All the ships were side-wheelers except for one, *San Jacinto*, which was powered by a screw propeller. None of the vessels ever participated in the war.

After bombarding the forts protecting Veracruz, Perry put General Winfield Scott's twelve-thousand-man army ashore in a single day, after which the navy mopped-up coastal towns with small amphibious expeditions. Marines joined Scott's attack on Mexico City, which enabled them to add a half-stanza to their spirited anthem—"From the halls of Montezuma to the shores of Tripoli."

INSET BELOW: Historian George Bancroft (1800–1899) founded the United States Naval Academy during his 1845–1846 term as secretary of the navy under President James K. Polk. Bancroft later became ambassador to Great Britain, Prussia, and Germany.

George Bancroft (1800–1899)

On March 11, 1845, George Bancroft of Massachusetts became President James K. Polk's secretary of the navy. Bancroft never admitted knowing much about the navy, but he fully appreciated a good education. At Polk's bidding, Bancroft spent his first year in office involved in the annexation of Texas and preparing for war with Mexico. He posted Commodore David Conner's Home Squadron off Veracruz and sent Commodore John D. Sloat's squadron to the Pacific. On March 31 Mexico broke diplomatic relations, and in April the U.S. administration issued preparatory orders for the navy to transport General Zachary Taylor's army to Texas.

As the United States and Mexico moved toward war, Bancroft made his greatest contribution to the navy and founded the United States Naval Academy. For more than ten years Congress had opposed the idea because they doubted whether academic training was of value to a naval officer. They also believed the United States was immune from wars and simply refused to spend the money.

Bancroft snubbed Congress by not asking for funds. He solved the site problem by obtaining Fort Severn, at Annapolis, Maryland, from the army. He then raised $28,200, enough to transfer eighteen of the navy's twenty-five professors on waiting orders at half pay to teach at the academy. He named Commander Franklin Buchanan superintendent, and in early 1846 fifty-six students reported for instruction, half being midshipmen returning from sea and the other half being new appointees, soon to be called cadets.

Even as the nation approached war with Mexico, Bancroft remained

ABOVE: The brig USS Somers had been used to train midshipmen until Secretary of the Navy George Bancroft secured the U.S. Army post at Fort Severn in Annapolis, Maryland, and in October 1845 opened the school as the United States Naval Academy.

more interested in improving the quality of the navy than increasing its size. President Polk became distressed by Bancroft's parsimonious requests for new construction, guns, and manpower. Bancroft eventually admitted that he opposed going to war with Mexico, so Polk removed him and on July 10, 1846, replaced him with John Young Mason, the previous secretary of the navy. Mason had opposed the establishment of a naval academy, but thereafter supported it.

From the Mexican War the navy learned something about the difficulties of maintaining a lengthy blockade in enemy waters. Little did sailors realize that in fourteen years they would be at sea again, patrolling 3,500 miles of their own coastline in a section of the south called the Confederate States of America.

You Have gained yourself a lasting name, and have won it without shedding a drop of blood or inflicting misery on a human being. What naval commander ever won such laurels at such a rate?

Washington Irving to Matthew C. Perry in A History of the United States Navy, by Edgar S. Maclay.

A Decade of Exploration

Although Matthew Perry's opening of Japan may have been the diplomatic highlight of the 1850s, the navy launched a series of expeditions to explore the world. Lieutenant Matthew F. Maury, superintendent of the U.S. Naval Observatory, had begun tracking the winds and currents of the oceans and established routes that became the world's commercial highways of the seas. In 1851 he sent Lieutenant William L. Herndon over the Andes of South America to explore the basin and navigability of the Amazon, which opened commercial opportunities with Brazil.

In May 1850 the navy sent the first of two "Grinnell" expeditions into the polar waters of Greenland in search of British Captain Sir John Franklin, who had disappeared in 1847 while searching for the Northwest Passage. Though both missions failed to find Franklin, Dr. Elisha Kent Kane made discoveries in what became the Lincoln Sea that opened the way for future Arctic expeditions.

ABOVE: On March 8, 1847, after the Mexican government refused to surrender, General Winfield Scott disembarked 8,600 soldiers from Commodore Perry's Home Squadron, and with naval gunfire support, captured the city of Veracruz.

In January 1854, Lieutenant Isaac G. Strain led an expedition across the Isthmus of Panama and reconnoitered the route that eventually became the Panama Canal.

In July 1958 the steam frigate *Niagara*, commanded by Captain William L. Hudson, cooperated with the HMS *Agamemnon* to lay the first telegraphic cable across the Atlantic Ocean. The cable soon failed, but the work had begun and in 1866 succeeded, putting the United States in telegraphic communication with

ABOVE: On June 15, 1847, Commodore Matthew C. Perry leads the second expedition of 1,173 bluejackets in 47 boats up the Tabasco River before putting the men ashore at Seven Palms and capturing the city of Tabasco the following day.

Matthew C. Perry (1794–1858)

Born in Rocky Brook, Rhode Island, Perry joined the navy as a mid-shipman in 1807 and served in the Barbary Wars of 1815-16. Promoted to master commandant in 1826, he commanded the New York Navy Yard, where he championed the adoption of steam propulsion. He helped Secretary of the Navy Bancroft establish the United States Naval Academy, and was perhaps best remembered for assisting General Winfield Scott during the Mexican War, but Perry's greatest contribution was yet to come.

In 1852 Perry commanded the East India Squadron based at Hong Kong, where Secretary of the Navy James C. Dobbin had sent him to open trade with Japan. On July 8, 1853, Perry sailed into Edo (Tokyo) Bay and sent an emissary ashore with a letter from President Millard Fillmore to the emperor. Perry promised to return the following year for an answer.

On February 13, 1854, Perry reentered Edo Bay with a larger force and resumed negotiations with the Japanese. Between entertaining and exchanging gifts, talks continued, and on March 31 Perry signed the Treaty of Kanagawa, giving the United States access to Japanese ports for wood, water, supplies, and refuge. Perry used no intimidation during the discussions: the presence of the steamers *Mississippi* and *Susquehanna*, on which Japanese officials were feasted, were enough. Perry opened Japan to foreign trade, capping a brilliant success beyond the reaches of the most polished diplomats.

LEFT: On March 8, 1854, Commodore Matthew C. Perry returned to Yokohama harbor with a squadron of eight ships to meet with Japanese commissioners. Applying masterful diplomacy, Perry opened the island to commerce by signing the Treaty of Kanagawa.

LEFT: After Perry entered Yokohama harbor, nothing impressed the Japanese more than the big guns on the side-wheel steamer Mississippi and the great deck where people could sit and listen to American music played by the ship's band.

RIGHT: On May 30, 1853, the U.S. Navy approved a second polar expedition privately financed by Henry Grinnell and led by Elisha Kent Kane to search for the missing British explorer Sir John Franklin. The unsuccessful expedition's steamer Advance became trapped in ice until the summer of 1855.

Europe. However, America's Civil War caused an eight-year interregnum in cable-laying efforts.

Secession

On November 6, 1860, Abraham Lincoln's election as the sixteenth president of the United States set the stage for the secession of South Carolina on December 20. By February 1, 1861, six more states of the Deep South had followed. When Lincoln took office on March 4, the Confederate States had already been formed with Jefferson Davis as president and Stephen R. Mallory as secretary of the navy. As the former U.S. Senator from Florida, Mallory had been the powerful chairman of the Naval Affairs Committee. He knew considerably more about the weak condition of the U.S. Navy than did Gideon Welles, who entered Lincoln's cabinet on March 5 as the Union's secretary of the navy.

> I believe this government cannot endure, permanently half slave and half free….It will become all one thing, or all the other.
> *Abraham Lincoln's campaign speech for the Senate, June 16, 1858.*

The weakness of the navy and naval administration became manifest on the first official day of the Civil War. On April 12, 1861, Confederate batteries in Charleston's harbor opened on Fort Sumter. A naval relief expedition consisting of the steamship *Baltic*, the USS *Pawnee*, and the revenue cutter *Harriet Lane,* all under the command of Gustavus Vasa Fox, arrived late because of miscommunication over another expedition bound for Pensacola, Florida. Major Robert Anderson surrendered the fort on April 13, and two days later President Lincoln called for 75,000 ninety-day volunteers. (There were only sixteen thousand men in the regular army, and most of them were stationed in the

West.) On April 19, two days after Virginia seceded and joined the Confederacy, Lincoln declared a blockade of southern ports, even though the navy lacked the ships for such an enterprise. The idea for a blockade actually came from enfeebled General Winfield Scott, whose Anaconda Plan called for the strangulation of the Confederacy by cutting the South off from the resources of the outside world.

On April 20 the situation became worse when bumbling sixty-eight-year-old Captain Charles S. McCauley, charged with defending the Norfolk (Gosport) Navy Yard, abandoned it to Virginia militia, leaving nine vessels that Welles dearly needed in the yard, plus the remains of the screw frigate *Merrimac*, which the Confederates later raised and converted into an ironclad menace. McCauley also failed to destroy more than a thousand pieces of ordnance, which soon found employment in the forts and ships of the Confederacy.

After the seizure of Norfolk, Captain George S. Blake, superintendent of the Naval Academy, became so concerned that Maryland would secede that he packed up his faculty and midshipmen, put them on the frigate *Constitution*, and moved the school to Newport, Rhode Island, for the duration of the war.

ABOVE: Fort Sumter stands near the entrance to Charleston, South Carolina's harbor, and in April 1961 the American flag flying over the ramparts represented the last symbol of the federal government in the newly formed Confederacy.

ABOVE: Confederate Secretary of the Navy Stephen R. Mallory had the daunting task of creating the South's naval strategy. Having few resources, he opted to build a fleet of ironclads and high seas commerce raiders.

TOP: Ship's officers and crew gather on the deck of the 10-gun side-wheel steamer USS Mendota. The former blockade-runner was purchased by the navy from New York contractors and put into service on February 1, 1864, shortly before this picture was taken.

ABOVE: During exercises on the USS Brooklyn, an officer (left) watches a gun crew composed of marines and sailors go through the convolutions of manning the ship's 11-inch pivot gun.

Gideon Welles (1802–1878)

Born in Glastonbury, Connecticut, Gideon Welles spent most of his life as a journalist and editor of the *Hartford Times.* He eventually turned to politics, and made three unsuccessful attempts to achieve elective office as a Democrat. In 1836 President Andrew Jackson rewarded Welles's fidelity by naming him postmaster of Hartford. During the Mexican War, President Polk put Welles in charge of the Naval Bureau of Provisions and Clothing. When in 1861 Lincoln named him secretary of the navy, Welles's knowledge of naval matters remained limited.

Welles's predecessor, Isaac Toucey, came from the South. Though in 1857 he had pressed for funds to build seven steam sloops to suppress the slave trade and money to install 9-inch and 11-inch smoothbore guns designed by Commander John A. B. Dahlgren on all fighting ships, Toucey slowed everything down after Lincoln's nomination. When Welles took office, he had only ninety ships, of which forty-eight were laid up or rotting in navy yards. Thirty others were spread around the world on foreign duty. Many of the ships were still driven by sail rather than steam. One half of the navy's officer corps, more than three hundred and fifty officers from captain to midshipman, joined the Confederacy, and half of the clerical staff in the navy department remained sympathetic to the South.

In 1861, Welles confronted an enormous task of building a navy and blockading three thousand five hundred miles of southern coast. He surmounted many of his other problems by engaging, though with reluctance at first, Gustavus Vasa Fox as assistant secretary of the navy. Fox understood ships, men, and the navy. They shared the work, Welles attending to administrative matters, Fox to operational matters. The division of responsibilities worked, and by the end of the Civil War the United States owned the strongest navy on earth.

[The blockade] shut the Confederacy out from the world, deprived it of supplies, weakened its military and naval strength, and compelled exhaustion….
J. Thomas Scharf, History of the Confederate States Navy.

Welles purchased or leased any ship that would float and armed it with old guns to perform blockade duty. For many months the feeble Union blockade functioned ineffectively, but by the end of 1861 Welles had increased his fleet to 260 ships with hundreds more on the way. Confederate blockade runners, mostly fast steamers operating out of England and manned by British sailors, slipped through the sparsely manned blockading squadrons, delivering tons of arms and ammunition to the South.

Blockade Running Attempts

Year	Ratio of Success
1861	9 of 10
1862	7 of 8
1863	3 of 4
1864	2 of 3
1865	1 of 3

The situation evolved into diametrically opposite strategies for Confederate Secretary of the Navy Mallory and Welles, his Union counterpart. Welles had to build a huge navy to blockade the South and strangle it like a coiled anaconda into submission. Mallory wanted a small navy capable of driving away the Union blockaders with a few extremely powerful ships and a separate seagoing squadron of armed steamers to prey on the American merchant fleet. Both strategies made sense, but could either be implemented?

The Evolution of Ironclads

Mallory faced a greater problem than Welles because he had to find a way to break the flimsy Union blockade before it became stronger, but the South had no shipyards, few factories or trained workmen, and no funds. Aware of the U.S. Navy's traditional resistance to building ironclads, Mallory believed the only way to keep southern ports open was to launch an ironclad program before the North changed its mind. The opportunity came unexpectedly when Virginians captured the Norfolk Navy Yard and raised the partly burned hulk of the USS *Merrimac*.

In June 1861 Mallory took his ironclad plan to the Confederate Congress, promising that if he were permitted to build ironclads the Union's frigates, sloops, and gunboats would become useless. He hired former Union naval constructors to overhaul the machinery on the *Merrimac*, build an ironclad casemate on her deck, fit her out with ten heavy guns, and fix an iron prow to her bow for ramming. Manufacturing the iron for *Merrimac* consumed almost all the capacity of Richmond's Tredegar Iron Works for two months.

Welles soon learned of Mallory's project and in September 1861 began investigating ironclads for the Union navy. Though not particularly impressed by the proposals he received, he issued contracts for two experimental ironclads. Cornelius Bushnell of Connecticut received a contract to build the *Galena*, and Swedish inventor John Ericsson, an eccentric engineer with wild ideas about shipbuilding, received a contract for the *Monitor*.

The CSS *Virginia*, formerly the *Merrimac*, and the *Monitor* reached the final stages of completion in

ABOVE: Launched February 14, 1862, the screw-steamer USS Galena (actually an ironclad) once competed for navy contracts with the USS Monitor. She carried eight 9-inch Dahlgren smoothbores, two of which can be seen protruding from her ports.

ABOVE: Lieutenant John Lorimer Worden will always be remembered for commanding the USS Monitor during her momentous battle with the CSS Virginia on March 9, 1862. Though partially blinded during the fight, Worden rose in rank to rear admiral.

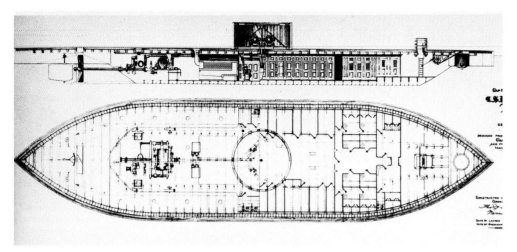

RIGHT: Rear Admiral David Dixon Porter reclines against one of the 20-pounder Dahlgrens on the deck of the USS Malvern, his flagship while commanding the Union North Atlantic Blockading Squadron off the Cape Fear River.

ABOVE: The design of marine engineer John Ericsson's USS Monitor, with her revolving turret, air make-up system, and unique propeller drive, introduced technological concepts that immediately rendered obsolete every other warship in the world.

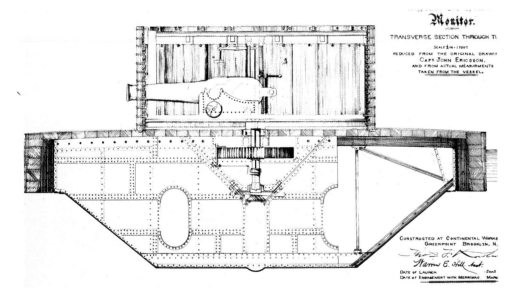

ABOVE: The traverse section of the USS Monitor shows the gearing amidships that rotated the turret, in which there were actually two 11-inch Dahlgren guns opposite each other. As one gun rotated into firing position, the crew reloaded the other.

Take the little thing home and worship it, as it would not be idolatry, because it was in the image of nothing in the heaven above or on earth beneath or in the waters under the earth.

Captain Charles Henry Davis's reaction to seeing Ericsson's wooden model of the Monitor.

February 1862. Structurally, they had nothing in common. The bulky 275-foot *Virginia* looked like the roof of a barn drifting on the water, and the oblong 172-foot *Monitor* looked like a "cheese box on a raft." The *Virginia*'s battery consisted of two 7-inch rifles on pivots, and two 6-inch rifles and six 9-inch Dahlgrens in broadside. The *Monitor* carried only two 11-inch Dahlgrens in a revolving turret that resembled a pillbox. For the first time in naval history, neither fighting ship carried a sail.

War on the Rivers

With the exception of eight Confederate commerce raiders on the high seas, the naval battles of the Civil War were fought mainly on inland waterways. The Mississippi River and its southern watershed became the most important link unifying the western states of the Confederacy (Texas, Arkansas, and most of Louisiana) with the other eight southern states. The Confederates were as aware of the dangers of losing control of the Mississippi as was the Union of the importance of controlling the river.

Duel Between the First Ironclads

On March 8, 1862, Captain Franklin Buchanan steamed down the Elizabeth River and headed the *Virginia* into Hampton Roads. Directly across the James River, near Newport, Virginia, lay two sailing ships of the Union blockading squadron. After ramming and sinking the 32-gun sloop *Cumberland*, Buchanan turned on the 52-gun frigate *Congress* and destroyed her with incendiary shells. When the 43-gun steamer USS *Minnesota* attempted to join the battle, though no match for the *Virginia*, she ran aground. Because Buchanan had suffered a wound, executive officer Lieutenant Catesby ap R. Jones withdrew, intending to finish off *Minnesota* and the rest of the Union squadron in the morning.

During the evening the *Monitor* slipped into Hampton Roads, and her commander, Lieutenant John L. Worden, moored her beside the grounded *Minnesota*. When the *Virginia* reappeared on the morning of March 9, Worden's *Monitor* met her before Jones could get in range of the *Minnesota*. For four hours the two ironclads fought each other "mercilessly, but ineffectively," neither ship doing serious damage to the other. Early in the afternoon the *Virginia* withdrew to Sewell's Point, leaving *Monitor* in possession of Hampton Roads and *Virginia* in possession of the river approaches to Norfolk. On that day, every wooden warship in the world became obsolete.

ABOVE: Lieutenant Catesby ap R. Jones assumed command of the CSS Virginia **after Captain Franklin Buchanan suffered a wound on March 8. Jones tried every way imaginable to defeat the USS** Monitor **and, finding his efforts useless, retired from the battle.**

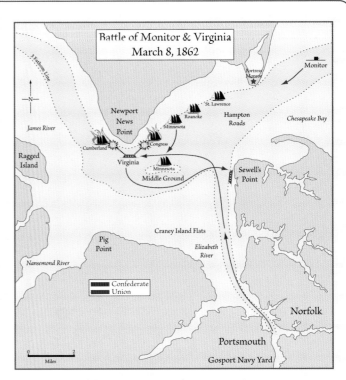

ABOVE: Union ships in Hampton Roads were poorly prepared when the CSS Virginia **exited the Elizabeth River. After destroying the USS** Cumberland **and the USS** Congress, **the** Virginia **returned to Sewell's Point, unaware that the USS** Monitor **was on the way.**

In August 1861, Welles put Flag Officer Andrew Hull Foote in command of naval forces on the upper Mississippi. During the winter of 1862, Foote very ably assisted General Ulysses S. Grant in the capture of Fort Henry on the Tennessee River and Fort Donelson on the Cumberland River. Foote had the advantage on the upper Mississippi, thanks to the efforts of James B. Eads of St. Louis, who in sixty-five days built seven shallow-draft ironclad gunboats for service on western waters. Designed with hump-backed silhouettes by constructor Samuel M. Pook, the gunboats became known as "Pook's Turtles." During the spring of 1862, Foote used two of Eads's gunboats, *Carondelet* and *Pittsburgh*, to run the batteries at Island No. 10 and open the upper Mississippi to Fort Pillow, Tennessee.

On the lower Mississippi, Flag Officer David G. Farragut, commanding a seventeen-ship squadron of wooden ocean-going ships, began working his deep draft vessels over the bar at the mouth of the Mississippi. With Farragut came a squadron of wooden mortar schooners led by Commander David Dixon Porter. On April 18 Porter's mortars opened on Forts Jackson and St. Philip, two massive structures capable of pouring a crossfire into any ships attempting to steam upriver to New Orleans, the South's most wealthy and populous city. At 2:00 A.M. on April 24, Farragut accomplished the seemingly impossible. He led his squadron through a gauntlet of fire from the forts, destroyed a weak force of Confederate gunboats, continued up the river to New Orleans, and on April 25 took possession of the city. The campaign led to the destruction of three Con-

The Confederate Submarine *Hunley*

Conceived in New Orleans by Horace L. Hunley, but built in Mobile as a privateer, a submarine was moved to Charleston by its inventor at the invitation of Confederate General Pierre G. T. Beauregard, who sought a weapon capable of dismantling the Union blockade and reopening Charleston to foreign trade. Hunley had reconfigured the boat by reshaping and tapering a large boiler, on which he rigged conning towers, diving planes, ballast tanks, a keel, and a bow-mounted spar capable of carrying a 90-pound torpedo. For propulsion, seven crewmen cranked the propeller by hand. After two ironclads built in Charleston failed to break the Union blockade, Hunley's submarine became the city's last hope of reopening the harbor.

The boat sank three times in all, twice during testing at Charleston. During the first sinking, on August 29, 1863, the skipper, Lt. John A. Payne, and two other men escaped while five others drowned. All were volunteers. *Hunley* was recovered, but during further trials on October 15, 1863, this time with her inventor as skipper, she sank again, and all aboard drowned.

On the night of February 17, 1864, the ocean became dead calm and all the tidal variables seemed right for a live attack. The *Hunley*, running on the surface, partially submerged after sighting the sloop USS *Housatonic* dead ahead. Detecting the submarine off the beam of the Union ship, *Housatonic* slipped her cable and began backing at the same time that *Hunley* changed course. The motion swung *Housatonic* into the submarine. *Hunley*'s torpedo exploded between *Housatonic*'s main and mizzenmasts, and the sloop sank minutes later. *Hunley* became caught in the *Housatonic*'s descent. Years later it was located lying on the bottom near her victim.

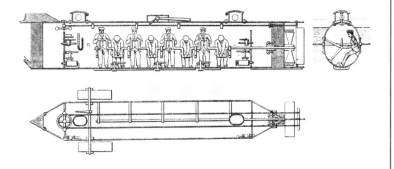

*ABOVE: The **Hunley** was powered by seven men (not eight as depicted in this early drawing) turning a crank. She sank twice during trials but on each occasion was recovered and returned to service. Finally, she sank after her attack on the USS **Housatonic** in February 1864.*

federate ironclads, the *Manassas* and the powerful *Mississippi* and *Louisiana*. Farragut's occupation of New Orleans shut the Mississippi off from the Gulf of Mexico and began the process of squeezing the life from the Confederacy.

"Damn the Torpedoes"

Torpedoes came in many shapes and sizes, but most of them, commonly referred to as Confederate "infernal machines," were actually mines that either exploded on contact or were cabled to galvanic batteries on shore and detonated by an operator. In the entrance channel to Mobile Bay, Alabama, and a few feet below the surface of the water, Confederates had anchored several rows of contact mines between Fort Morgan on the eastern side of the channel and Fort Gaines on the western side. Only a small width of the channel directly under the heavy guns of Fort Morgan remained free of mines and obstructions. Roving inside Mobile Bay was the CSS *Tennessee*, the strongest Confederate ironclad ever built, and a small flotilla of gunboats. Admiral Franklin Buchanan, who had commanded the CSS *Virginia* at Hampton Roads, now commanded the Mobile Bay squadron. These were the obstacles Rear Admiral David Farragut faced when on August 5, 1864, he determined to fight his way into Mobile Bay.

Farragut admired his stately wooden steam-powered sloops and despised the ugly monitors, which was one of the reasons he made the 26-gun USS *Hartford* his flagship. Altogether he had fourteen wooden ships and four monitors when he gave the orders to advance into Mobile Bay. He placed the monitors on the right to engage Fort Morgan, hoping it would draw fire away from his wooden ships. The monitor *Tecumseh*, however, veered to port to engage the CSS *Tennessee*, cut across the path of the wooden ships, struck a mine, and went down in minutes. The sinking stultified the captain of the leading ship, the USS *Brooklyn*, and threatened to pile up the column of wooden ships steaming into the bay on the left.

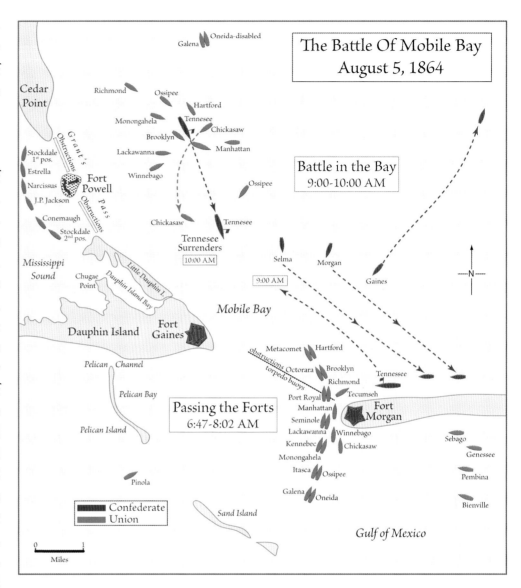

Farragut, in his favored position in the tops from where he could see over the smoke of battle, noticed that the column was both easing into the minefield and halting under the guns of Fort Morgan. He shouted down to the helm, "Damn the torpedoes. Full speed ahead!" The *Hartford* veered to the left and plowed through the minefield, the others following. Men below listened to inactive mines damaged by water ominously scraping against the hulls of their ships.

Once inside the bay, the mighty CSS *Tennessee* put up a valiant fight against Farragut's fleet. After a two-hour battle, during which Farragut's heavy sloops

ABOVE: The Battle of Mobile Bay was fought with mostly wooden sloops-of-war, but the outcome was decided by ironclads. To win in Mobile Bay, Admiral Farragut needed three monitors to defeat the powerful CSS Tennessee. His wooden ships were useless.

RIGHT: During the passage of Fort Morgan at the mouth of Mobile Bay, Rear Admiral David G. Farragut (top right) ascended into the tops to get a better view as the USS Hartford steamed through a minefield planted in the channel.

ABOVE: During the Battle of Mobile Bay, the USS Richmond fires a broadside at the CSS Tennessee. The projectiles from Richmond's 11-inch Dahlgren smoothbores merely fractured into pieces when striking the casemate of the Confederate ironclad.

No officer in the Union navy participated in more important battles or earned more laurels for exceptional victories than David Farragut. After the war, Congress recognized Farragut by making him the nation's first full admiral.

The Fall of Fort Fisher

In the aftermath of Mobile Bay, Welles attempted to give Farragut command of the North Atlantic Blockading Squadron because he wanted Fort Fisher captured and the port of Wilmington, North Carolina, shut down as a sanctuary for blockade-runners. Farragut declined because of poor health, so Welles called Rear Admiral David Porter from the Mississippi and gave the task to him.

Porter made two attempts to force the surrender of Fort Fisher, which guarded the main entrance to the Cape Fear River. The first assault failed because Major General Benjamin Butler disembarked only part of his force and then abandoned it. The second attempt, under a different army commander, included a landing party of marines, sailors, and infantry. Without monitors firing 11- and 15-pound shells near shore, the giant earthen fortress might never have been penetrated. The attack on Fort Fisher was the last amphibious operation of the war. It was never as well coordinated as Farragut's assault on the defenses of New Orleans or Mobile Bay, but it did the job. Five years later, after the death of the heroic Farragut, Porter became the navy's second full admiral.

repeatedly rammed the Confederate ironclad while the monitors pummeled her with 11-inch and 15-inch shells, the *Tennessee* finally lost her steering mechanism. Buchanan had been wounded during the fighting and the *Tennessee* could no longer make way, so she was forced to surrender, but she was the toughest Confederate ship ever built during the Civil War and stood off Farragut's entire squadron until immobilized but only slightly damaged.

The anaconda had, at last, wound its fatal folds around us.
Rear Admiral Raphael Semmes, CSN, on the surrender of Fort Fisher, Official Records of the Navy.

The Postwar Navy

In September 1861, when the navy department authorized the construction of the *Monitor* and the *Galena*, Welles added the experimental *New Ironsides* almost as an afterthought. Unlike the *Monitor* design, the *New Ironsides* began to resemble the shape of the battleships and cruisers soon to come. The navy still maintained the silly idea that iron ships should carry sails, and the 230-foot, dual-engine, 3,486-ton heavily armed behemoth carried a full stand of bark-rigged sails.

On September 18, 1865, the 250-foot, double-turreted, 3,815-ton *Miantonomoh* went into commission with four 15-inch guns. Welles sent the ship to Great Britain in an effort to settle claims caused by Confederate commerce raiders against the American carrying trade. A correspondent for the London *Times* newspaper took a close look at the ship and wrote, "There was not one [British warship] that the foreigner could not have sent to the bottom in five minutes, had his errand not been peaceful…not one of these big ships…could have avenged the loss of its companion, or saved itself from sharing its fate. In fact, the wolf was in the fold, and the whole flock was at its mercy."

The moment marked the beginning of the end of the world's sailing navies. Although Congress quickly suspended appropriations for modernizing the U.S. fleet, and ships once again returned to navy yards to rot, Japan and the nations of Europe took notice while the U.S. Navy lapsed from being the strongest in the world to among the weakest. But not for long.

CHAPTER 3

A FLEXING OF POWER 1898–1939

After the end of the Civil War, the navy remained in virtual limbo until 1881, when Chester A. Arthur became the twenty-first president and William E. Chandler became the thirtieth secretary of the navy. During those years there had been problems in Uruguay, China, Formosa, Korea, Panama, Egypt, and elsewhere, all of which required the presence of the navy. A look at the British squadron that bombarded Alexandria, Egypt, in 1882 convinced Chandler that drastic measures were required to upgrade the navy's antiquated fleet. Chandler also believed the navy needed more than ships. In 1884, after making an effort to get ship construction revived, he also established the Naval War College at Newport, Rhode Island, and directed Rear Admiral Stephen B. Luce, the college's first president, to infuse naval officers with a higher degree of professionalism.

"Remember the Maine"

On January 25, 1898, Captain Charles D. Sigsbee conned the armored cruiser USS *Maine* into the harbor of Havana, Cuba, ostensibly on a goodwill mission. His actual purpose was to protect Americans whose lives were being threatened by Cuba's revolt against Spain. On February 15 an explosion of unknown cause blew the ship to pieces, killing 253 of the 358 officers and men comprising the crew. After examining the wreck, Captain William T. Sampson declared that the effects of the blast "could have been produced only by...a mine situated under the bottom of the ship." A later study blamed a fire in the coalbunker for igniting the

The American Republic has no more need for its burlesque of a Navy than a peaceful giant would have for a stuffed crab or a tin sword.
Henry George, social commentator, 1882.

RIGHT: On the USS Colorado, Captain McLane Tilton, USMC, stands with Medal of Honor recipients Private Hugh Purvis (center) and Corporal Charles Brown (left), who captured the pictured Korean military flag during an assault on June 1, 1871.

The Evolution of the Battleship

Under Secretary of the Navy Chandler's guidance, Congress appropriated $1.3 million for construction of what became known as the ABCD ships—the protected (meaning deck-armored) 3,000-ton cruisers *Atlanta* and *Boston*, the 4,500-ton cruiser *Chicago*, and the 1,500-ton dispatch ship *Dolphin*. They were the first modern ships to enter the U.S. fleet since the Civil War and, despite their ability to steam at up to seventeen knots, the old sages of the navy insisted they still carry a pair of masts, three tiers of brig-rigged sails, and a jib. The ships were still powered by Civil War engine technology, and though they carried 5-inch, 6-inch, and 8-inch breechloaded rifles of good range, the navy still used inaccurate open sights for aiming. Before the ships reached sea, Chandler discovered that Great Britain had built the *Esmeralda* for the Chilean Navy; it was a protected cruiser with 18-knot capability and 10-inch breechloaders that outclassed everything in the ABCD group.

In 1885 William C. Whitney became the new secretary of the navy, and he discovered that the British had sent Brazil the armored cruiser *Riachuelo*, a ship capable of destroying the entire U.S. fleet. Whitney took the problem to Congress and received funds to build the first American battleships, the 6,682-ton *Maine* with four 10-inch guns and the 6,315-ton *Texas* with two 12-inch guns. By then, sails had finally fallen out of favor. In June 1890 Congress authorized the construction of America's new first-class battleships, the 10,000-ton *Indiana* (BB-1), *Massachusetts* (BB-2), and *Oregon* (BB-3) with four 13-inch guns mounted in centerline turrets, thereby downgrading the *Maine* and *Texas* to armored cruisers (ACRs).

Without the new building program, bolstered by those that followed, the United States would not have been prepared for the Spanish American War.

ABOVE LEFT: The protected (armored) cruiser Chicago *(left), flagship of the Squadron of Evolution, leads the ABCD ships to sea. The flotilla includes the dispatch ship* Dolphin *(far center), and to her left the protected cruisers* Boston *and* Atlanta.

ABOVE: The 6,682-ton USS Maine *looked more like a royal yacht than a battleship. The ship carried only four 10-inch guns, two in the bow and two in turrets placed diagonally on the starboard bow and the port quarter.*

LEFT CENTER: In 1890 Congress authorized three more battleships, the Indiana *(BB-1), the* Massachusetts *(BB-2), pictured, and the* Oregon *(BB-3). The identical 10,000-ton battleships were a third again larger than the* Texas *and the* Maine.

LEFT: On August 15, 1895, the United States launched its first battleship, the USS Texas. *Unlike with the now decade-old protected cruisers, the navy finally abandoned sails, and* Texas *went to sea with only two stubby observation masts.*

RIGHT: On February 15, 1898, while on a goodwill visit to Cuba, the protected battleship USS Maine is blown to pieces while anchored in Havana harbor. President William McKinley blames Spain for the catastrophe and leads America to war.

RIGHT: With the wreck of the Maine on the bottom of Havana's harbor, Captain William T. Sampson told a naval court of inquiry that the effects of the blast "could have been produced only by... a mine situated under the bottom of the ship."

Admiral Dewey in the Philippines

The ink had barely dried on President McKinley's April 20, 1898, declaration of war when sixty-one-year-old Commodore George Dewey, commanding the Asiatic Squadron, received a cable from Secretary of the Navy John D. Long: "Proceed at once to Philippine Islands. Commence operations…against Spanish fleet. You must capture vessels or destroy."

After midnight on May 1, Dewey led the Asiatic Squadron past Spanish shore batteries and into Manila Bay without suffering damage to a single ship. At dawn, Dewey located the Spanish fleet commanded by Rear Admiral Patricio Montojo y Parasón lying at anchor off the Cavite Navy Yard. The odds were distinctly in Dewey's favor. His squadron consisted of the protected cruisers *Olympia* (C-6), *Baltimore* (C-3), *Boston,* and *Raleigh* (C-8), the gunboats *Concord* (PG-3) and *Petrel* (PG-2), the revenue cutter *Hugh McCulloch*, and two transports. The combined broadsides of Dewey's ships could hurl 3,700 pounds of projectiles. Admiral Montojo chose to fight at anchor. His fleet consisted of an unseaworthy steel cruiser, an old wooden cruiser, five small cruisers, and a few gunboats with a combined broadside of 1,273 pounds. By circling off Cavite and firing broadsides, Dewey's squadron sank three of Montojo's cruisers, disabled the other vessels, silenced the Spanish forts, and by noon enjoyed full possession of Manila Bay. Dewey informed Secretary Long of the naval victory and requested that troops be sent to take possession of Manila. Major General Wesley Merritt did not arrive with his ten-thousand-man army until July 25. By then, Captain Henry Glass had captured the island of Guam in the Mariana Islands where Spanish colonial authorities had not yet been informed of the war.

ABOVE: While maintaining a vigil in Manila Bay, Admiral George Dewey and his dog "Bob" rest comfortably on the protected cruiser Olympia (C-6), flagship of the Asiatic Squadron, during a practice session by the ship's musicians.

ship's magazine. No one questioned Sampson's conclusions. Americans became enraged, shouting, "Remember the *Maine*! To hell with Spain!" On March 8 Congress appropriate $50,000,000 for national defense. Reacting to public pressure, on April 11 President William McKinley asked Congress for permission to intervene in Cuba. The American objective, however, was not Cuba but securing Spain's Philippine Islands, which lay on China's doorstep.

> …ultimately those who wish to see this country at peace with foreign nations will be wise if they place reliance upon a first-class fleet of first-class battleships….
> *Theodore Roosevelt, 1897.*

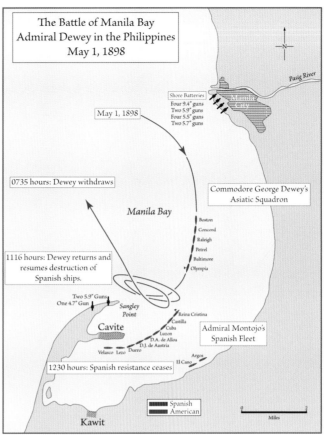

The Battle of Manila Bay
Admiral Dewey in the Philippines
May 1, 1898

Pasig River

Shore Batteries
Four 9.4″ guns
Two 5.9″ guns
Four 5.5″ guns
Two 5.7″ guns

May 1, 1898

Commodore George Dewey's
Asiatic Squadron

0735 hours: Dewey withdraws

Manila Bay

Boston
Concord
Raleigh
Petrel
Baltimore
Olympia

1116 hours: Dewey returns and
resumes destruction of
Spanish ships.

Two 5.9″ Guns
One 4.7″ Gun

Sangley
Point

Reina Cristina
Castilla
Cuba
Luzon
D.A. de Alloa
D.J. de Austria
Velasco Lezo Duero

Cavite

Admiral Montojo's
Spanish Fleet

Argos
El Cano

1230 hours: Spanish resistance ceases

Spanish
American

Kawit

Miles

Battle of Santiago

Commodore Dewey had no battleships when he took his squadron into Manila Bay, but Admiral Sampson's squadron in the Atlantic contained the battleships *Indiana* and *Iowa* (BB-4), the armored cruiser *New York* (ACR-2), two unarmored cruisers, two monitors, and two auxiliaries. Samson struck a course for Puerto Rico, where he hoped to find Rear Admiral Pascual Cervera y Topete's Spanish squadron. A second flotilla, Commodore Winfield Scott Schley's Flying Squadron, with the battleships *Massachusetts* and *Texas* and several cruisers, swung south around Cuba and began looking for Cervera's squadron at Cienfuegos. Schley eventually worked east along Cuba's southern coast and found the Spanish fleet bottled up in Santiago harbor. On June 1 Sampson arrived with his squadron and assumed overall command of Schley's flotilla. Sampson shelled the fortifications guarding the channel, but he could not take his ships through to Santiago. Meanwhile, marines went ashore at Guantanamo and, supported by fire from the battleships *Oregon* and *Texas*, began moving with the V Army Corps by land to Santiago.

On July 3, two days after the battle of San Juan Hill, Admiral Cervera expected Santiago to be assaulted by land and attempted to escape from the harbor. Led by the flagship *Infante Maria Teresa*, Cervera's squadron turned west along the Cuban coast. Sampson smoth-

ered the Spanish ships with fire from the *Indiana, Iowa, Oregon*, and *Texas* and drove most of them ashore. Only the cruisers *Vizcaya* and *Cristobal Colón* broke free, pursued and overhauled by the *Oregon, Brooklyn* (ACR-3), *Texas*, and *Iowa*. By 1:10 P.M. that day, Sampson dispatched a cable to Secretary Long: "The fleet under my command offers the nation as a Fourth of July present the whole of Cervera's fleet." On July

When in 1890 Alfred Thayer Mahan, who became the second president of the Naval War College, published *The Influence of Sea Power Upon History, 1793-1812,* Kaiser Wilhelm II began building battleships and placed copies of Mahan's book on every ship in the German Navy.

TOP: To keep pace with European dread-noughts, in 1906 the navy introduced an entirely new class of battleships. Unlike earlier designs, the USS Connecticut (BB-18) carried 12-inch guns, placed on the ship's quarterdeck.

ABOVE: After a 46,000-mile tour of the world, the Great White Fleet returned to Hampton Roads. On February 22, 1909, President Teddy Roosevelt visited the USS Connecticut (BB-18) and expressed his appreciation to the officers and crew.

17 Santiago surrendered, and on August 13 Dewey reported the surrender of Manila.

On December 10, 1898, the United States signed a treaty of peace with Spain, paid $20,000,000 for Guam, Puerto Rico, and the Philippines, and became an instant empire. Only a battle fleet could defend such far distant territories, thus ensuring America's commitment to sea power: once so aptly expressed in Alfred Thayer Mahan's treatise on controlling the seas.

Foreign Affairs

The cost of empire building came high. On February 4, 1899, eight weeks after signing the peace accord with Spain, an insurrectionary army under General Emiliano Aquinaldo attacked American forces in the Philippines. The navy's ships in Manila Bay detached a battalion of marines to quash the rebellion. The insurrection ended on March 23, 1901, with the capture of Aquinaldo, but another insurrection broke out on the Muslim-infested islands of Samar, Mindanao, and Jolo and lasted another year. To add more confusion, a tribal uprising in Samoa threatened American interests and a landing party from the USS *Philadelphia* (C-4) went ashore to protect consulate employees.

On May 18, 1900, while Americans were still fighting in the Philippines, the Boxer (Righteous Society of Heavenly Fists) Rebellion erupted in China, and the Asiatic Squadron received a call for help. Marine Colonel R. W. Meade did not have enough troops to answer the call, so he borrowed sailors from the navy.

Nor were matters quiescent in the western hemisphere. In the early 1900s the navy became involved in sending peacekeeping forces into Nicaragua, Panama, Honduras, and Cuba.

In 1901 Theodore Roosevelt became president, and his plan for the navy included more battleships. By 1907, twenty-two were afloat. Roosevelt had paid close attention to the Russo-Japanese War (1904-1905) during which an upstart Japanese Navy defeated the

powerful Russian fleet. The impressive victory surprised Roosevelt, so he made arrangements to demonstrate America's naval strength to the world. On December 16, 1907, he sent the Great White Fleet of sixteen steel battleships, colliers, and auxiliaries, on a fourteen-month worldwide goodwill tour. After a 46,000-mile cruise, the fleet returned to Hampton Roads; the ships had already been made obsolete by Great Britain's 17,900-ton, 21.6-knot HMS *Dreadnought*. The British ship carried ten 12-inch guns in twin turrets, three of which were on centerline, and a new state-of-the-art steam turbine propulsion system.

The Dreadnoughts

The Germans were among the first to recognize that the *Dreadnought* had reduced every other battleship in the world to second-class status. In 1908 Roosevelt still had three more undersize battleships coming out of shipyards before tackling his first dreadnought. Before he left office in 1909, work started on America's own

dreadnoughts, the 16,000-ton *Michigan* (BB-27) and *South Carolina* (BB-26) and the 20,000-ton *Delaware* (BB-28) and the *North Dakota* (BB-29). Though they carried two fewer 12-inch guns, they could match the *Dreadnought*'s firepower because all the guns were piggybacked in turrets on centerline.

The new American battleships had an additional advantage that traced back to 1901. At that time Lieutenant William S. Sims had formed a friendship with British Captain Percy Scott, who commanded the HMS *Terrible*. Scott demonstrated a gunnery system of his own design called "continuous aim," which scored eighty percent success rate on hits. Sims concluded that *Terrible* could out-fire the entire U.S. Navy. When nobody in the navy department listened to his advice to adopt the system, Sims took his proposal directly to Roosevelt. He also told the president that the battleships of the Great White Fleet had serious defects in design and construction: their freeboards were too low to fight in stormy seas, and powder rooms

ABOVE: The USS Michigan (BB-27) went into commission on January 4, 1910, as the first American dreadnought and the first to employ super-imposed turrets so that all eight of her 12-inch guns could be trained on either side of the ship.

were so close to turrets that wayward sparks could ignite the charges and blow up the ships.

At Roosevelt's insistence, the navy retrofitted its battleships with Sims's improved "continuous aim" system, and when new dreadnoughts went into commission in 1910, they all incorporated more freeboard and improved powder handling.

TOP: After several attempts to interest the navy in submarines, John P. Holland's Plunger, commissioned in 1897, officially became the navy's first acceptable prototype. However, Holland abandoned the design because the navy demanded a 15-knot running speed.

ABOVE: John P. Holland (1840–1914) stands in the conning tower of a concept submarine he built for the navy. He produced a number of practical submarines before winning the navy department's competition for design in 1888.

Mr. Holland's Submarine

Irish-born John P. Holland hatched an idea that traced back to the days of David Bushnell and Horace Hunley—a submersible vessel that could creep unseen upon an enemy ship and destroy it with a torpedo. While the navy concentrated on methods to launch Whitehead torpedoes from destroyers, Holland went to work building an 85-foot submarine with two torpedo tubes. In 1897 he launched the *Plunger*. When submerged, *Plunger* drew her power from batteries, but when on the surface, the navy demanded fifteen knots, an impossible task for 1897 engines.

The frustrated Irishman abandoned the *Plunger* and in 1900 introduced the 64-ton *Holland* (SS-1). Fifty-four feet in length, *Holland* carried a single torpedo tube and three Whitehead torpedoes, and was powered by a gasoline engine when on the surface. She had a maximum range of fifteen hundred miles and operated at a maximum depth of seventy-five feet. Because she had no periscope, the commander had to surface frequently to get his bearings through small glass ports in the conning tower. Teddy Roosevelt recommended that *Holland* be purchased, and for $150,000 the navy bought its first submarine. Admiral Dewey inspected the craft and remarked that if the Spaniards "had two of these things in Manila, I could never have held it with the squadron I had."

Germany did not adopt the submarine until 1906, but after the perfection of the gyrocompass in 1908, submarines became the commerce menace of World War I.

ABOVE: Rear Admiral Bradley Allen Fiske (1854–1942) took an early interest in flying machines and in 1911 flew a biplane off a ship. Convinced that aircraft had a future, he designed a device for carrying aerial torpedoes.

The Flying Navy

In 1903 Teddy Roosevelt became immensely curious about "flying machines" after Orville and Wilbur Wright put an engine-powered contraption in the air at Kitty Hawk, North Carolina. Roosevelt turned to the most brilliant innovator in the navy, Captain Bradley Allen Fiske, and asked if a plane could fly off a navy ship. On November 14, 1910, Fiske watched as civilian barnstormer Eugene B. Ely flew a Curtiss pusher plane from an inclined platform hastily erected over the bow of the cruiser *Birmingham* (CL-2). Five minutes later, Ely landed safely on the nearby beach. In 1911 Fiske, now an admiral, squeezed into the cockpit of a Curtiss, flew it off a platform, circled, and landed back on the ship. Sold on the tactical importance of aircraft, Fiske went to work drafting plans for the first aerial torpedo.

By December 23, 1910, Glenn Curtiss had solved several major problems in aeronautic design and invited the navy to send men for flight training to his school at San Diego, California. Lieutenant T. Gordon Ellyson attended Curtiss's school and became Naval Aviator Number One. The new airborne technology caught the navy's attention. On May 8, 1911, Captain Washington Irving Chambers officially awarded the first contracts for aircraft to Curtiss, marking the birthday of naval air. Chambers established the first naval air station at Annapolis, Maryland, with Ellyson as his first test pilot.

Gearing Up for World War I

Wars in Europe were not new, and in August 1914 when another conflict began, Americans shrugged their shoulders indifferently. President Woodrow Wilson cautioned against involvement, believing the war would be short. He appointed pacifist Josephus Daniels secretary of the navy. Daniels knew more about raising hogs than battleships or aircraft. Senior naval officers lamented Wilson's choice and were surprised when Daniels chose thirty-one-year-old Franklin Delano Roosevelt, a cousin of the former president, assistant secretary. Daniels had probably never heard of Mahan, who died in 1914, but Roosevelt knew the man by his work and had become a disciple.

> I am running the real work [of the Navy].
> *Franklin Roosevelt to his wife, August 2, 1914.*

When Daniels took office, the navy had eight dreadnoughts afloat and two 32,000-ton *New Mexico*-class battleships mounting twelve 14-inch guns under construction. Though this gave the United States a lead over Japan, Britain's Royal Navy had twenty-nine dreadnoughts and the German navy had twenty battlecruis-

ers. As long as America remained neutral, Daniels expected no trouble, although Japan was rapidly gobbling up German possessions in the Pacific. When Roosevelt asked for another twenty thousand men for the navy, Daniels balked and rejected the request. Roosevelt soon established himself among the admirals as the navy's "good guy," and Daniels the "bad guy."

Wilson, however, enjoyed the commercial benefits of America's neutrality boom. The war renewed the United States' economy, but the conflict also assumed a

ABOVE: On November 14, 1910, civilian barnstormer Eugene B. Ely proved to the navy that a Curtiss pusher biplane could take off from the deck of a ship by flying off a platform built over the bow of the scout cruiser USS Birmingham (CL-2).

LEFT: President Roosevelt (right) stands with Admirals Sims (center) and Burrage (left) in front of a painting titled "The Return of the Mayflower," which symbolically depicts a squadron of U.S. destroyers arriving in Ireland.

ABOVE: Long American escorted convoys steam through the North Atlantic towards Great Britain during World War I. The George Washington (right) is followed by the America and the DeKalb, with a destroyer centered in the distance.

RIGHT: The Lusitania, filled with 1,198 men, women, and children, departs from New York for Great Britain. On May 17, 1915, the German submarine U-20 sank the liner off the coast of England, killing all passengers, including 128 Americans.

Congress became skeptical of Wilson's appeasement policy and urged him to prepare for war. Wilson asked Daniels to prepare a five-year plan, and Daniels asked the navy's first chief of naval operations (CNO), Rear Admiral William S. Benson, to prepare the plan. Benson, a conventional officer with little imagination, turned the task over to Admiral Dewey's General Board. Dewey had been waiting for such an opportunity and came back with a proposal for building a hundred and fifty-six ships, including ten battleships, six battle-cruisers, ten scout cruisers, fifty destroyers, and sixty-seven submarines. The $500,000,000 proposal stunned Benson and dazed Congress. On May 31, 1916, while Congress was debating the navy bill, the British and German navies fought the Battle of Jutland in the most confused naval engagement of the war. Concerned by the Royal Navy's heavy losses, Congress acted on August 29 and passed the Naval Act of 1916. Work began on the 32,600-ton battleships *Colorado* (BB-45), *Maryland* (BB-46), *Washington* (BB-56), and *West Virginia* (BB-48), all armed with the navy's newest 16-inch guns.

The U-boat War

Convoys crossing the North Atlantic consisted of twenty to thirty freighters guarded by cruisers. Together they zigzagged across the ocean to the danger zone, which began about two hundred miles west of the British Isles. From Queenstown, Ireland, Commander Joseph K. Taussig's Destroyer Division 8, fitted with anti-submarine devices, intercepted the convoys and covered the flanks. The destroyers carried depth charges, also known as "ash cans," which were loaded with 300 pounds of TNT and could be set to explode at predetermined depths. During the war, American escort ships operating in European waters participated in more than two hundred attacks on U-boats and sank at least twenty-three submarines. Five or six U-boats made it to the eastern seaboard of the United States, but their mis-

new dangerous character in 1815 when Germany declared the waters around Great Britain a war zone and authorized U-boats to sink without warning any ships entering the area. Wilson warned Germany that any loss of American life would lead to dire repercussions. As Americans continued to travel through the war zone on Allied vessels carrying munitions, lives were lost, and Wilson did nothing until May 7, 1915, when the *U-20* sank the Cunard liner *Lusitania* and took the lives of 1,198 men, women, and children, including 128 Americans. He protested to Germany and won a few concessions. Kaiser Wilhelm ordered U-boat commanders to take passenger liners off the hit list.

TOP LEFT: An officer on watch from the bridge of a destroyer scans the harbor of an English port for the telltale plume created by the periscope of a roving German submarine.

TOP RIGHT: Skirting an incoming freighter, an American SC405 submarine chaser from the wooden-hulled "splinter fleet" returns from a patrol and heads into port at Brest, France.

BOTTOM LEFT: On November 17, 1917, the USS Fanning (DD-37), commanded by Lieutenant Arthur S. Carpender, forces the U-58 to the surface with depth charges and rescues her crew before she plunges to the bottom.

BOTTOM RIGHT: The crew of an escort destroyer at sea loads a depth charge into the ship's Y-gun and sets the firing mechanism on the end of the charge to explode when reaching a specific depth.

sions were primarily diversionary and created more alarm and anxiety than their presence warranted.

To augment the destroyers, the navy built four hundred submarine-chasers, which were 100-foot, 60-ton, gasoline-powered wooden craft armed with 3-inch guns and a "Y" for launching depth charges off the beam. Ensigns commanded the ships of the so-called "splinter fleet," and most of the twenty-five-man crews were drawn from reservists and college men looking for excitement. The crews worked in squadrons of three, motored about listening on hydrophones for submarine activity, and, after locating their prey, triangulated on the U-boat's position and dropped depth charges.

During 1918, thirty-six American sub-chasers operating out of Corfu, a Greek island in the Ionian Sea off the coast of Albania, shut down German and Italian submarine activities by blockading the Straits of Otranto with constant twenty-four-hour Adriatic patrols.

Without the cooperation of the American Navy, the Allies could not have won the war.
Admiral William S. Sims

ABOVE: *When the transport* **Mercury** *prepared to shove off for France on June 30, 1918, her decks were crowded with the 105th Regiment, Field Artillery. By the time the ship arrived in Europe, the war had reached its closing weeks.*

RIGHT: *Although the photograph suggests that "Yeomanettes," the forerunner of the WAVES, joined the navy to have fun, they helped boost the nation's Victory Loan campaign and served in clerical posts that released men for active duty.*

officers and forty-five thousand sailors. It was all that four navy boot camps at Norfolk, Great Lakes, Newport News, and San Francisco could do to assimilate some forty-five thousand recruits processed through training centers every eight weeks.

The navy solved a small part of its manpower problem on March 17, 1917, when it authorized "Yeomanettes," forerunners of the WAVES. Some 11,275 women served in clerical jobs during the war.

The production of battleships quickly gave way to the mass production of 273 destroyers for convoy and U-boat suppression duty. They were all 1,200-ton, 35-knot four-pipers carrying four 4-inch guns, a 3-inch antiaircraft gun, twelve 21-inch torpedo tubes, and two depth charge racks. The destroyers became the backbone of the navy. Although many were not finished until after the war, they became an important factor twenty-two years later by sustaining Great Britain during World War II.

Crossing the Atlantic

During World War I the U.S. Navy fought no battles at sea. On December 17, 1917, Rear Admiral Hugh Rodman joined the British Grand Fleet with the battleships *Delaware*, *Florida*, *Texas*, *Wyoming*, and *New York*, but there was little to do other than to patrol the North Sea and protect commerce. The roughest and most tedious work fell on the sailors escorting convoys and troopships across the North Atlantic.

On April 26, 1917, twenty days after Wilson declared war on Germany, Congress created the Emergency Fleet Corporation to replace more than seven million tons of Allied shipping sunk by U-boats. During the next eighteen months, the corporation impressed, built, or bought nine million tons of shipping. By the end of the war, Rear Admiral Albert Gleaves had assembled forty-five troopships and a squadron of twenty-four cruisers and other escort vessels to carry the two-million-man American Expeditionary Force (AEF) to France. During the same period, the Naval Overseas Transportation Service grew from seventy-two vessels in 1917 to a fleet of 453 ships with five thousand naval

ABOVE: In 1916, eighteen naval air cadets became the first aviators to graduate from the new Pensacola Naval Air Station in Florida. Parked in the center is the Curtiss and Wright "hydroaeroplane" on which they flew solo.

ABOVE: Marc A. Mitscher took an early interest in aviation. He learned to fly a Curtiss and Wright "hydroaeroplane" in 1916, became navy "Aviator No. 33," and during World War II became the nation's most gifted aircraft carrier commander.

Naval Aviation

World War I ushered in naval aviation. The design of aircraft changed drastically after Eugene Ely proved that planes could fly from the decks of ships. In 1916 Marc A. Mitscher, who was to command a carrier task force in the Pacific during World War II, learned to fly a Curtiss "hydroaeroplane" and became Naval Aviator No. 33. In April 1917, when the United States entered the war, the navy had thirty-nine qualified pilots, and the marines five. Between them were fifty-four planes suitable for training. During the war the Naval Air Corps grew to 2,500 officers, of which 1,656 were pilots, and 22,000 enlisted men. Those not serving on ships flew from twenty-seven bases in Europe; American aircraft carriers capable of launching aircraft on combat missions were not perfected in time for World War I.

On June 7, 1917 the first American force to reach France, other than medical teams, were seven officers and 122 men of the United States Flying Corps, products of the Naval Reserve Flying Corps. The pilots flew seaplanes, which during the war evolved from single-

ABOVE: During air operations over northern France, Lieutenant David S. Ingalls destroys a German hydrogen-filled observation balloon.

seat scouting planes to huge flying boats powered by Liberty engines built in America. More than five hundred Curtiss flying boats saw service in Europe. Navy planes escorted convoys to Scandinavian countries, flew reconnaissance missions, and attacked German U-boats. In France, the Northern Bombing Group flying out of Dunkirk struck German submarine bases at Zeebrugge and Ostend.

Navy pilots also won a few laurels. On August 21,

ABOVE: Nineteen-year-old Lieutenant David S. Ingalls, flying a British Sopwith Camel on temporary duty with 213 Squadron, RAF, scored his fifth aerial victory in northern France and became the navy's only ace in World War I.

RIGHT: Sailors and marines on the USS New Mexico (BB-40) watch with great interest as Germany's capital ships steam through the North Sea en route to Scapa Flow, Scotland, where they are to be surrendered to the Allies.

1918, Ensign Charles H. Hammann of the Naval Reserve Flying Corps, while returning from a mission over Italy, landed his flying boat on the Adriatic while under attack to pick up a downed pilot, and earned the Medal of Honor. On September 24 the same year, nineteen-year-old Lieutenant David S. Ingalls, flying a Sopwith Camel on temporary duty with Britain's Royal Air Force in northern France, scored his fifth kill and became the navy's first and only World War I ace.

Surrender of the German Fleet

On November 11, 1918, at 11:00 A.M., the cease-fire ending World War I went into effect. Ten days later, in accordance with the armistice agreement, fourteen German capital ships—nine battleships and five battle-cruisers—crossed the North Sea to be interned at the British naval base at Scapa Flow in Scotland's Orkney Islands. Thirty-three Allied dreadnoughts waited in two parallel columns six miles apart with an open lane in between. The U.S. Navy's Sixth Battle Squadron stood in line with the dreadnoughts of the Royal Navy, the men half-expecting to become engaged in the last and most horrific naval battle of World War I, but the German

Navy Medals

Until 1908 the navy had no award system for gallantry because decorations were considered a throwback to the British Empire that the colonists had left behind in 1776. After Teddy Roosevelt created a series of badges for the army in 1905, the navy followed suit and began a system of retroactive awards dating back to the Civil War.

Three major medals were awarded to sailors, all of which were officially codified after World War I.

Navy Medal of Honor: Conceived as the highest award by Secretary of the Navy Gideon Welles during the Civil War, it was first available only to enlisted men who had shown "conspicuous gallantry and intrepidity at the risk of life, above and beyond the call of duty." In 1915, Congress made naval officers eligible for the award, and in 1919 the navy adopted the Tiffany Cross version for non-combat valor. Since the Civil War, more than seven hundred and fifty sailors have received the award.

Navy Cross: The second-highest decoration in the navy went to sailors demonstrating heroism in the face of great danger but not to the extreme of those receiving the Medal of Honor. Created in 1919, more than 4,200 navy personnel have received the decoration since World War I.

Navy Distinguished Service Medal: Once the second highest navy decoration, but now the third, it is given to sailors or marines who distinguish themselves by "exceptionally meritorious service to the Government in a duty of great responsibility." Thousands have received the award.

LEFT: During World War I, sailors and flyers earned their share of Congressional Medals of Honor (pictured). The war revealed the need for other decorations, and in 1919 the navy authorized the Distinguished Service Medal and the Navy Cross.

ships passed peacefully into Scapa Flow. While the Allies discussed the disposition of the German vessels, German Vice Admiral Ludwig von Reuter scuttled the fleet. A few hours later, only smokestacks and masts marked the graves of the once powerful German Navy.

Emergence of the Aircraft Carrier

During World War I, Great Britain led the way in designing ships capable of carrying seaplanes. In 1917 the HMS *Furious*, the first prototype of the modern aircraft carrier, went to sea with Sopwith Pups fitted on skids. In 1918 the RAF commissioned the HMS *Argus*, the first carrier with an end-to-end 550-foot flight deck capable of handling wheeled aircraft. Japan quickly responded and in 1919 laid down the 7,500-ton *Hosho* with a 519-foot flight deck.

ABOVE: After Great Britain fitted out two experimental aircraft carriers during World War I, Congress grudgingly authorized the USS Langley (CV-1) and told the navy to use her to justify their request for four attack carriers.

BELOW: Commissioned on December 14, 1927, the carrier USS Lexington (CV-2), known to her crew as "Lady Lex," begins a series of trials before joining her sister ship, the USS Saratoga (CV-3), for fleet maneuvers off Guantánamo, Cuba.

ABOVE: After converting the Langley (CV-1) from the collier Jupiter, the navy stacked her deck with planes, took her to sea, proved the need for aircraft carriers, and in July 1922 obtained authorization to build the Lexington and the Saratoga.

In 1920 the U.S. Navy Board decided to get into the aircraft carrier business after Commander Kenneth Whiting, assistant director of naval aeronautics, suggested converting the collier *Jupiter* to a full flight deck carrier. On April 21, 1920, after her conversion, the navy renamed her *Langley* (CV-1), for Professor Samuel Langley of the Smithsonian Institute, who in 1898 had produced an experimental model of a flying machine that never flew. Commissioned as a carrier on March 20, 1922, *Langley's* 523-foot flight deck stretched from bow to stern with a single smokestack protruding from

YORKTOWN

ABOVE: In 1933, with an arms race heating up, Congress authorized two identical 19,800-ton aircraft carriers, the Yorktown (CV-5) (pictured) and the Enterprise (CV-6). Four years later they went into commission, serving with distinction in the Pacific.

RIGHT: Appearing at his court-martial, Brigadier General Billy Mitchell, one of the earliest advocates of air power, sacrificed his career to prove that ships, even battleships, could be sunk by aircraft armed with bombs.

the starboard beam aft. Because of her appearance, sailors called her "the old covered wagon." She was never more than an experimental carrier, and on July 1 that year, when Congress authorized the conversion of two unfinished battle-cruisers as the navy's first fast carriers—*Saratoga* (CV-3) and *Lexington* (CV-2)—*Langley* became the guinea pig for testing catapults, arresting lines, aircraft handling, and the design of carrier planes.

Between the Wars

As was customary after every war, Congress could not decide what to do with its immense battle fleet, and put most of it in mothballs. Decisions came easier when on February 6, 1922, the United States, Great Britain, Japan, France, and Italy signed the Washington Naval Treaty limiting the

construction, size, and armament of capital ships (battleships and aircraft carriers) on a ratio of 5:5:3:1¾:1¾ respectively. The Five-Power Treaty called for a ten-year moratorium ("naval holiday") on laying down vessels of more than ten thousand tons and provided for the scrapping of sixty capital ships and the limitation of capital ships to thirty-five thousand tons with 16-inch guns. Although the United States and Great Britain honored the treaty and built fewer than the number of ships allowed, Japan eventually refused to sign renewal treaties and in the 1930s began preparing for war.

In 1921, while Americans looked ahead to a century of peace, marine Lieutenant Colonel Earl H. "Pete" Ellis produced a remarkable document titled "Advance Base Operations in Micronesia," which evolved into the "Orange Plan" prepared by the navy in the event of war with Japan. When the navy sent Ellis into the Japanese-mandated islands of the Pacific to refine his observations, he mysteriously died of poisoning.

In 1921 Brigadier General William "Billy" Mitchell, chief of the U.S. Army Air Service, proved that battleships could be sunk by aircraft. Instead of placing close attention on the need to improve and perfect aircraft carrier tactics, the navy criticized Mitchell for breaking the rules of engagement by using 2,000-pound bombs

> Air power has completely superseded sea power or land power as our first line of defense.
> *General Billy Mitchell, 1921.*

instead of the agreed-upon 500-pound bombs. The Japanese took notice of the experiment and twenty years later proved its effectiveness at Pearl Harbor.

On June 16, 1933, after President Herbert Hoover cancelled further shipbuilding, President Franklin D. Roosevelt, an old navy man, took the reigns of government during the Great Depression and scrounged $238,000,000 from the National Industrial Recovery Act to build thirty-two ships over the next three years. Into the mix went the aircraft carriers *Yorktown* (CV-5) and *Enterprise* CV-6). During the six years before the 1939 outbreak of war in Europe, the navy built two more carriers, six battleships, three heavy cruisers, thirteen light cruisers, eighty-three destroyers, and thirty-eight submarines. Without them, it would have been impossible to hold a defensive line in the Pacific during the early months of 1942. Had the men of the navy been able to see the nature of the war that lay ahead, they would have built more carriers and improved the capabilities of carrier aircraft, which sadly lagged behind the speed and nimbleness of Japanese planes.

Without Roosevelt looking after the navy, Japan might still have control of the Far East, the Netherlands East Indies, and the Pacific.

ABOVE: During World War I the navy built K-, L-, R-, and O-class submarines. Like the others, the K-8 had inadequate range and could not keep up with the fleet. After receiving six German U-Boats, the navy began building the S-class.

CHAPTER 4

WORLD WAR II IN THE PACIFIC 1941–1945

RIGHT: Two months before Japan struck Pearl Harbor, the five ships of Destroyer Squadron 3 (Desron 3) of Destroyer Division 6 (Desdiv 6) lay peacefully parked at the end of a wharf at the San Diego Naval Station in California.

During June 1940 the German *blitzkrieg* overran France and created an entirely new set of problems for the United States. Ever since the mid-1920s Britain's Royal Navy had dominated the Atlantic, allowing the U.S. Navy to concentrate on monitoring Japanese activities in the Far East. Now the British government stood virtually alone against the Axis. If Great Britain were to fall, America could be faced with fighting a two-ocean war or subordinating its economic interests to those of Germany and Japan. As the price of preparedness increased, President Franklin Delano Roosevelt did not like the options, but abandoning Great Britain was not an acceptable alternative.

On June 17, 1940, Admiral Harold R. Stark appeared before Congress and asked for $4 billion, enough to double the size of the combat fleet by adding 257 ships and fifteen thousand naval aircraft. Included in the Two-Ocean Navy Bill were fast battleships, heavy cruisers, and the first ten of twenty-seven *Essex*-class aircraft carriers. On July 19 Roosevelt signed the bill. Six weeks later he sent fifty World War I destroyers to Great Britain in exchange for the use of British bases. Meanwhile the threat from Japan only intensified.

> Before we're through with 'em the Japanese language will only be spoken in hell!
> *Admiral William F. Halsey, USN.*

Japanese Imperialism

In 1931 Japan took the first step toward world war by invading Manchuria in northeast Asia. Six years later the Japanese broke the arms limitation treaty and began building the largest and most modern navy in the Pacific, including ten aircraft carriers and the 68,000-ton battleships *Yamato* and *Musashi,* both armed with 18.1-inch guns. Japan also built a huge army, and in 1937 invaded Mainland China. After four years of fighting, Japan needed new sources for oil and minerals, and during the summer of 1941 the Imperial Japanese Army (IJA) occupied Indochina to establish bases for launching strikes into the oil-rich islands of Malaysia and the Dutch East Indies.

On March 27, 1941, six months after Japan signed a tripartite pact with Germany and Italy, the United States signed the ABC-1 staff agreement with Great Britain. The latter pact stipulated that if the United States became

LEFT: *During the Pearl Harbor strike, a Japanese bomb pierces the deck of the destroyer USS* Shaw *(DD-373) and tears the ship to pieces after exploding in the magazine.*

drawn into the war, efforts would first be directed to defeating Germany. In the interim the U.S. Atlantic Fleet would render immediate assistance to the Royal Navy in safeguarding convoys. Through an active Japanese espionage network in the United States, Admiral Osami Nagano, chief of the Imperial Japanese Navy's general staff, learned of the U.S. agreement to attack Germany first and decided to attack the Philippines before Roosevelt changed his mind. During discussions among the general staff, Admiral Isoroku Yamamoto, commander in chief of the Imperial Japanese Navy, proposed sending a carrier force to first destroy the U.S. Pacific Fleet at Pearl Harbor, thereby ridding the Pacific of Japan's only menace. "If we are to have war with America," he cautioned, "we will have no hope of winning unless the U.S. fleet in Hawaiian waters can be destroyed."

Yamamoto believed that, with the Pacific Fleet crippled, Japan would have an uncontested period of six months to seize a vast section of the Far East and the Pacific. Although he questioned the wisdom of attacking the United States, he calculated that Americans might lack the will to sustain a two-ocean war.

Remember Pearl Harbor

On November 26, 1941, a Japanese strike force under the command of Vice Admiral Chuichi Nagumo steamed from the Kurile Islands with two battleships, three cruisers, sixteen destroyers, and six carriers jammed with four hundred and twenty-five fighters, dive-bombers, and torpedo planes. The timetable had been carefully set. Nagumo's squadron would arrive two hundred and fifty miles north of the island of Oahu, Hawaii, before dawn on December 7.

On November 27 Admiral Husband E. Kimmel, commanding the U.S. Pacific Fleet, received a message from Admiral Stark: "Japan is expected to make an

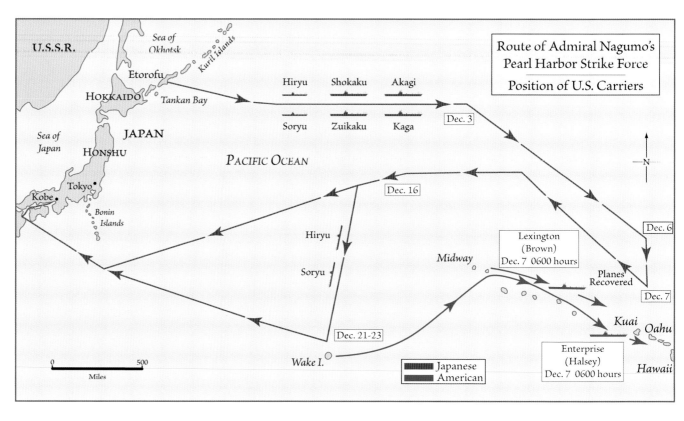

aggressive move within the next few days." The warning mentioned the Philippines and the Dutch East Indies. Because Stark omitted Hawaii, Kimmel failed to put Pearl Harbor on alert. By dumb luck, Kimmel happened to have the carriers *Lexington* (CV-2) and *Enterprise* (CV-6) at sea delivering aircraft to Wake and Midway Islands, and a third carrier, the *Saratoga* (CV-3), on the West Coast for maintenance. The rest of the Pacific Fleet, eighty-six combat and auxiliary ships, lay tranquilly anchored in neat order on the oil-slicked waters of Pearl Harbor.

At 7:40 A.M., December 7, 1941, the first Japanese wave of forty-five Zero fighters, a hundred and four Val dive-bombers, and forty Kate torpedo planes droned over Oahu. At 7:55, while Zeroes strafed Wheeler, Ewa, and Hickam airfields, torpedo planes swung around Pearl Harbor and at forty feet above the water approached Kimmel's venerable battleships. Behind the Kates came dive–bombers, swooping down from two thousand feet. An hour later a second wave of thirty-six

fighters and a hundred and thirty-five dive-bombers appeared over the island, adding to the devastation. By 9:00 A.M. the battleships of the once proud Pacific Fleet lay burning.

Of eight battleships in the harbor, five sank. Only three, *Pennsylvania* (BB-38), *Maryland* (BB-46), and *Tennessee* (BB-43), were able to limp to the West Coast under their own power. Struck by a bomb that detonated her magazine, the *Arizona* (BB-33) blew up, killing 1,103 of 1,400 men on board. *Oklahoma* (BB-37) capsized, taking 415 of her 1,354 officers to the bottom. *California* (BB-44), *West Virginia* (BB-48), and *Nevada* (BB-36)—the only battleship to get underway—settled to their superstructures. Of two hundred and two serviceable navy planes on Oahu, only fifty-two could fly. Altogether, 2,403 American servicemen were killed and 1,178 wounded. Naval personnel suffered the greatest loss.

The Japanese gravely underestimated the psychological effect the sneak attack would have on Americans.

LEFT: *After being clobbered by Japanese bombs and torpedoes, the USS Arizona (BB-39) is engulfed in flames and lists to starboard just before a bomb detonates her forward magazine and sends her to the bottom.*

FAR LEFT TOP: *After taking several hits during the Japanese attack on Pearl Harbor, the USS Nevada (BB-36) made a courageous run from her berth in Battleship Row. Her crew finally beached the ship to keep her from sinking and blocking the harbor.*

FAR LEFT CENTER: *Smothered in smoke and her decks shattered with debris, the battleship West Virginia (BB-48) slowly sinks. A small rescue boat approaches, looking for bodies and survivors who may have escaped the holocaust.*

FAR LEFT BOTTOM: *Japanese pilots targeted the battleships first, which gave the heavy cruiser USS Phoenix (CL-46) an opportunity to get underway in the harbor and find enough maneuvering room to avoid serious damage.*

President Roosevelt called December 7 "a day that will live in infamy," partly because Nagumo's planes attacked Pearl Harbor an hour before Japanese envoys terminated diplomatic relations with the United States. Instead of demoralizing the people, as Japan had hoped, the attack galvanized the nation, and "Remember Pearl Harbor" became the battle cry.

> In all my fifty years of public service, I have never seen a document with infamous falsehoods and distortions…on a scale so huge that I never imagined until today that any government on this planet was capable of them.
> *Secretary of State Cordell Hull to Japanese Ambassador Kichisaburo Nomura, December 7, 1941.*

Revitalizing the Navy

Japan had planned well and caught the United States poorly prepared for war. A few days after attacking Pearl Harbor, Japanese forces landed on the Philippines and Guam, but were temporarily repulsed at Wake Island. Guam fell on December 10 and Wake Island surrendered thirteen days later. General Douglas MacArthur's forces on the Philippines withdrew to the Bataan Peninsula and for several days fought against time.

President Roosevelt realized something had to be done to revitalize the navy and restore confidence. On December 17, after a hurried review of what went wrong at Pearl Harbor, CNO Admiral Stark relieved Kimmel at Roosevelt's request and recalled him to Washington. Kimmel had been struck in the chest by a spent bullet during the attack. Later he lamented, "Too bad it didn't kill me."

Three days later Stark, again at Roosevelt's request, named sixty-three-year-old Admiral Ernest J. King commander-in-chief, U.S. Fleet. In March, King would take Stark's job and wear a second hat, chief of naval operations, making him the navy's ranking officer. Few men had King's experience. He had been an aviator, a submariner, a carrier division commander, chief of the Bureau of Aeronautics, and commander-in-chief of the Atlantic Fleet.

One of King's first decisions involved the replacement of Kimmel in the Pacific. On December 31, King jumped fifty-six-year-old Admiral Chester W. Nimitz over the heads of twenty-eight senior officers and named him commander-in-chief, U.S. Pacific Fleet. As naval historian Samuel Eliot Morrison observed, two more dissimilar men could not have been chosen. He described King as "a hard man with little sense of humor…more respected than liked in the Navy," and

The way to victory is long. The going will be hard. We will do the best we can with what we've got. We must have more planes and ships—at once. Then it will be our turn to strike. We will win through—in time.

Admiral King, on being named commander-in-chief, U.S. Fleet.

Nimitz as "the most accessible, considerate and beloved of fleet commanders." Despite a great contrast in personalities and the distance between them—King in Washington and Nimitz at Pearl Harbor—they complemented each other on matters involving strategy.

Fighting Back

Nimitz found that six of the damaged battleships in Pearl Harbor—*California, Maryland, Nevada, Pennsylvania, Tennessee*, and *West Virginia*—could be repaired, but until they were he would have to depend upon aircraft carriers and cruisers. Admiral King drew a line on the map of the Pacific that began at Midway and tracked south through the Marshall and Gilbert Islands to Australia. Pointing to everything east of the line, which included Samoa and the Fijis, he told Nimitz to "hold what you've got and hit them where you can." Nimitz turned loose Vice Admiral William F. Halsey's task force, formed around the *Enterprise* and the *Yorktown* (CV-5). On February 1, 1942, planes from *Enterprise* struck Japanese air bases at Kwajalein in the Mar-

Admiral Chester W. Nimitz (1885–1966)

Chester William Nimitz grew up in Fredericksburg, Texas, and in 1905 graduated from the U.S. Naval Academy. He spent his early career commanding submarines, developing diesel engine technology, and during World War I he commanded the Atlantic Fleet's submarine division. In 1938 he commanded of a cruiser division, became a rear admiral, and in 1939 took charge of a battleship division. During his career, Nimitz had been short-changed in only one command category—aircraft carriers—which had become the portable airfields of the seas, and World War II in the Pacific would be all about aircraft carriers.

On December 17, 1941, after Admiral King completed his inquest on the lack of vigilance at Pearl Harbor, he named Admiral Nimitz commander-in-chief of the Pacific Fleet. Despite Nimitz's lack of experience with aircraft carriers, King picked the right man. Nimitz had also been the choice of Admiral Stark, who King replaced. King and Nimitz shared a common characteristic—they were both brilliant strategists and tacticians, despite having distinctly different personalities. Nimitz, a battleship man, was amiable and sociable; King, a carrier man, could only be blunt. "Ernie King always thought he was God Almighty," one officer recalled. Yet the two admirals made one of the greatest teams in naval history.

When a navy flying boat landed Nimitz on debris-strewn Pearl Harbor, he expressed deep dismay, muttering, "This is a horrible sight." His task was daunting. He had to swiftly reorganize the loose defensive structure of the Hawaiian Islands, repair and rebuild the shattered Pacific Fleet, and find a way to check the advance of Japanese forces, which had already invaded the Philippines, captured

Guam and Wake Island, were plunging into Malaysia, and headed towards the Dutch East Indies, New Guinea, and the Solomon Islands.

On March 30, 1942, Admiral King unified Nimitz's command to include all the sea, land, and air forces in the Pacific Ocean area. Samuel Eliot Morrison credited Nimitz with having "an almost impeccable judgment of men, and a genius for making prompt, firm, decisions." By capitalizing on the superb naval intelligence cryptanalysts at Pearl Harbor, Nimitz designed the strategy and chose the men that ultimately defeated Japan.

ABOVE: Admiral Chester W. Nimitz (center) was not a man to sit in his office at Pearl Harbor. He was often at sea boosting carrier pilots' morale, often flying from one carrier to another to do so.

RIGHT: The destroyer USS Fanning (DD-385), part of Vice Admiral William F. "Bull" Halsey's Task Force 16, guards the carriers transporting Lieutenant Colonel James H. Doolittle's B-25 Mitchell bombers within range of Japan.

RIGHT: The destroyer USS Fanning (DD-385), part of Vice Admiral William F. "Bull" Halsey's Task Force 16, guards the carriers transporting Lieutenant Colonel James H. Doolittle's B-25 Mitchell bombers within range of Japan.

shall Islands while the *Yorktown* hit the Gilberts. Halsey swung the *Enterprise* north and on returning to Pearl Harbor bombed Japanese positions on Wake Island and Marcus Island. *Yorktown* joined Vice Admiral Wilson Brown's task force, which included the carrier *Lexington*, twelve Allied cruisers and sixteen American destroyers. Brown intended to strike the Japanese base at Rabaul in the Solomons but turned back after being spotted by

enemy planes. In the dogfight that followed, Lieutenant Edward H. "Butch" O'Hare, flying a Grumman F4F Wildcat, shot down five Kate torpedo planes, thus becoming the navy's first ace in World War II and its first recipient of the Medal of Honor in the war.

Carrier strikes were mere pinpricks in the Pacific but made good publicity at home. More serious problems were developing in the Dutch East Indies. In December 1941, Admiral Thomas C. Hart, commanding the U.S. Asiatic Squadron, had lost his base when the Japanese invaded the Philippines. Hart withdrew to the Dutch East Indies and on January 15 became part of the ABDA (American, British, Dutch, and Australian) command formally established to defend the southwest Pacific. Before the motley array of old warships—nine cruisers, twenty-six destroyers, and thirty-nine submarines—could unify communications, two powerful Japanese squadrons entered the area and began landing troops on Borneo.

On the night of January 24, 1942, Commander Paul Talbot, with four old American destroyers—*John D. Ford, Parrott, Paul Jones,* and *Pope*—sighted Japanese transports putting troops ashore on Balikpapan. Silhouetted by burning oil tanks ashore, the Japanese ships made good targets. With Hart's approval, the

U.S. Navy Ship Designations

AO	Oiler
BB	Battleship
C	Cruiser
CA	Heavy Cruiser
CL	Light Cruiser
CV	Fleet Aircraft Carrier
CVA	Attack Aircraft Carrier
CVE	Escort Aircraft Carrier
CVL	Light Aircraft Carrier
DD	Destroyer
DE	Destroyer Escort
PT	Motor Torpedo Boat
SS	Submarine

four-pipers dashed into Makassar Strait, launched torpedoes, fired 4-inch projectiles, and scurried away after sinking four transports and a patrol boat. On February 4 Japanese aircraft replied and severely damaged the ABDA division under Dutch commander Rear Admiral Karel Doorman. By March 1, the Japanese had finished off the balance of the ABDA force in a series of air and sea encounters. America's first carrier, the *Langley*, now designated as an aviation transport, became caught in the melee and was sunk by Japanese planes near Java.

The Tokyo Surprise

The most spectacular of the early American raids occurred when Colonel James H. Doolittle and his army pilots flew sixteen twin-engined B-25 bombers off the flight deck of Captain Marc A. Mitscher's carrier *Hornet* (CV-8) and headed towards Tokyo. Army planes were chosen because no navy bomber had the range. Naval officers trained Doolittle's men in short takeoffs but not deck landings, so the game plan was for the B-25 pilots to fly another eleven hundred miles after bombing Tokyo and land in China. Halsey used the *Enterprise* task force (TF-16) to provide defensive cover because *Hornet* had no room on deck for fighters to fly combat air patrol (CAP). Halsey's mission was to get the *Hornet* within five hundred miles of Tokyo before launching Doolittle's bombers, but Japanese picket ships discovered the task force. Halsey could not afford to lose his carriers, so Doolittle launched the bombers from further out, 668 miles from Japan. The greater distance unfortunately cut deeply into the bombers' chances of reaching China.

At 8:24 A.M., April 18, the first B-25 wobbled off the deck of the *Hornet* as tense observers stood by. Flying low over Tokyo, Yokohama, Kobe, and Nagoya with 2,000-pound payloads, Doolittle's raiders achieved complete surprise. The psychological effect of the raid overshadowed the small amount of damage done. It

LEFT: On board the carrier USS Hornet (CV-0), Lieutenant Colonel Doolittle (standing left) and Rear Admiral Marc A. Mitscher (standing right) pose with the pilots and crews of the B-25s about to make the first air attack on Tokyo.

boosted American morale and embarrassed Japan's Imperial General Headquarters, which had promised but failed to keep the home islands safe from attack. The Japanese searched in vain to locate the B-25 base. In a radio broadcast, Roosevelt claimed the bombers flew from "Shangri-La," the fictional Tibetan hideaway in James Hilton's popular novel, *Lost Horizons*.

BELOW: On April 18, 1942, the first army B-25 takes off from the USS Hornet (CV-8) in the first U. S. air strike on Japan. Fifteen Mitchells will land or crash-land in occupied China, and one will seek refuge in Vladivostok, USSR.

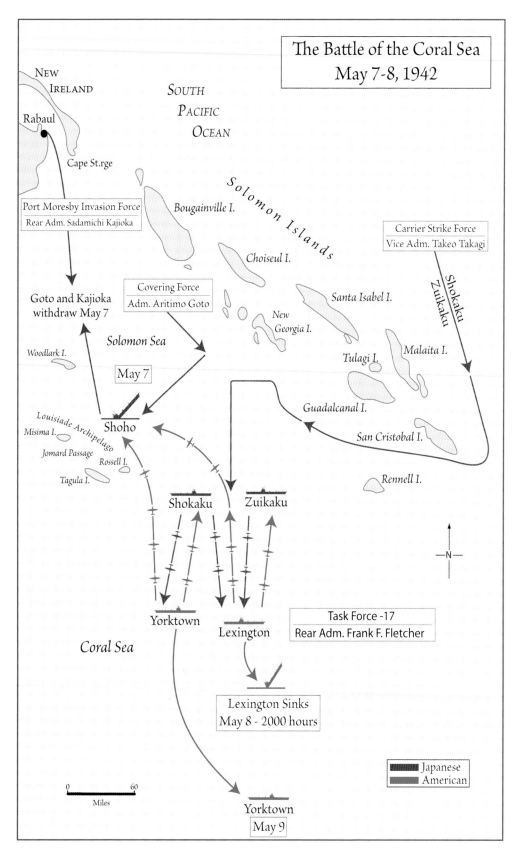

The Battle of the Coral Sea
May 7-8, 1942

NEW IRELAND

Rabaul

Cape St.rge

SOUTH PACIFIC OCEAN

Port Moresby Invasion Force
Rear Adm. Sadamichi Kajioka

Bougainville I.

Solomon Islands

Carrier Strike Force
Vice Adm. Takeo Takagi

Choiseul I.

Shokaku
Zuikaku

Goto and Kajioka withdraw May 7

Covering Force
Adm. Aritimo Goto

Santa Isabel I.

Solomon Sea

New Georgia I.

Woodlark I.

May 7

Tulagi I.

Malaita I.

Louisiade Archipelago
Misima I.

Shoho

Guadalcanal I.

Jomard Passage

Rossell I.

San Cristobal I.

Tagula I.

Shokaku   Zuikaku

Rennell I.

—N—

Yorktown

Lexington

Task Force -17
Rear Adm. Frank F. Fletcher

Coral Sea

Lexington Sinks
May 8 - 2000 hours

0   60
Miles

Japanese
American

Yorktown

May 9

Stepping up the Ante

Flush with victory in the Dutch East Indies, Japanese strategists turned their attention to a campaign that would extend their conquests to the Solomon Islands and New Guinea, thus providing them with a launching platform into Australia. American cryptanalysts at Pearl Harbor, however, had broken the Japanese naval code and learned the enemy intended to attack Port Moresby, New Guinea, with a large amphibious force.

Nimitz worked fast. He mustered all the ships he could spare from the Pacific Fleet and in early May sent them to Rear Admiral Frank J. Fletcher, commanding the *Yorktown* group, and to Rear Admiral Aubrey W. Fitch, commanding the *Lexington* group. Fletcher formed Task Force 17 (TF-17) around the two carrier groups and spent two days searching the Coral Sea southwest of Guadalcanal for the Japanese amphibious force. On May 7 search planes over the Solomon Sea spotted a carrier among a Japanese squadron screening the column of troop transports. A few hours later, dive-bombers from the *Lexington* and *Yorktown* sank the Japanese light carrier *Shoho*.

Scratch one flattop! Dixon to carrier,
scratch one flattop!
*Lieutenant Commander Robert E. Dixon
on destroying the Shoho.*

The following morning aircraft from TF-17 located a second Japanese squadron in the Coral Sea with two heavy carriers, the *Shokaku* and the *Zuikaku*. Japanese planes had also spotted Fletcher's carriers. All four carriers launched attacks at roughly the same time, leaving only a few fighters behind for CAP. Navy dive-bombers damaged *Shokaku*'s flight deck, forcing her returning planes to ditch, but Japanese dive-bombers damaged *Yorktown* and *Lexington*. With all four carriers damaged, both squadrons withdrew, but later two tor-pedoes launched from a Japanese submarine finished off the gallant old *Lexington*. Captain Frederick C. Sherman ordered her abandoned, saving most of the ship's three thousand men.

Though the Japanese destroyed the greater tonnage by sinking *Lexington*, the Battle of the Coral Sea scored as an American victory because the fight turned back the Port Moresby invasion force. Startled by the loss of the *Shoho* and damage to the *Shokaku* and *Zuikaku*, the Japanese commander, Vice Admiral Takeo Takagi, limped back to Truk for repairs. The battle marked the first major naval action in history where surface ships never exchanged a shot. The Coral Sea affair also produced consequences for the Japanese by depriving Yamamoto of the services of *Shokaku* and *Zuikaku* in the forthcoming Battle of Midway.

FAR LEFT: *Often called the "Battle of Errors" because of many mistakes made, the Battle of the Coral Sea did turn back the Port Moresby Invasion Force and inflicted enough damage on Japanese carriers to prevent them from participating in the forthcoming Battle of Midway.*

LEFT: *During the battle of the Coral Sea, on May 8, 1942, bombers and torpedo planes from the Shokaku and Zuikako strike the USS Lexington (CV-2), igniting gasoline and smothering her in smoke and flames.*

LEFT: *A destroyer rushes to the side of the burning USS Lexington (CV-2) to haul survivors from the Coral Sea. During the afternoon of May 8, 1942, carrier escorts pulled 2,735 sailors from the Lexington to safety.*

The Battle of Midway

The repulse in the Coral Sea disturbed Yamamoto. He had wanted one great naval battle to remove the menace of the U.S. Pacific Fleet and bring the war to a victorious conclusion. This could not be accomplished without the destruction of the American carriers. New American battleships were already going into commission, *South Dakota* (BB-57) in March, *Indiana* (BB-58) in April, and *Massachusetts* (BB-59) in May, but it was the *Essex*-class carriers in production that troubled the Japanese admiral more. So in early May, Yamamoto conceived a complex plan to expand the Japanese defensive perimeter by seizing the island of Midway, eleven hundred and fifty miles west of Honolulu, thereby drawing out and destroying the remnants of the Pacific Fleet.

Once again, through hard work and deception, Commander Joseph J. Rochefort's Pearl Harbor code-breakers discovered Yamamoto's plans. Nimitz responded with alacrity and ordered Fletcher's TF-17 with *Yorktown* and Halsey's TF-16 with *Enterprise* and *Hornet* to Midway.

Battle Forces at Midway

	U.S.	Japan
Aircraft Carriers	3	6
Carrier Aircraft	233	303
Battleships	0	11
Cruisers	8	12
Destroyers	14	46
Seaplane Carriers	0	2

Yamamoto also sent a diversionary force to attack the Aleutians in an effort to compel Nimitz to take counter-measures and possibly draw the Pacific Fleet away from Midway. Nimitz retained a few cruisers to delude Yamamoto into believing the bait had been taken.

Nagumo's carrier strike force—*Akagi, Kaga, Hiryu,* and *Soryu*—had been reduced from six to four flattops because *Shokaku* and *Zuikaku* had been damaged in the Coral Sea. Nimitz had intended that Halsey lead the task force, but the admiral became hospitalized with a bout of shingles. With some reluctance, Nimitz put fifty-five-year-old Vice Admiral Raymond A. Spruance, a cruiser man, in charge of Halsey's TF-16. So on the morning of June 4, 1942, the only three serviceable American carriers in the Pacific were searching for Nagumo's carriers when Midway reported the first wave of Japanese strike planes approaching.

At sunup, a PBY search plane spotted Nagumo's carrier strike force two hundred miles northwest of Midway. Nagumo also had planes searching to the east, looking for the Pacific Fleet, but mechanical problems delayed the aircraft assigned to the sector occupied by the American carriers. Feeling reasonably secure, Nagumo launched his planes against installations on Midway. While antiquated navy and marine aircraft at Midway met the Japanese air attack, search planes from *Yorktown* obtained a fix on Nagumo's carriers. About this time Japanese planes began returning to their car-

BELOW: *During the Battle of Midway on June 4, 1942, the aircraft carrier USS* Enterprise *(CV-6) steams at high speed toward the point of recovery for incoming aircraft.*

Admiral Raymond Ames Spruance (1886–1969)

Born in Baltimore, Maryland, Spruance graduated from the U.S. Naval Academy in 1906 and served with Admiral George Dewey in the round-the-world voyage of the Great White Fleet. During World War I he served first at sea and later in staff assignments. Promoted to rear admiral in 1939, Spruance continued working with gunships and, at the outbreak of World War II, commanded Cruiser Division 5 of the Pacific Fleet. Though Spruance had virtually no experience with aircraft carriers or air tactics, Admiral Nimitz put him in charge of Halsey's task force (TF-16) after the latter fell ill.

Spruance's performance during the Battle of Midway earned him a third star and made him among the top fleet commanders in the Pacific. Some questioned whether Spruance ever completely understood the tactical aspects of America's growing fleet of fast attack carriers, but the admiral's distinguished record of success in the island-hopping campaigns leading up to the Marianas assault marked him as a man of superb administrative, organizational, and strategic ability. Those who knew Spruance best described him as a quiet and unassuming, extremely effective fleet commander who in tense situations always remained composed and unruffled.

Spruance earned his fourth star in 1944, after which he directed operations at Iwo Jima and Okinawa. Before retirement in 1948, Spruance spent his postwar years as president of the Naval War College.

LEFT: Admiral Chester W. Nimitz (center) stands on the deck of the battleship USS New Jersey (BB-62) with Admiral Raymond A. Spruance (left) and Rear Admiral Forrest P. Sherman (right) during discussions about future operations in the Pacific.

riers. As Nagumo prepared another air assault on Midway, a Japanese search plane reported a single carrier, Fletcher's *Yorktown*, to the east. Nagumo now had a dilemma. With another wave beginning to return from Midway, he paused to consider whether to change the ordnance on the planes on the flight deck to attack *Yorktown* instead of Midway. He had just begun the changeover when planes from *Enterprise* and *Yorktown* appeared over the Japanese carriers. During the next hour, and with amazingly good luck, the Spruance-Fletcher strike force sank Nagumo's four carriers. *Hiryu*, the last Japanese carrier to go down, managed to get off enough planes to severely damage the *Yorktown*. Spruance attempted to save Fletcher's *Yorktown*, but a Japanese submarine finished her off.

Having lost four carriers, all his planes, and a number of other vessels, Yamamoto turned solemnly away and

LEFT: After snuffing out most of the fires on the USS Yorktown (CV-5), sailors make a valiant attempt to keep her afloat, but a prowling Japanese submarine frustrated their efforts by finishing her off with two torpedoes.

RIGHT: In an effort to save the listing USS Yorktown, destroyers converge with more fire-fighting equipment and to take off the wounded.

RIGHT: In an effort to save the listing USS Yorktown, destroyers converge with more fire-fighting equipment and to take off the wounded.

withdrew to Japan. The Imperial Japanese Navy had not been defeated since 1592, and Yamamoto understood the consequences of failing at Midway. The U.S. Navy had prevailed. He had predicted in September 1940 that if America could not be driven out of the Pacific in six to twelve months, the war for Japan would become one of attrition. Exactly six months had passed since Pearl Harbor, and at Midway the attrition began.

Guadalcanal

On July 2, 1942, Admiral King unleashed Nimitz and told him to go on the offensive in the Pacific. The decision came three weeks before the Japanese landed on the northeastern coast of New Guinea, from where they planned to cross the Owen Stanley Mountains and attack Port Moresby. King wanted to capture Japanese-held territory suitable for the construction of airfields somewhere near the outer perimeter of enemy penetration in the Solomon Islands. The Joint Chiefs of Staff (JCS) approved King's plan to employ Major General Alexander Vandegrift's 1st Marine Division, already en route to the South Pacific, in an amphibious assault against Guadalcanal and the small Japanese seaplane bases across Sealark Channel at Tulagi, Gavutu, and Tanambogo. Nimitz put Rear Admiral Richmond

ABOVE: Vice Admiral Richmond Kelly Turner, whose fiery temper earned him the nickname "Terrible Turner," commanded the amphibious forces that put the marines ashore on Guadalcanal in August 1942 and for many of the later campaigns.

Kelly Turner in charge of amphibious operations and Admiral Fletcher in charge of the strike force.

On August 7, the 1st Marine Division, supported by planes from the *Enterprise, Saratoga,* and *Wasp* (CV-7), and the services of the new battleship *North Carolina* (BB-55), six cruisers, and sixteen destroyers, landed nineteen thousand men from seventy-five ships on Guadalcanal and the three small islands across the channel. It marked the first amphibious undertaking by the U.S.

Navy since 1898 and went off smoothly because it took the Japanese completely by surprise. The enemy on Guadalcanal, numbering no more than two thousand, fled, abandoning a partially completed airstrip. Next day, marines secured the Japanese seaplane bases on Tulagi, Gavutu, and Tanambogo. Ten days later the first marine F4F Wildcats touched down on Guadalcanal's newly named Henderson Field. Over the next six months, the Japanese would expend all the military and naval resources they could spare to retake Guadalcanal.

At Guadalcanal, Admiral Fletcher made a tactical mistake that would haunt him for the rest of his life.

After delivering the marines to Guadalcanal, he worried about being attacked by Japanese planes from Rabaul and pulled his carriers out of harm's way. On orders from Yamamoto, Vice Admiral Gunichi Mikawa came through "the Slot" in the Solomon Sea on the night of August 8 and sank four of Fletcher's cruisers and damaged a fifth, without losing a ship. The attack forced Admiral Turner's virtually defenseless amphibious squadron to withdraw before moving all the provisions and ammunition ashore, leaving the marines in a perilous situation for weeks without adequate supplies or naval protection.

Mikawa did not get away cleanly. On August 9 Commander John R. Moore in the antique submarine *S-44* (SS-155), commissioned in 1925, sent a spread of torpedoes into the heavy cruiser *Kako,* marking the sinking of the first major Japanese warship by an American submarine.

Naval Operations in the Solomons

After marines landed on Guadalcanal, hell broke loose in the Solomons. The Japanese vowed to win back the island and began drawing military and naval reinforcements from other areas. Yamamoto organized a two-prong strategy for driving the marines off Guadalcanal

LEFT: The USS North Carolina (BB-55) was the first battleship to go into commission since 1923 and the first to reach the South Pacific after the devastating attack on Pearl Harbor.

I'll never forget it: One minute we were too limp with malaria to crawl out of our foxholes; the next, we were running around whooping like kids.

One officer's response to news that Halsey was taking over the South Pacific Fleet, quoted from E. B. Potter, Nimitz, *198.*

ABOVE: The Japanese submarine I-19 interrupted a Guadalcanal-bound convoy by firing a spread of torpedoes into the carrier USS Wasp (CV-7) and set her on fire, forcing her commander, Captain Forrest P. Sherman, to abandon her.

RIGHT: During the naval battle of Guadalcanal on November 14-15, 1942, land-based carrier planes from Henderson Field pulverized Admiral Raizo Tanaka's Tokyo Express, a convoy of transports attempting to reinforce Guadalcanal.

and ridding the Solomons of American warships. Using two squadrons coming from different directions, he sent Admiral Nagumo's three carriers with three battleships down the eastern Solomons, and a cruiser-destroyer force with three transports carrying fifteen hundred troops down the Slot. On August 24 Admiral Fletcher's task force, consisting of the carriers *Enterprise*, *Saratoga*, and *Wasp*, and the battleship *North Carolina*, clashed with Nagumo's strike force during the Battle of the Eastern Solomons. Although planes from the *Enterprise* sank the light carrier *Ryujo*, Fletcher had mishandled the tactics by having sent the *Wasp* away to refuel on the eve of battle, which depleted air cover and enabled Nagumo's planes to damage the *Enterprise*. Fletcher succeeded in turning back the Japanese strike force but lost the opportunity to destroy it.

On October 18, 1942, Nimitz put Vice Admiral Halsey in charge of the South Pacific and recalled Admiral Robert L. Ghormley, the area commander, and

Fletcher, the fleet commander. During the same period, Yamamoto marshaled Japan's Combined Fleet of four carriers, four battleships, fourteen cruisers, and forty-four destroyers to settle the naval issue in the Solomons. The *Wasp* had been torpedoed on September 15, and the loss cut the number of Halsey's carriers to two. Once again informed by Pearl Harbor's code-breakers of Yamamoto's plans, on October 26-27 Halsey met Nagumo's strike force off Santa Cruz Islands with the two carriers *Enterprise* and *Hornet,* the new battleship *South Dakota* (BB-57), six cruisers, and fourteen destroyers. During the Battle of Santa Cruz Islands, Halsey lost the *Hornet* but severely damaged the Japan-

ese carriers *Shokaku* and *Zuiho,* and the heavy cruiser *Chikuma,* and shot down more than a hundred enemy planes. Nagumo won the tactical battle but lost the strategic victory by turning back and leaving Halsey in possession of the South Pacific and Guadalcanal.

On November 12 Yamamoto tried once more to reinforce Guadalcanal. In early morning darkness, Admiral Hiroaki Abe's so-called Tokyo Express, led by the battleships *Hiei* and *Kirishima,* steamed down the Slot to shell American positions on Guadalcanal and put ten thousand fresh troops ashore near Henderson Field. Halsey had no ships in the area other than Rear Admiral Daniel J. Callaghan's two heavy cruisers, three light cruisers, and eight destroyers. Callaghan spotted the Japanese force off Lunga Point and courageously offered battle, informing his skippers, "We want the big ones." Callaghan lost his life trying to sink the *Hiei* with his flagship, the cruiser *San Francisco* (CA-38), in what Admiral King described as "one of the most furious sea battles ever fought." Though the battle lasted only twenty-four minutes, Callaghan's division cut through the wedge-shaped enemy formation and compelled the overwhelmingly superior Japanese squadron to turn away without shelling Guadalcanal. Callaghan lost two cruisers, three destroyers, and his life. In the morning, planes from *Enterprise* located the crippled *Hiei* and sank her.

Two days later Yamamoto tried once again and sent ships through the Slot with ten thousand troops loaded into eleven high-speed transports. American planes sank six of the transports and damaged a seventh. In a separate action, Rear Admiral Willis A. Lee's Task Force 64, formed around the battleships *South Dakota* and *Washington* (BB-56) and four destroyers, met the Japanese battle group shortly before midnight and sank the battleship *Kirishima*. On December 31, Imperial General Headquarters conceded defeat and arranged to take the remaining Japanese troops off Guadalcanal, but thousands withered away on the island and died of disease in the jungle.

U.S. Navy Carrier Aircraft

Squadrons on fleet aircraft carriers consisted of fighters (VF), dive-bombers (VSB), torpedo planes (VT), and observation planes (VS). At the beginning of the war, the fighters were F4F-3 or F4F-4 Grumman Wildcats powered by 1,100-horsepower engines that delivered a top speed of 298mph. Wildcats carried six .50-caliber machine guns and an external bomb load of two hundred pounds. In mid-1942 Grumman F6F Hellcats began replacing Wildcats and became the carrier pilot's preferred fighter. An F6F-5 Hellcat generated a maximum speed of 380mph, carried ten .50-caliber machine guns, and either a 1,000-pound bomb load or six 5-inch rockets.

The two-man Douglas Dauntless SBD dive-bombers became the most important aircraft in the navy's inventory at the beginning of the war. Every fleet carrier had a VS squadron of Dauntlesses for scouting and bombing and a VSB squadron strictly for bombing. At the beginning of the war the navy flew Douglas SBD-3s, which by 1944 were progressively improved to SBD-6s. Speeds remained around 250mph, but load capacity improved from 1,000 to 2,250 pounds of bombs or depth charges. When in 1943 the slightly faster Curtiss SB2C Helldivers became available, many navy pilots still preferred flying a Dauntless.

The worst carrier aircraft during the early months of the war were Douglas Devastator TBD-1 torpedo planes, which were slow (221mph) and carried either one torpedo or 1,200 pounds of bombs. In 1943, General Motors began replacing Devastators with three-man TBM-3 Avengers, which could fly at 272mph and carry one torpedo or 2,000 pounds of bombs. Many TBMs were later fitted with search radar and adapted for night fighting.

Although American carrier aircraft had neither the range nor the speed of most Japanese planes, the armored cockpits, protected oil and fuel lines, and other safety features kept the pilots and planes flying while Japanese aircraft often burst into flames after being struck.

ABOVE: The carrier USS** Monterey **(CV-26), commissioned on June 17, 1943, begins exercising her aircraft squadrons in preparation for orders directing her to U.S. Fifth Fleet in the Pacific.

ABOVE: The gull-winged Chance-Vought F-4U Corsair became the finest navy fighter developed during the war. Because of the aircraft's speed, carriers had trouble handling the plane, so the Marine Corps took the Corsairs and the navy kept the Hellcats.

Admiral Isoroku Yamamoto (1884–1943)

In 1941, few Japanese officers understood the American culture better than Yamamoto. After graduating from the Japanese Naval Academy in 1904 and fighting in the 1905 Russo-Japanese War, he attended the U.S. Naval War College, studied at Harvard University, and became Japan's naval attaché in Washington. Being a skillful gambler gave him an opportunity to study the American mind. He also understood America's immense untapped industrial capacity, and in September 1941 he warned Japanese Prince Kanoye, "If I am to fight regardless of consequences, I shall run wild considerably for the first six months or a year, but I have utterly no confidence for the second or third year." On December 7, 1942, on the eve of Japan abandoning Guadalcanal, the second year of the war in the Pacific began. For Yamamoto, the end came swiftly.

In April 1943, Pearl Harbor cryptanalysts decoded a transmission containing Yamamoto's itinerary for a planned inspection tour of Japan's naval forces. When Nimitz received the information, he said, "It's down in Halsey's bailiwick. If there's a way he'll find it." Admiral Mitscher, commanding Air Solomons, arranged a reception. On April 18, sixteen Lockheed P-38 Lightnings from Henderson Field intercepted two bombers that were transporting Yamamoto and his staff to Kahili, Buin, and shot them down, killing everyone on board. More than six months passed before the Japanese appointed a successor. Yamamoto's death knocked the aggressiveness out of the Japanese Navy. Oddly enough, Yamamoto's successor, Admiral Mineichi Koga, suggested that the Americans had broken the Japanese code, but Imperial General Headquarters insisted the code was unbreakable. Yamamoto did not live to see the rapid collapse of the Japanese Empire, which after a year of war he had predicted.

ABOVE: Admiral Isoroku Yamamoto masterminded Japanese naval strategy. He warned that Japan could not prevail without destroying the U.S. Pacific Fleet, and planned the strike on Pearl Harbor during the summer of 1941.

BELOW: In 1944 the navy invaded the Palaus and converted Ulithi Atoll into a naval base. Prior to the invasion of the Philippines, the USS Ticonderoga (CV-14) (bottom) joined a row of fast attack carriers moored in the harbor.

The Expanding Navy

On December 31, 1942, the *Essex* (CV-9), the first of nine 27,100-ton, hundred-plane *Essex*-class carriers, went into commission, followed by the light carriers *Independence* (CVL-22) in January; the new *Lexington* (CV-16) and *Princeton* (CVL-23) in February; the *Belleau Wood* (CVL-24) in March; the new *Yorktown* (CV-10) in April; and in May, the *Bunker Hill* (CV-17), *Cowpens* (CVL-25), and *Monterey* (CVL-26). New battleships also came on line, *Iowa* (BB-61) in February and *New Jersey* (BB-62) in May, and they all joined the Pacific Fleet. By mid-1943 the navy operated eighteen thousand aircraft, and most of the planes were in the Pacific.

Navy personnel had also expanded from 325,000 officers and men in 1941 to 3.4 million, including a hundred thousand enlistees of the Women Accepted for Voluntary Emergency Service (WAVES), which had been organized on June 20, 1942. Instead of four, there were now seven boot camps and a thousand schools training three hundred thousand men and women every day of the week.

The Island-hopping Campaign

In 1943, as Halsey began mopping up the Solomon Islands and General MacArthur commenced operations against Japanese forces on New Guinea, Admiral King obtained approval from the president to initiate an island-hopping campaign for the purpose of obtaining air bases in the Central Pacific. The step-by-step strategy resembled aspects of the Orange Plan, originated in 1921 by marine Lieutenant Colonel Earl H. Ellis.

The first step involved landings on Betio, Makin, and Apamama on Tarawa Atoll in the Gilbert Islands. Nimitz gave the assignment to Vice Admiral Spruance's Fifth Fleet with Admiral Mitscher commanding the carrier force, Rear Admiral Turner commanding the naval assault force, and Major General Holland M. "Howling Mad" Smith of the marines commanding the V Amphibious Corps. The operation, which began on November 20, 1943, and lasted four days, proved to be a learning experience for everyone involved. Major General Julian C. Smith's 2nd Marine Division lost 990 killed and 2,391 wounded in a seventy-six-hour engagement on Betio during which all but seventeen of 4,836 Japanese naval troops fought to the death. Spruance admitted confusion on the beaches, citing the need for more pre-landing bombardment, improvements in communication and air support, and better tracked landing vehicles (LVTs).

Nimitz waited until January 31, 1944, before taking the next hop. On January 29 Admiral Mitscher's Task Force 58 had begun bombing Japanese airfields on Eniwetok and Kwajalein in the Marshalls. Once again

Spruance led the Fifth Fleet with Turner's assault force, Smith's Amphibious Corps, Major General Harry Schmidt's 4th Marine Division, and army Major General Charles H. Corlett's 7th Infantry Division. On Kwajalein the Japanese fought to the death, but the marines, having learned harsh lessons on Tarawa, used vastly improved landing techniques and suffered fewer casualties.

With the Japanese outer defensive perimeter penetrated in the Marshall and Gilbert Islands, Nimitz decided to move into the Marianas and strike Saipan, Tinian, and Guam. By doing so, he would circumvent the strong enemy naval base at Truk—as Halsey had done with Rabaul in the Solomons—and let the enemy

ABOVE: The USS Iowa (BB-61) went into commission on February 22, 1943, and became one of Vice Admiral Willis A. Lee's gunships in the Pacific. During World War II, battleships played second fiddle to carriers and that relationship has not changed.

BELOW: The new Iowa-class battleships became the last of the war. The USS New Jersey (BB-62) became the second to go into commission, followed by the USS Missouri (BB-63) and the USS Wisconsin (BB-64).

RIGHT: During operations under General Douglas MacArthur in 1944, Australian solders disembark from LST-560 and wade ashore at Labuan Island, Brunei Bay, Borneo.

BELOW LEFT: In February 1944, immediately following the capture of Kwajalein in the Marshall Islands, marines come ashore with thousands of tons of supplies in preparation for operations against Eniwetok.

BELOW RIGHT: Three commanders involved in the Iwo Jima assault were old hands at amphibious landings. They consisted of Vice Admiral Richmond Kelly Turner (left) Major General Harry Schmidt (center), and Lieutenant General Holland M. Smith.

Landing Ship & Craft Designations

LCI	Landing Craft, Infantry
LCM	Landing Craft, Mechanized
LCP	Landing Craft, Personnel
LCR	Landing Craft, Rubber
LCS	Landing Craft, Support
LCT	Landing Craft, Tank
LCV	Landing Craft, Vehicle
LSD	Landing Ship, Dock
LSM	Landing Ship, Medium
LST	Landing Ship, Tank
LSV	Landing Ship, Vehicle
LVT	Landing Vehicle, Tracked
DUKW	Amphibious Trucks

wither away in their island fortress. The Marianas were important because once secured, the seven-hundred-mile leap across the Pacific would bring B-29 Superfortresses within reach of Japan and provide handier bases for submarines. Nimitz could not completely ignore Truk. On February 17-18 Mitscher's carrier planes from TF-58 flew more than twelve hundred sorties, destroying the cruiser *Naka*, three destroyers,

and two hundred and sixty-five Japanese aircraft. On February 23 TF-58 steamed back to the Marianas and launched air strikes against enemy airfields on Saipan, Rota, Tinian, and Guam while Admiral Lee's battleship group shelled shore installations.

The Marianas "Turkey Shoot"

Imperial General Headquarters could not afford to lose

the Marianas. In desperation, the Japanese Navy assembled a huge fleet of nine carriers, five battleships, seven cruisers, and thirty-four destroyers, and attempted to muster more than sixteen hundred planes to stop the invasion. Japanese Admiral Jisaburo Ozawa did not have enough refined fuel for his ships and had to delay his departure by filling up with volatile crude oil from storage tanks at Borneo.

On June 15 Holland Smith (by now lieutenant general of the marines) put the 2nd and 4th Marine divisions ashore on Saipan against 29,662 Japanese defenders. Throughout the operation, Mitscher's TF-58 carrier pilots divided their time between providing close air support over the beaches and pulverizing airfields on Saipan, Guam, and Tinian. Four days passed before Ozawa's fleet came within range of Mitscher's fleet. American submarines had monitored Ozawa's departure from the time it exited through the Philip-

ABOVE: *During the Marianas Turkey Shoot, Commander David McCampbell flew a Grumman F6F Hellcat and shot down seven Japanese planes. He would later shoot down nine more in a single day during the Battle of Leyte Gulf.*

LEFT: *Another desperate effort by the Japanese to curb U.S. progress in the Pacific occurred during the Marianas campaign. Admiral Mitscher's carrier aircraft literally destroyed every Japanese plane and would have completely wiped out the enemy fleet had Admiral Spruance not delayed the attack.*

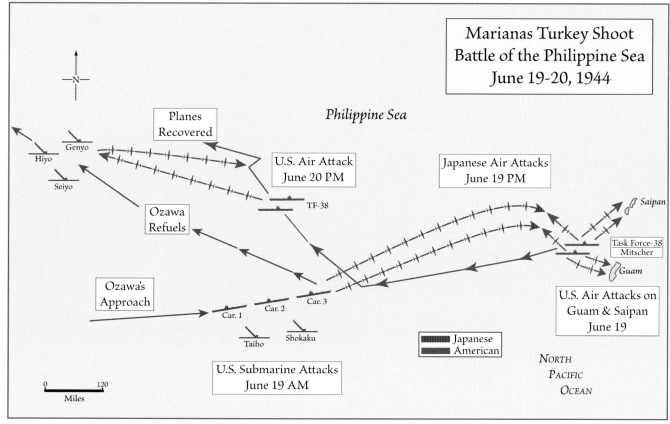

Marianas Turkey Shoot
Battle of the Philippine Sea
June 19-20, 1944

ABOVE: Although Admiral "Bull" Halsey is often remembered as the carrier commander of World War II, nobody understood carrier tactics better than Vice Admiral Marc A. Mitscher (pictured), who actually commanded the carrier task force.

Admiral Marc A. Mitscher (1887–1947)

Born in Hillsboro, Wisconsin, Mitscher graduated from the U.S. Naval Academy in 1910. Though he began his naval career on armored cruisers, Mitscher took an early interest in flying and in June 1915 earned his wings at Pensacola's Naval Air Station, after which he became involved in improving aircraft catapults. In May 1919 he earned his first Navy Cross by trying to fly solo across the Atlantic, though he only made it to the Azores.

In 1926 Mitscher served on the *Langley* (CV-1), and in 1934 he became the executive officer on the *Saratoga*. He could not get airplanes and aircraft carriers out of his system, and in July 1941 he became captain of the *Hornet*. Nine months later he launched Jimmy Doolittle's B-25 bomber attack on Tokyo, and in June 1942 he commanded the *Hornet* in the make-or-break Battle of Midway. When promoted to rear admiral and made commandant of land-based Fleet Air in the South Pacific, Mitscher yearned to get back on carriers. When Nimitz began looking for a fast carrier task force commander, he chose Mitscher, who soon became the outstanding carrier-commander of the war.

Mitscher served as vice admiral under both Spruance, a gunship man, and Halsey, a carrier man. At times he disagreed with both of them. Spruance, though a brilliant tactician, never quite understood the purpose of the fast carrier force and, as demonstrated during the Marianas campaign, kept the carriers in position to aid ground troops when they were not needed and missed the opportunity to destroy Ozawa's fleet. When Halsey, who prided himself as the war's greatest carrier commander, took command of the fleet, he suppressed Mitscher, and as a consequence made mistakes during the 1944 Philippines campaign by not listening to Mitscher's advice.

Mitscher became deputy chief of naval operations in June 1945, was promoted to full admiral and commanded the 8th Fleet in March 1946, became commander-in-chief, U.S. Atlantic Fleet, in September that year, but suffered poor health and died from a heart attack in February 1947.

pines. As Ozawa approached the Marianas, Commander James W. Blanchard, captain of the *Albacore* (SS-218), fired a spread of torpedoes into the carrier *Taiho*, Ozawa's flagship. The resulting fires ignited volatile oil fumes that eventually blew her up. Later, Lieutenant Commander Herbert J. Kossler of the *Cavalla* (SS-244) sank the carrier *Shokaku*, reducing Ozawa's carrier force to seven.

Ozawa launched his planes beyond the range of American aircraft, intending to attack Mitscher's carriers, land on Saipan and Guam airfields, refuel and rearm, and attack a second time while returning to the fleet. When Ozawa launched his planes on June 19, he did not know that the Japanese airfields had been clobbered and all the land-based planes destroyed. Mitscher's Hellcats intercepted Ozawa's incoming air strikes and literally ripped the enemy planes to pieces. At one point, a pilot from *Lexington*'s VF-16 shouted over the radio, "Hell, this is like an old time turkey shoot." Commander David McCampbell, leading nine F6F Hellcats from *Essex*'s VF-15, grumbled over the radio, "The sky is getting short of enemy planes." During the Marianas Turkey Shoot, McCampbell knocked down seven planes. By war's end he had become the navy's leading ace with thirty-four confirmed kills, earning him the Medal of Honor.

During the air battle, which virtually wiped out Ozawa's aircraft, Mitscher implored Spruance for permission to pursue the Japanese fleet. Spruance hesitated, and precious hours passed before he granted Mitscher's request. Because of the delay, the Battle of the Philippine Sea became one of the war's missed opportunities. Most of his pilots were flying on low gas when at sunset on June 20 they sighted the Japanese fleet. *Belleau Wood* pilot Lieutenant (jg) Warren R. Omark, flying one of the few Avengers armed with torpedoes, sank the light carrier *Hiyo*, but the other Japanese flattops slipped away in the dark. When the naval phase of the campaign ended, the Japanese had lost

more than five hundred planes during the "Turkey Shoot," as well as three aircraft carriers. Mitscher lost only twenty planes in dogfights, but eighty ran out of gas returning from the air strike on Ozawa's fleet and were forced to ditch in the Philippine Sea. Mitscher's destroyers rescued most of the pilots.

Setting Sights on the Philippines

While in July and August 1944 Admiral Spruance concentrated on securing Saipan, Guam, and Tinian, and General MacArthur completed the conquest of New Guinea, Admiral Halsey worked with Nimitz's Pearl Harbor staff in preparation for taking over the Third Fleet. The Fifth Fleet under Spruance merely became the Third Fleet under Halsey and, on paper, Mitscher ran them both, including Admiral Lee's battle fleet.

MacArthur also operated his own navy, Vice Admiral Thomas C. Kinkaid's Seventh Fleet, which consisted of battleships, cruisers, destroyers, escort car-

ABOVE: Ships of the Seventh Fleet assemble at Seeadler Harbor off Manus Island in the Admiralties prior to General Douglas MacArthur's invasion of the Philippines.

LEFT: General Douglas MacArthur (left) and Admiral Chester W. Nimitz (right), the two men who will bring the war in the Pacific to a successful conclusion, flank President Roosevelt on the USS Baltimore (CA-68) In Honolulu.

ABOVE: At Rendova in the Solomon Islands, PT boats go onto a floating drydock for maintenance. The boats' wooden hulls take a severe beating, especially when operating in tropical war zones.

riers, submarines, PT boats, and a collection of transports and other vessels.

When in August Halsey took over the Third Fleet, Mitscher's TF-58 automatically became TF-38. Halsey had always wanted to accelerate the Pacific War, and here was his opportunity to do it. Mitscher's carriers went wild, bombing the Caroline Islands and airfields in the Philippines. When Mitscher finished, Halsey recommended that MacArthur forego the planned invasion of Mindanao and assault Leyte on October 20 instead of waiting until December. Another operation involved the Palaus, which Halsey preferred to bypass, but Nimitz wanted the islands secured to provide air

and naval bases closer to the Philippines. On September 15 marines ran into stiff opposition on Peleliu, but eight days later Rear Admiral W. H. P. Blandy's Task Group from TF-38 put troops ashore on Ulithi, which provided an advance base for the Pacific Fleet. With that accomplished, Halsey planned to clobber all the airfields on the Philippines and Formosa, obtain air superiority, and open the way for MacArthur's October landing on Leyte.

RIGHT: During the Battle of Leyte, Admiral Halsey went after a squadron of Japanese decoys. Off Cape Engaño on October 25, 1944, planes from the USS Enterprise (CV-6) photographed the camouflaged deck of the Zuiho before sinking her.

Naval Actions at Leyte

Imperial General Headquarters expected MacArthur to invade the Philippines or Formosa and began concentrating aircraft at both locations. They also developed a complicated SHO-1 plan to eliminate the American naval threat and smash MacArthur's landing. To this end, and without fully appreciating the strength of the U.S. Navy, the Imperial Japanese Navy staked everything on one big battle. Japan had little choice. Losing either the Philippines or Formosa would cork the transportation of oil from the Dutch East Indies. On October 10, 1944, Mitscher's carrier planes launched a six-day bombing campaign against Okinawa, Formosa, and Luzon that destroyed hundreds of enemy aircraft. The Japanese delayed launching SHO-1 because Mitscher's strikes caused temporary confusion over MacArthur's actual intentions.

SHO-1 involved three Japanese squadrons. Admiral Ozawa commanded the "Northern Force" of four carriers, two hybrid battleship-carriers, three light cruisers, and eight destroyers. Ozawa planned to provide a decoy force to draw off Halsey's Third Fleet while Vice Admiral Takeo Kurita's "Center Force" of five battleships, twelve cruisers, and fifteen destroyers attacked through San Bernardino Strait as a third "Southern Force" composed of the squadrons of Vice Admirals Shoji Nishimura and Kiyohide Shima—two battle-

Navy Submarines in the Pacific

When Japan struck Pearl Harbor, the U.S. Navy had twenty-two old submarines operating out of Hawaii and twenty-nine stationed at Subic Bay, near Manila. The latter went to sea to attack the Japanese fleet during the invasion of the Philippines, but with defective torpedoes. Many exploded prematurely, others failed to explode at all, and some ran in circles because of faulty gyroscopes. Finally, on January 27, 1942, the *Gudgeon* (SS-211) scored the navy's first kill by a submarine, sinking the Japanese submarine *I-173* west of Midway. Seldom during the first six months of the war were more than a dozen navy submarines on patrol for offensive operations.

In 1943 Vice Admiral Charles A. Lockwood took command of the Pacific Fleet's submarines. By then the vastly improved 1,526-ton, ten-tubed *Gato*-class submarines with improved torpedoes, instrumentation, and night radar began appearing in the Pacific, followed a year later by the *Balao*-class. With navy code-breakers at work, the submarines began targeting Japanese convoys, racking up two hundred thousand tons a month. Convoys departing from the oil-rich Dutch East Indies made spectacular targets. Three or four submarines working in teams destroyed tankers faster than they could be replaced. In October 1944, sixty-eight submarines operating off Japan sent 320,000 tons of enemy shipping to the bottom.

Tankers were not the only prey. In June 1944, during the Marianas campaign, *Gato*-class submarines sank the Japanese carriers *Taiho* and *Shokaku*. On November 21, the *Balao*-class *Sealion* (SS-315) torpedoed *Kongo* in Formosa Strait, the first Japanese battleship to be sunk by a submarine. Six days later *Archerfish* (SS-311) put four torpedoes into the largest aircraft carrier in the world, the 59,000-ton *Shinano*, and sank her off Honshu.

At war's end, Lockwood had 288 submarines operating in the Pacific. Notwithstanding other duties, such as the rescue of downed pilots, American submarines sank 4,861,000 tons of Japanese shipping, including one battleship and six carriers.

TOP: After Lieutenant Colonel Evans C. Carlson's 2nd Marine Raider Battalion made a commando raid on Makin Island in August 1942, the transport submarine USS Argonaut (APS-1) picked up the survivors and returned them to Pearl Harbor.

ABOVE CENTER: Following a war patrol in Japanese home waters, the Gato-class USS Tinosa (SS-283) steams to her berth at Pearl Harbor, flying her battle flag and several small Japanese flags, each representing a kill.

BOTTOM : The diving officer and two enlisted men prepare the USS Batfish (SS-310) to submerge. James L. Garnet mans the stern planes while Robert T. Craig (background) handles the bow planes. Ensign Herman W. Krets supervises the operation.

Escort Carriers

During 1942, while naval appropriations were being discussed for 1943, Henry J. Kaiser approached the Bureau of Ships and offered to mass produce in six months thirty or more escort carriers of his own design. Admiral King did not like the idea, but Roosevelt approved it. From C-3 cargo ship hulls, Kaiser eventually built fifty *Casablanca*-class 7,700-ton escort carriers, all 512 feet 3 inches long with a 108-foot beam, a 22-foot 4-inch draft, and a speed of 19 knots. Though they were about half the length of a fleet carrier, the Japanese had trouble distinguishing one from the other. The ships carried twenty-eight planes (Hellcats and Avengers) and a complement of eight hundred and sixty officers and men. King later admitted, "When the Kaisers really got started, they did quite well."

ships, four cruisers, and eleven destroyers—attacked through Surigao Strait to smash MacArthur's landing on Leyte. The fallacy of the plan occurred when MacArthur, supported by the Seventh Fleet, landed on Leyte before the Japanese launched SHO-1. Kinkaid's battleships, relics salvaged from Pearl Harbor and ably commanded by Rear Admiral Jesse B. Oldendorf, decimated Nishimura's squadron, and Rear Admiral Thomas L. Sprague's Escort Carrier Group, while losing two carriers and two destroyers, turned back Kurita's powerful battleship group.

Through miscommunication caused by Kinkaid serving MacArthur and Halsey serving Nimitz, the latter pursued Ozawa's decoys instead of guarding San

Admiral William F. "Bull" Halsey, Jr. (1882–1959)

Born in Elizabeth, New Jersey, Halsey graduated from the U.S. Naval Academy in 1904. He served under Admiral George Dewey during the world cruise of the Great White Fleet (1907–1909), and during World War I he became a destroyer man. Halsey finally moved up to battleships, but he could see the future of aircraft carriers. In 1935 he completed flight training at Pensacola and in July took command of the *Saratoga*. Promoted to vice admiral in 1940, Halsey assumed command of the Aircraft Battle Force as well as Carrier Division 2.

One of Halsey's greatest disappointments was missing the Battle of Midway because of being smitten with an outbreak of shingles. Midway made Spruance's reputation, and Halsey had to work hard for his. There was not a better carrier commander in World War II apart from Marc A. Mitscher, who served under both Halsey and Spruance. The navy never completely forgave Halsey for being decoyed by Admiral Ozawa during the Leyte campaign, although Halsey had been correct in assuming that Admiral Kinkaid had force enough to take care of himself. Nor did it help Halsey's reputation when two months later his Third Fleet sailed into a typhoon that sank three of his destroyer escorts and blew dozens of planes into the sea.

Halsey turned the fleet over to Spruance for the Okinawa campaign, but when Spruance could not find a way to stop *kamikaze* attacks, Nimitz gave the carriers back to Halsey with orders to terminate the menace. Promoted to fleet admiral in 1945, Halsey retired two years later but frequently became involved in defending his policy of perpetual aggressiveness. Regardless of what some senior navy officials thought, Halsey became the most popular admiral in the navy.

ABOVE: Early in the war, Vice Admiral William "Bull" Halsey replaced Admiral Robert L. Ghormley as commander of the South Pacific Area. The news of his appointment produced a wave of jubilation among South Pacific forces.

ABOVE LEFT: During operations off the east coast of Luzon on October 24, 1944, Japanese planes broke through combat air patrol (CAP) and bombed the USS Princeton (CVL-23). Efforts to save her failed, and the light carrier went to the bottom.

FAR LEFT: During efforts to keep the stricken USS Princeton afloat, one of the cruisers in the carrier task group stands off the beam and pours streams of water into the gasoline fires pouring through gaping holes in the flight deck.

ABOVE: As part of the preparation for the invasion of Okinawa, Admiral Halsey's Third Fleet carrier planes swung over the island of Hokkaido and pulverized the railroad yards and military installations at Kushiro.

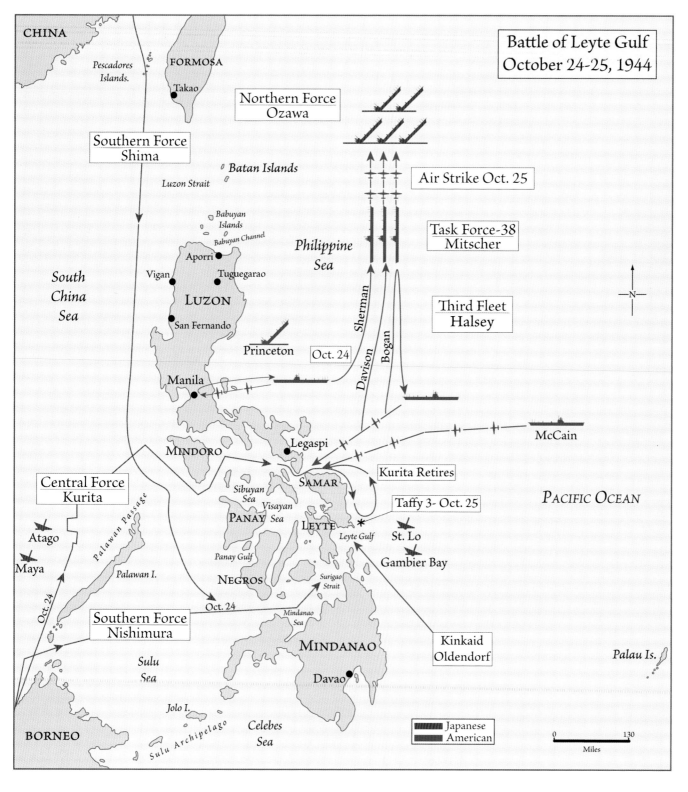

**Battle of Leyte Gulf
October 24-25, 1944**

CHINA

Pescadores Islands.

FORMOSA

Takao

**Northern Force
Ozawa**

**Southern Force
Shima**

Batan Islands

Luzon Strait

Air Strike Oct. 25

Babuyan Islands

Babuyan Channel

Philippine Sea

**Task Force-38
Mitscher**

Aparri

Vigan

Tuguegarao

LUZON

South China Sea

San Fernando

Sherman

**Third Fleet
Halsey**

Princeton

Oct. 24

Davison

Bogan

Manila

MINDORO

Legaspi

McCain

**Central Force
Kurita**

Sibuyan Sea

Visayan Sea

SAMAR

Kurita Retires

PACIFIC OCEAN

Palawan Passage

PANAY

LEYTE

Taffy 3- Oct. 25

Atago

Leyte Gulf

St. Lo

Maya

Oct. 24

Panay Gulf

NEGROS

Surigao Strait

Gambier Bay

Oct. 24

Mindanao Sea

**Southern Force
Nishimura**

Palawan I.

MINDANAO

**Kinkaid
Oldendorf**

Palau Is.

Sulu Sea

Davao

Jolo I.

Celebes Sea

Sulu Archipelago

BORNEO

Japanese
American

0   130
Miles

LEFT: Anticipating General MacArthur's invasion of the Philippines, the Japanese pulled together every ship to prevent it. The only tactic that worked was luring Admiral Halsey's Third Fleet into a wild goose chase, which nonetheless resulted in the destruction of five Japanese carriers.

Bernardino Strait against the return of Kurita's fleet. Halsey had earlier repulsed Kurita and erroneously believed the Japanese squadron would not return.

Despite warnings from Mitscher and Lee that Ozawa's carriers were nothing but decoys, Halsey wanted the carrier battle that had always eluded him and vacated his coverage of San Bernardino Strait. The following morning, when Kurita came through the strait and attacked Sprague's escort carriers, Halsey's fleet was off Cape Engaño, more than three hundred miles to the north.

While Sprague's escort carriers and destroyers were fighting Kurita's battleships and cruisers, Mitscher's aircraft were attacking Ozawa's defenseless carriers. When Kinkaid radioed for help, Halsey ignored the message, convinced that Kinkaid had enough escort carriers and firepower to take care of the Leyte beachhead. Kinkaid panicked and notified Nimitz that naval operations off Leyte were in jeopardy, when in reality Sprague's escort carriers were handling the situation, though with some difficulty, and Oldendorf's battleships were on the way.

Nonetheless, Nimitz sent Halsey a scathing message and ordered him back to Leyte. Halsey left most of Mitscher's carriers off Cape Engaño to finish off Ozawa and returned to San Bernardino Strait with Lee's battleship group. By then, Kurita had escaped, chased off by escort carriers he mistook for being Halsey's fleet carriers. Thus ended the Battle of Leyte Gulf, which etched a small stain on Halsey's reputation for being decoyed away from MacArthur's beachhead. Mitscher's planes, however, destroyed Ozawa's four carriers, four destroyers, and one light cruiser.

The Last Campaigns

In February 1945, while MacArthur mopped up the Philippines, Mitscher took his carriers north and began striking military installations around Tokyo. Three days later the carriers were stationed off Iwo Jima, providing close air support for marines assaulting the eight-square-

LEFT: Rear Admiral Thomas L. Sprague commanded Task Group 77.4 during the October 24-25, 1944, battle off Samar. His escort carriers turned back Admiral Kurita's battleships, but the real surprise came when his ships were hit by the first kamikaze attacks.

LEFT: Off Mindoro in the Philippines, antiaircraft gun crews on an American cruiser spot an unidentified aircraft overhead and prepare to take measures against a possible kamikaze attack.

LEFT: *The invasion of Okinawa brought hundreds of kamikaze attacks. When one kamikaze pilot tried to strike the deck of the battleship USS* Missouri, *a photographer caught the plane's approach seconds before antiaircraft fire blew the aircraft apart.*

mile volcanic island. The naval bombardment became the heaviest of the Pacific war but failed to dislodge the Japanese defenders. Nimitz wanted Iwo because the island lay between Saipan and Tokyo and would provide emergency landing fields for damaged B-29s returning from bombing missions over Japan. Six thousand marines lost their lives securing the island, but before the war ended, 2,251 B-29s made emergency landings on the island, saving the lives of up to 24,761 crewmen.

On March 26, 1945, two days after securing Iwo Jima, Spruance's Fifth Fleet opened fire on Okinawa. On April 1 marines secured beachheads against light resistance. Five days later the sky became filled with *kamikazes*, Japanese suicide planes that had made their first official appearance over Leyte Gulf. The pilots were inexperienced. They were mostly young men who could get their aircraft off the ground and fly, but they

did not always know how to land. Admiral Soemu Toyoda, commander of the Japanese Combined Fleet, hoped to have four thousand five hundred planes available to repel the American attack, but because of Mitscher's pre-invasion strikes on Japanese airfields, Toyoda could muster only 699 planes, half of which were *kamikazes*. During the first attack, Mitscher's carrier planes shot down four hundred enemy aircraft, but they were partially replaced and kept on coming.

The navy weathered six *kamikaze* attacks, mainly because Spruance insisted on keeping the carriers chained to Okinawa. Mitscher complained when he began losing ships. The Okinawa campaign proved unnecessarily costly. *Kamikazes* sank thirty-four ships, damaged a further 368, killed 4,900 sailors, and wounded 4,800 more. Nimitz turned the fleet back to Halsey, who promptly took it out of harm's way.

OPPOSITE: *As the invasion of Okinawa begins and amtracs advance toward the beach, the battleship USS* Tennessee *(BB-43) opens with her 16-inch guns on enemy positions spotted by observation aircraft.*

LEFT: *Although* kamikaze *pilots were instructed to target capital ships, they often struck smaller ships. Most* kamikaze *pilots did not know the difference, and on April 6, 1945, one smashed into the destroyer USS* **Morris** *(DD-417).*

ABOVE: *The carrier USS* **Essex** *(CV-9) burst into flames after a* kamikaze *plunged into the venerable ship's flight deck and scattered debris several hundred yards across the water.*

Mitscher resumed strikes on Japanese airbases and ended the *kamikaze* threat.

In the last sortie of the war, the Japanese converted ships in their dwindling navy to surface *kamikazes* and sent them to Okinawa with only enough fuel for a one-way trip. During a span of two hours, Mitscher's carrier aircraft sank the 68,000-ton superbattleship *Yamato*, a light cruiser, and four destroyers.

After ground forces secured Okinawa on June 21, Halsey's Third Fleet with Mitscher's carriers roamed at will off the Japanese coast, sending strike after strike against airfields, railroads, supply dumps, and weapons industries. On August 6 the "Enola Gay" flew over Hiroshima and incinerated much of the city with the first atomic bomb. Three days later a second A-bomb leveled Nagasaki. On August 15 the Japanese surrendered.

On September 2 the USS *Missouri* (BB-63), the last battleship to be commissioned during World War II, lay at anchor in Tokyo Bay to host the signing of the Japanese surrender instrument. General MacArthur represented the Allied powers, and Fleet Admiral Nimitz signed for the United States. None of the signatories expected to be at war five years later.

LEFT: *Off Okinawa on May 4, 1945, a wave of 124 kamikazes struck the U.S. fleet and sank seven ships and damaged six others, among them the escort carrier USS* Sangamon *(CVE-26). Despite having her flight deck battered, the carrier survived the attack.*

BELOW: *In Tokyo Bay on September 2, 1945, men of the battleship USS* Missouri *(BB-63) give a cheer as the Japanese officials formally sign the instrument of surrender.*

CHAPTER 5

WORLD WAR II IN THE ATLANTIC 1940–1945

After Hitler attained power in Germany in 1933, tension mounted in Europe. The new chancellor intended to reverse the consequences of Germany's defeat in World War I and seize control of Europe. He renounced the limitations imposed on the German Navy by the Treaty of Versailles and in June 1935 signed the Anglo-German Naval Agreement, which allowed him to rebuild, though with restrictions, a surface fleet with U-boats. However, Hitler was a land-grabbing strategist and not a naval disciple. When Germany invaded Poland on September 3, 1939, Hitler had just forty-three combat-ready submarines, and only four a month in the schedule.

In 1939 Americans were not nearly as neutral as during World War I. The Allies were permitted to buy arms from the United States on a cash-and-carry basis, but under the Neutrality Act of 1937 American ships were not permitted to enter the war zone. Nor were Americans allowed to sail in Allied warships. To enforce

> We have sought no shooting war with Hitler. We do not seek it now. But neither do we seek peace so much that that we are willing to pay for it by permitting him to attack our naval and merchant ships.
>
> *Franklin D. Roosevelt, September 11, 1941, on the sinking of the American merchant ship* Steel Seafarer.

the regulations, Admiral Stark initiated a neutrality patrol consisting of the old battleships *New York* (BB-34), *Texas* (BB-35), *Arkansas* (BB-33), and *Wyoming* (BB-32), the carrier *Ranger* (CV-4), and an assortment of cruisers and destroyers.

The unexpected collapse of France in June 1940 created a crisis for the United States. Great Britain now stood alone against the German war machine, and Roosevelt understood the danger to the United States should Britain fall. He decided to help Britain avoid defeat and offered every assistance short of war. For eighteen months the U.S. Navy provided the shield while America mobilized.

The U-boat Menace

German U-boats operating from French ports in the Bay of Biscay began ripping British convoys apart. Prime Minister Winston Churchill appealed to Roosevelt for help, who promptly sent the Royal Navy fifty old four-piper destroyers for patrol duty. The destroyers proved too few. During the first six months of 1941, U-boats sank 756 and damaged 1,450 British merchantmen.

Safely elected to a third term, on March 11, 1941, Roosevelt pushed the Lend-Lease Act through Congress, thus ending the cash-and-carry practices of 1937 and promulgating a policy allowing the lending of arms, munitions, and supplies to those nations "whose defense the President deems vital to the defense of the United States." The Lend-Lease Act marked the end of America's fictitious neutrality and the beginning of an undeclared

OPPOSITE: Somewhere in the Arctic Sea north of Norway, a Type VIIC German U-boat surfaces while patrolling Allied convoy routes to the Soviet Union. The photograph looks forward from her 88mm/45 deck gun.

"shoot on sight" war against Germany. On September 16, 1941, the navy joined the Royal Canadian Navy in escorting convoys to the Iceland area, where the Royal Navy took over the responsibility of getting the ships into Great Britain. German U-boats reacted to the belligerency and in October torpedoed two destroyers, the USS *Kearney* (DD-432) and the USS *Reuben Jones* (DD-245). Congress responded on November 17 and authorized the arming of merchant ships.

> The Navy is already at war in the Atlantic, but the country does not seem to realize it.
> *Admiral Harold R. Stark, CNO, November 7, 1941.*

Liberty Ships

On September 27, 1941, the Maritime Commission, later superseded by the War Shipping Administration and commanded by Rear Admiral Emory S. Land, launched the *Patrick Henry*, the first Liberty ship. The design would eventually lead to Victory ships and other cargo vessels, which altogether became one of America's many "miracles of production." Eighteen new yards comprising 171 shipways, none of which existed before 1941, sprang up before the end of the year. The typical 441-foot, 4,380-ton EC-2 Liberty ship carried general cargo and could cruise seventeen thousand miles at eleven knots. The C-2 (3,733-ton) and C-3 (5,700-ton) general cargo ships that followed were twenty to fifty feet longer and faster, and could cruise up to seventeen knots. The Maritime Commission also built T2 (6,107-ton) and T3 (6,646-ton) tankers that cruised at fourteen-and-a-half and eighteen knots, respectively. The VC-2 4,555-ton Victory-type general cargo ships generated up to seventeen knots, which improved the speed at which a convoy could travel by 50 percent, and this added another factor to a convoy's ability to

ABOVE: The Liberty ship Francis Scott Key departed from Reykjavik, Iceland, on April 26, 1942, as part of Northern convoy PQ-15, and after dodging U-boats in the Arctic Ocean, tied up safely at Murmansk, Russia.

Bringing Home the War

The Japanese attack on Pearl Harbor on December 7, 1941, galvanized Americans, and Congress responded with unusual celerity. Except for one representative, the House and Senate voted unanimously for war with Japan. On December 11 Germany and Italy responded and declared war on the United States.

U-boat commanders prowling the Atlantic greeted the declaration with great enthusiasm. American coastal defenses did not exist, and lights from the cities lit up the ocean, silhouetting cargo ships offshore. During January–March 1942, sixty-four German submarines operating in American waters sank 112 ships totaling 927,000 tons. Because of increased operating distances, Germany's Admiral Erich Raeder solved the problem by sending 1,700-ton "milch cow" submarines across the Atlantic with fresh supplies of fuel and torpedoes. The ABC-1 Staff Agreement signed on March 27, 1941, contained Roosevelt's commitment to deal with Germany ahead of concentrating on Japan, and the first concern became getting convoys safely through to Great Britain and the Soviet Union.

> We cannot allow our goods to be sunk in the Atlantic. We must make good our promise to Great Britain.
> *Secretary of the Navy Frank Knox.*

elude U-boats, as the early eleven-knot Liberty ships were much too slow.

The *Patrick Henry* required 244 days' construction, but by 1944 the average time to build a Liberty ship was just forty-two days. Liberty ship production jumped from 139 (1,119,000 tons) in 1941 to 816 (6,135,000 tons) in 1942. By the end of 1943, one-and-a-half million men and women worked in ship construction.

During World War I, U-boats operated independently and without guidance systems. By World War II everything had changed. Admiral Raeder organized wolf-packs of up to twenty submarines and sent them into the North Atlantic to wait for radioed instructions on the location of approaching convoys. U-boat commanders surfaced at dark, received directions, and set their courses, using faster surface speeds to intercept convoys. After the attack, U-boats submerged to avoid surface detection but stayed on the heels of the convoy. After escort vessels gave up the hunt, U-boats struck again, often tracking a convoy over a thousand miles of ocean.

U-boat attacks intensified during the summer and fall of 1942, but so did Allied countermeasures, which included a combination of surface ships with improved tracking sonar, radar, and patrol aircraft (VP). Though Allied merchant losses in the Atlantic and Arctic in 1942 amounted to 1,027,000 tons, by year's end eighty-five U-boats had been sunk.

The Battle of the Atlantic

In January 1943 Hitler relieved Raeder and replaced him with Admiral Karl Dönitz, who immediately intensified an already accelerated wolf-pack campaign. He increased the goal for merchant ship sinkings from 500,000 tons to 1.3 million tons a month. For three months the number of U-boats operating in the North Atlantic averaged 116. They crisscrossed sea-lanes taking a heavy toll on merchant convoys during one of the worst years for winter storms on record, which added to the difficulties and dangers of surface craft.

The campaign reached its climax near the end of March with 108 merchantmen sunk against the sinking of only fifteen U-boats. Supplies in the United Kingdom fell to a three-month backlog, with civilians living hand-to-mouth. The turning point began around the end of April when Commander Peter W. Gretton of the Royal Navy picked up convoy ONS-2 of forty-two merchantmen off Iceland and fought a running battle across the North Atlantic against fifty-one U-boats. Though Gretton lost thirteen ships, the Germans lost seven U-boats.

Convoys to Murmansk, Russia, suffered fewer losses during the winter because ships moved through almost total darkness. After spring came, convoys to the USSR went through Iran to avoid exposure to German air attack.

ABOVE: Ever on alert, a North Atlantic convoy loaded with aircraft, artillery, munitions, and supplies for delivery to Great Britain zigzags silently through the sea, their silhouettes making easy targets on such a treacherous moonlit night.

LEFT: Sailors aboard the USS Greer in the cold, storm-lashed North Atlantic maintain a constant vigil for the telltale signs of an enemy periscope.

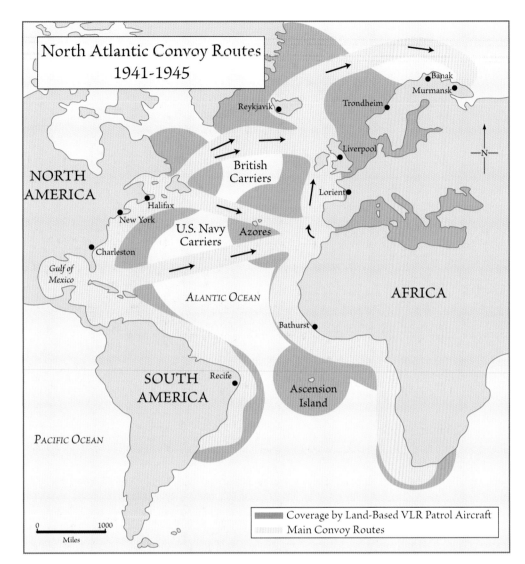

North Atlantic Convoy Routes 1941-1945

Coverage by Land-Based VLR Patrol Aircraft
Main Convoy Routes

LEFT: *The North Atlantic convoy routes became the hunting grounds for German wolfpacks. U-boats preferred to operate in ocean areas outside the range of land-based aircraft. The introduction of escort carriers marked the end of the U-boat threat.*

ABOVE: *Convoys crossing the North Atlantic during the summer were especially vulnerable to U-boat attack because the sun in the higher latitudes never sets. Air cover often involved blimps, which kept pace with the convoy.*

U-Boat Sinkings—1943

Month	CVEs	AAF	Air Patrol	Other	Total
May	1	1	4	2	8
June	2		2	1	5
July	7	7	11		25
August	6	1	3	1	11
September			1		1
October	6		1		7
November	2		4		6
December	3		2		5

In June the U.S. Navy's Tenth Fleet organized the first "killer groups," each with an escort carrier (CVE) equipped with a VC (composite) squadron of nine Wildcat FM-2 fighter-bombers and twelve TBF/TBM Avengers armed with bombs, depth charges, or torpedoes, and accompanied by either destroyers or destroyer escorts. Each group commander received wide discretion in hunting U-boats wherever a "fix" was reported, and the hunt extended from the far northern latitudes to the South Atlantic. German U-boat commanders fought back savagely, but between May and September 1943, after British cryptanalysts cracked the new German code, 3,546 merchantmen in sixty-two convoys crossed the Atlantic without a single casualty. The rate of Allied U-boat kills began to exceed Germany's ability to produce replacements, and by mid-summer 1943 the food crisis in the British Isles ended.

DD Destroyers/DE Destroyers Comparison

DD Destroyers

Class	Tons	Length (feet)	Speed (knots)	Guns	Torpedo tubes	Complement
Gleaves Class	1,630	347	33	Four 5in	5	276
Fletcher Class	2,050	376	35	Six 5in	10	329
Sumner Class	2,200	376	34	Six 5in	10	345

DE Destroyers

Class	Tons	Length (feet)	Speed (knots)	Guns	Torpedo tubes	Complement
Evarts Class	1,140	289	21	Three 3in	0	198
Butler Class	1,350	306	24	Two 5in	3	222
Buckley Class	1,400	306	23	Three 3in	3	213
Edsall Class	1,200	306	21	Three 3in	3	216

BELOW: Off Salerno, Italy, an American destroyer lays down a smoke screen during an enemy air raid. Note the stenciling of enemy aircraft silhouettes on the curtain of the ship, for identification purposes.

Destroyer Escorts

In 1940 the idea for a new ship, the destroyer escort (DE), came from President Roosevelt. None of the early designs met the approval of the navy board because they preferred building 2,000-ton conventional destroyers instead of 775-ton destroyer escorts. The navy solved the problem by increasing the size and armament of destroyer escorts.

One of the ironies of American naval history occurred when the navy obtained the first destroyer escorts by building them for the Royal Navy and then taking them back. Samuel Eliot Morison remarked, "Our first DE program was a back-handed gift to ourselves through lend-lease." On January 18, 1942, President Roosevelt floated a plan to build 1,799 ships and various types of landing craft for the Royal Navy, of which 250 were to be destroyer escorts. Of the latter built for Great Britain, the United States had taken 195 back by August 1943.

Under Secretary of the Navy James V. Forrestal took special interest in developing the industrial capacity required to produce destroyer escorts. In February 1943 he opened space in five navy yards, engaged a dozen

Admiral Ernest Joseph King (1878–1956)

Born in Lorain, Ohio, King returned to the U.S. Naval Academy after serving in the Spanish-American War and in 1901 graduated near the top of his class. From the deck of the USS *Cincinnati* (C-7), Ensign King watched with keen interest the naval action in the Russo-Japanese War and recognized Japan as an emerging naval power.

In 1917, when the United States joined the Allies in World War I, King served with the Atlantic Fleet and held the temporary rank of captain. His experience included everything the navy had to offer, from submarines and destroyers to battleships. In 1927, at the age of forty-eight, he became a pilot and three years later captain of the *Lexington* (CV-3). Following his promotion to vice admiral in 1938, King took command of the five-carrier Aircraft Battle Force. On February 1, 1941, Roosevelt raised him to full admiral. Following Pearl Harbor, King became commander-in-chief U.S. Fleet, and on March 12, 1942, he also became chief of naval operations, relieving Admiral Stark. Irascible and arrogant, purely professional and humorless, King ranked as one of the navy's most innovative and indispensable strategists. When told to wear two hats,

he merely remarked, "…when they get into trouble, they always call for the sons-of-bitches."

King played a major role in directing the undeclared antisubmarine war with Germany and later the war in the Pacific. He also participated significantly in all the important conferences with the Allies, and served with the Joint Chiefs of Staff and the combined chiefs of staff, which basically worked under Roosevelt and Churchill and directed the war. Oddly enough, King did not play a major role in the war in Europe because most of the naval task had been turned over to the Royal Navy. The lines of communication became muddled at times when entire fleets became assigned to commanding generals. This may have accounted for King's characteristic grumpiness, though he never said so.

ABOVE: During September 1941 Admiral Ernest J. King, commander-in-chief of the Atlantic Fleet, meets with Secretary of the Navy Frank Knox to discuss the beginning of convoy escort, as agreed to in the ABC-1 staff agreement with the Royal Navy.

private shipbuilders, pushed the project into mass production, and by December 5 had two hundred and sixty destroyer escorts in commission. The "Short Haul" version (*Evarts*-class) was the original British design. Some of the "Long Haul I" version (*Edsall*-class) ships went to the Royal Navy, but all of the "Long Haul II" versions (*Butler*- and *Buckley*-class) served the navy in the Atlantic and the Pacific, and for much of the war performed the duties of a fully fledged destroyer escorting convoys and escort carriers. By war's end, the navy had commissioned 421 destroyer escorts.

Desegregation

African-Americans had served on warships ever since the American Revolution. When the navy was formally established in 1798, the organizers attempted to ban both slaves and freemen, but the demand for manpower became so great during the wars that followed that black sailors slipped into the navy. They served in menial tasks, mostly in what became known as the "Messmen Branch."

WAVES

On July 30, 1942, Congress authorized the establishment of the WAVES (Women Accepted for Volunteer Emergency Service). The idea was not completely new: on March 17, 1917, Congress authorized the navy to enlist women to perform yeoman's clerical duties, giving rise to the "Yeomanettes." Joy Bright became a yeoman-F, for female, one of the 11,275 enlisted women who filled clerical positions during the Great War. Unlike most Yeomanettes who left the service at war's end, Bright continued to work for the navy as a civilian. She married, lost both husbands in flying accidents, and retained her second husband's name, Hancock.

When Lieutenant Commander Mildred H. McAfee became the WAVES' first commandant on August 2, 1942. Hancock gave up her civilian job and rejoined the service as a lieutenant. The goal had been to recruit ten thousand women and a thousand officers, but by October the first of more than seventy-eight thousand women and eight thousand officers had volunteered for duty. They reported to colleges and received training in non-combatant skills to replace men needed for combat duty. Women learned typing, shorthand, and stenography as well as advanced courses in history and naval communication. The person who worked hardest to develop careers for women was not McAfee but Hancock, who by 1945 had risen to the rank of commander. In July 1946 she became director of the WAVES and received promotion to captain.

Secretary of the Navy James Forrestal claimed the WAVES released enough men for active duty to man ten battleships, ten aircraft carriers, twenty-eight cruisers, and fifty destroyers. Without WAVES, the navy's fighting force would have been that much smaller and weaker. The program was discontinued in 1945 because

the number of women who answered the call far exceeded expectations, but Hancock stuck with the job, lobbied two years for legislation that led to the Women's Armed Forces Integration Act of June 1948, and that October she was among the first eight of 288 women officers sworn into the regular navy.

Sailors watch with amusement as a pretty WAVE on the dock gives the navy man she has replaced in a shore billet a hand in getting his gear aboard a warship.

On December 7, 1941, Mess Attendant Second Class Doris Miller was serving as an officer's steward on the battleship *West Virginia* (BB-48) when the Japanese struck Pearl Harbor. He helped carry the wounded captain from the bridge and then returned to the deck to man a machine gun, though he had never been trained. Miller earned the Navy Cross that day, and this worked wonders for other African-Americans seeking careers in the navy.

After World War II began, the navy soon recognized that the talents of African-Americans were being wasted, and in 1942 Bernard Robinson became the first ensign in the navy. The navy opened the way for other blacks to apply for commissions, and in September

Samuel L. Gravely, Jr., of Richmond, Virginia, became the first to do so, although he knew the problems he would face among the traditionally all-white officers' corps. The navy needed thousands of officers and men to operate auxiliary ships, and blacks made up about ten percent of the crews.

In 1945 the Naval Academy began accepting African-Americans, and in 1948 Wesley A. Brown became the first of his race to graduate. Racial inequality persisted, diminishing slowly as each decade passed. The breakthrough picked up momentum in 1971 when Gravely became the first black rear admiral. Today, thanks to men like Doris Miller and Admiral Gravely, the navy shaped the way for racial equality in the services.

ABOVE LEFT: After attaching the American flag to U-505, a captured German Type 1XC-class submarine, a salvage crew holds on while spectators on the escort carrier USS Guadalcanal *(CVE-60) watch. Refurbished, U-505 became the USS* Nemo.

Operation Torch

The chain of command in the Atlantic worked much like that in the Pacific, where General MacArthur controlled the forces in the western sector (Australia, New Guinea, the Philippines, etc.). The combined chiefs of staff divided the Atlantic in half at 40 degrees west. King commanded the western half and British Admiral Sir Andrew Cunningham commanded the eastern half. During Operation Torch, the invasion of North Africa, Cunningham reported to General Dwight D. Eisenhower, the supreme commander. Admiral Royal E. Ingersoll reported to King as commander-in-chief of the U.S. Atlantic Fleet, and Vice Admiral H. Kent Hewitt, commander of the Western Naval Task Force,

reported to Ingersoll. Once Hewitt passed eastward of 40 degrees west, he with his ships full of soldiers and sailors became responsible to Cunningham. Once the soldiers went ashore, Hewitt's responsibilities changed again, and he and his sailors came under the command of Major General George S. Patton. The arrangement worked quite well, though some found the organization changes confusing.

In 1941 the British had already laid plans for the invasion of French North Africa before America became involved. With the United States in a position to provide ground forces, the combined chiefs of staff projected the invasion of Morocco and Algeria for the summer of 1942. The operation would serve as a prelude to opening

Navy Nurse Corps

Women had served as nurses in the navy as far back as the War of 1812, but not until August 29, 1908, was the Navy Nurse Corps officially established. During World War I nurses were never given an opportunity to make a career in the navy. In 1919 they were all released from active duty and a generation passed before they were invited into the ranks again. Since that time, the corps has continued to grow. During World War II more than eleven thousand nurses served in the navy.

Since the corps revitalization in World War II, nurses have gone wherever the navy went, tending to sick and wounded in war zones in every engagement. Today, along with wartime and peacetime duties, the corps trains the nurses of the future, keeping current with the always-evolving medical technology. The corps handles navy health care on an ongoing basis and oversees clinics, nursing schools, and mobile hospitals all over the world. In June 1971, during the selection of several new flag officers, Alene B. Duerk became the first rear admiral in charge of the Navy Nurse Corps.

a second front by securing bases in the Mediterranean. The combined chiefs also expected the expedition to be useful in correcting defects in amphibious operations before major landings began in Europe. A major concern facing the Allies involved Admiral Jean Darlan, commanding the French Navy and Vichy ground troops. Would these men fight or surrender?

In late October 1942, Admiral Hewitt's Western Task Force of ninety-nine ships with thirty-seven thousand troops steamed to sea from Hampton Roads, Virginia. On November 7, after taking a circuitous route south to avoid U-boats, the battleships *Massachusetts* (BB-59), *New York*, and *Texas*, and the carrier *Ranger* with four escort carriers and a host of other ships,

appeared off the west coast of French Morocco. On the same day, the Center and Eastern task forces—170 ships carrying 49,000 Americans and 23,000 British troops—passed through the Strait of Gibraltar and approached Oran and Algiers.

At dawn next day, covered by cruisers, destroyers, and rocket boats, American troops went ashore on French Morocco at Fedala, Lyautey, and Safi. Many of the flat-bottomed boats carrying troops reached shore without being observed. A few French planes attempted to strafe the landing force but were quickly put out of action by twenty carrier-borne Wildcats. A naval action fought off Casablanca, involving the *Massachusetts*, quickly sank a French light cruiser and four destroyers. By November

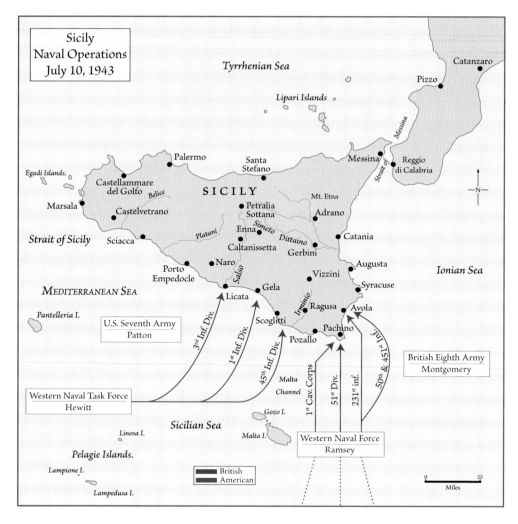

Sicily Naval Operations July 10, 1943

ABOVE: Coming from two different directions, one task force commanded by the U.S. Navy and the other by the Royal Navy, each making feints while en route to Sicily, came together on July 10, 1943, and invaded Europe.

10 the navy had put a hundred and sixty thousand troops and seventy tanks ashore, all of which moved toward Casablanca. The following day the French naval commander at Casablanca surrendered the remnants of his fleet and everything else.

In the Mediterranean the prize was Admiral Darlan's French fleet, which was anchored inside the fortified port of Oran. On November 8 thirty-nine thousand American troops flooded ashore and flanked the city while the Center Task Force blocked the harbor. Darlan surrendered two days later, after which he ordered the small French squadron at Toulon to scuttle their ships rather than allow them to fall into German hands. The Eastern Task Force encountered heavier resistance at Algiers, mainly from Germans, but soon captured the city.

The Learning Curve

The marines had learned something about amphibious operations in the Pacific when in August they assaulted the undefended beaches of Guadalcanal, but the navy learned a lot more when they waded ashore near Algiers. More than half of the invasion force landed on the wrong beach, and 94 percent of the landing craft were lost or damaged due to mishandling. The experience sent the navy back to the drawing board to develop an entirely new series of landing craft, from LSTs to LCIs (see Chapter Four).

While the army fought the enemy in North Africa's deserts and reversed a temporary setback at Kasserine Pass, the navy used the time to plan for the invasion of Sicily. Over a period of eight months the navy transported 2,500 vessels (including new landing craft), 4,000 aircraft, and 250,000 troops to newly established bases in North Africa. For the first time, LSTs, LCIs, and LCTs would put the landing force ashore without the problems of transferring troops to small boats.

Invasion of Sicily (Operation Husky)

The naval phase of Operation Husky fell under the command of Admiral Cunningham of the Royal Navy and involved more than fourteen hundred ships and landing craft. While Cunningham put British Lieutenant General Sir Bernard L. Montgomery's Eighth Army ashore on the southeastern side of Sicily, Vice Admiral Hewitt put Lieutenant General Patton's Seventh Army ashore along the southern coast. General Sir Harold Alexander, overall commander of the ground forces, committed 470,000 men to the operation, pitting them against 300,000 Italian and 50,000 German troops under General Alfredo Guzzoni, but only the Germans demonstrated a will to fight.

On the eve of the invasion, Admiral Hewitt's mile-deep formation stretched for sixty miles across the

Mediterranean. Rounding Cape Bon off Tunis, the long column feinted south before turning north. On the night of July 8 the squadron crossed the Mediterranean to Malta and sub-divided into three attack forces. During naval maneuvers, army special forces parachuted into Sicily to direct naval gunnery, and Allied planes bombed enemy airfields and fortified positions in an effort to disrupt communications between Sicily and Italy.

Shortly after midnight on July 10, the navy launched the largest amphibious assault in its history in terms of the number of men put ashore and the breadth of coastline under attack. During the first phase of the operation, landing craft fanned across a hundred miles of coastline and put three Seventh Army divisions under General Patton ashore at Licata, Gela, and Scoglitti, and General Montgomery's XIII and XXX Corps ashore between Pozzallo and Syracuse. During a span of forty-eight hours, the Allied naval force landed eighty thousand troops, seven thousand vehicles, six thousand tanks, and nine hundred artillery pieces. Cruisers laid down a heavy barrage on coastal batteries and smashed an armored attack by the Hermann

Goering Division as it rumbled toward Gela. Axis losses in Sicily led to the overthrow of Benito Mussolini, and on July 25 King Victor Emmanuel III began restoring non-Fascist Italy.

After the Germans threw fifty thousand reinforcements against Montgomery and stalled the British advance, General Alexander acceded to Patton's request to break from the British left flank and spread his American divisions across Sicily. Patton moved fast, and on July 22, using cruisers and destroyers roving off shore for supporting fire, captured Palermo. The navy patrolled the northern coast, preventing the enemy from landing reinforcements and supplies. While the Seventh Army rumbled east along the Tyrrhenian Sea, Patton used the navy to leapfrog forces over German defensive positions in his race to Messina. On August 17 Patton arrived in Messina, two hours ahead of the British, to complete the conquest of Sicily. During the thirty-nine-day campaign, Allied forces killed, wounded or captured 167,000 Axis troops against losses of 25,000, but 39,500 Germans and 62,000 Italians succeeded in escaping across the Straits of Messina to Italy.

Fire Support Group 81.5 at Salerno

Rear Admiral Lyal A. Davidson, commanding Fire Support Group 81.5 from the light cruiser *Philadelphia* (CL-41), thought he knew what to expect when on September 9 his squadron of five light cruisers and four destroyers appeared off Salerno's beaches. Davidson was a tall, lanky flag officer known as a man of few words, firm and decisive in his actions. No one ever recalled Davidson losing his temper until Salerno, where he became furious with General Clark. The general made two mistakes: first by forbidding a bombardment of German positions prior to the landing because he mistakenly thought it would jeopardize the element of surprise, and second by waiting so long

to call for help from the navy when beachheads were in danger of being thrown back into the sea. On coming ashore, the infantry was delayed by mines, confused when they reached shore, and pinned down by German Mark IV tanks, 88mm artillery, and machine guns.

Around 8:00 A.M. Davidson received an urgent call for help and immediately moved into firing position with his flagship *Philadelphia*, the light cruiser *Savannah* (CL-42), the monitor HMS *Abercrombie*, and four destroyers. Because fire-control parties had not gotten into position ashore, he used his own SOC (observation) floatplanes for spotting. At 8:25

the monitor got into action and at twenty-five thousand yards blew up an enemy artillery position, while around 9:30 *Savannah* silenced a bothersome railway battery. At 10:25, after observation planes spotted a concealed tank concentration, the *Abercrombie's* 15-inch guns drove it into the open where the *Philadelphia's* 6-inch guns ripped it apart and sent the tanks scurrying to the rear. Soon afterwards a SOC plane reported *panzer* units crossing a bridge, so Davidson shifted fire, tore up the bridge, and turned back the column.

At 10:57 he launched another spotter plane to get his destroyers into the action. Pilots soon located new targets in the

town of Capaccio. The *Abercrombie,* while steaming into position, struck a mine, took a 10-degree list, and retired to Palermo. At 2:00 P.M. the second spotter plane located another pocket of thirty-five enemy tanks, and the *Philadelphia's* 6-inch guns knocked out seven as they backpedaled.

Brigadier General John W. Lange, commander of the 36th Division's artillery, was one of many who appreciated the services of Davidson's Fire Support Group. "Thank God for the fire of the blue-belly Navy ships," he radioed. "Probably could not [otherwise] have stuck out Blue and Yellow beaches. Brave fellows these: tell them so."

RIGHT: On D-Day at Normandy, naval shellfire formed a screen for the first American landing parties wading through the surf at Utah Beach. Four thousand naval ships participated in the Normandy landings.

BELOW: U.S. Coast Guard cutters (right) served as rescue craft during the Normandy landings. Here a cutter ties up to an LCV (Landing Craft, Vehicle) while making a stop at a troop transport.

The Invasion of Italy

After the fall of Sicily, Allied forces did not wait long before moving into Italy. On September 3, 1943, the same day that Italy secretly surrendered to the Allies, the navy transported two divisions of the British Eighth Army across the Straits of Messina and landed them at Reggio on the toe of the Italian boot. While British forces began working northward and toward the naval base at Taranto, an Anglo-American force under Rear Admiral Frank J. Lowry moved towards the Gulf of Salerno on the ankle of the Italian boot.

General Eisenhower had hoped to throw the Germans into confusion by following the formal announcement of Italy's surrender on September 8 by executing Operation Avalanche (the invasion of Salerno) the following day. The Germans were not surprised. After stripping the Italians of arms, they had taken control of defenses and communications and had four divisions posted in the vicinity of Salerno. They also anticipated where Lieutenant General Mark W. Clark's seventy-thousand-man Fifth Army would come ashore and occupied strong defensive positions on the ridges overlooking Salerno's harbor. By nightfall, and because Clark had withheld naval gunfire support, the Allies held only four narrow, disconnected beachheads.

D-Day at Normandy (Operation Overlord)

While Allied forces worked through Italy with another suspenseful and problematical landing at Anzio, the greatest invasion force in history came together on the British Isles for the assault of Normandy in northern France. The decision to implement the assault had been made in January 1943, during the Casablanca conference between Roosevelt and Churchill. General Eisenhower called it the "Great Crusade."

With the majority of the U.S. Fleet in the Pacific, Rear Admiral Alan G. Kirk, commanding the Western Naval Task Force, scraped together Assault Force "U" under Rear Admiral Don P. Moon for Utah Beach and Assault Force "O" under Rear Admiral John L. Hall for Omaha Beach. The big battleships taking part were mostly relics from World War I. The *Nevada* (BB-36) had been repaired after being bombed at Pearl Harbor. *Texas* and *Arkansas* had been around since 1914. The heavy cruisers *Augusta* (CA-31), *Tuscaloosa* (CA-37), and *Quincy* (CA-39) were more modern ships, but there were too few of them. Admiral Sir Bertram H. Ramsey, commanding the naval phase of the operation, augmented Kirk's force with cruisers, monitors, and destroyers from the British and the French navies.

Normandy would be the first major landing without an aircraft carrier because planes could operate from British airfields. The Allied air force had already taken the sting out of the *Luftwaffe* by pulverizing German airfields, aircraft factories, and communications. Eisenhower's commanders had also deluded the enemy into believing the invasion of France would likely occur at Calais, though coastal fortifications along some sections of the Normandy beaches still remained strong.

At 4:45 A.M. on June 6, 1944, Kirk's 911-ship task force and Admiral Sir Philip Vian's 1,796 ships of the Eastern Naval Task Force began bombarding German coastal defenses on Utah and Omaha beaches in the U.S. First Army sector and on Gold, Juno, and Sword beaches in the British Second Army sector. As Kirk's

ABOVE: As soon the beaches were secured at Normandy, the first concrete temporary docks, called Mulberries, were delivered into position along the shore. A few days later, they were all swept away by a violent storm and were later replaced.

LEFT: During preparations for D-Day, army M-4 Sherman tanks and other equipment are loaded on an LCT. Moored alongside, LCT-213 is also ready to move. LSTs wait in the harbor, every man on board expecting orders to come at any moment.

gunships pounded Utah and Omaha, two hundred thousand Allied infantry swarmed aboard amphibious landing craft and bounded through the rollers as they headed for the beach. Lieutenant General Omar Bradley's First Army encountered weak opposition on Utah beach as 21,000 men from the 4th Infantry Division waded ashore with 1,700 vehicles and thousands of tons of supplies.

ABOVE: On D-Day, as soon as American infantry secure Omaha Beach, the first wave of navy Seabees head for shore with all their tools and equipment packed on a Rhino ferry.

Omaha proved to be heavily fortified, and for several hours German firepower pinned the 1st Infantry Division to the beach. Hitler's prediction that if the Allies invaded the French coast they would stay "exactly nine hours" came close to proving true at "Bloody Omaha." Navy ships shelled German pillboxes for hours, and a freshening wind made it difficult to get tanks ashore. When the 1st Infantry Division approached the point of being swept off the beach, Kirk's destroyers moved close to shore, risked ground-

ing, and with "their bows against the bottom" began demolishing artillery, tanks, bunkers, and everything else at point blank range. By evening, the beaches from Utah to Sword were secured and 250,000 men began pouring ashore. When Major General Leonard Gerow arrived on Omaha beach to establish V Corps head-quarters, he fired off a message, "Thank God for the U.S. Navy."

Though largely unheralded, navy demolition teams, Seabees, and naval beach battalions hit the coast and suffered heavy casualties right along with their army counterparts. They cleared obstacles and directed the flow of landing craft bringing troops ashore. After securing the beach, they changed routines and helped doctors and corpsmen evacuate the wounded.

During the period June 6-25, the navy lost 165 ships, the majority being landing craft. Only three destroyers were sunk, and those by mines. The most damage occurred on June 18-22 when a violent storm destroyed more than three hundred small craft and wiped out two artificial harbors known as "Mulberries."

Southern France (Operation Dragoon)

On August 15, after General Bradley's breakthrough in western France, Admiral Hewitt's Western Naval Task Force in the Mediterranean landed three American divisions and two French divisions between St.-Tropez and Cannes on the southern coast of France. The landing had been planned to coincide with the Nor-mandy offensive, but Eisenhower did not have enough ships and landing craft to carry out both operations simultaneously. Many of the American gunships that participated in Operation Dragoon, such as the battle-ships *Arkansas*, *Nevada,* and *Texas*, and several cruisers and destroyers had also participated in Overlord. Lieu-tenant General Alexander Patch's Seventh Army went ashore on the French Riviera, moved quickly into the interior, and on September 12 connected with Patton's Third Army north of Dijon.

RIGHT: Prior to Operation Dragoon, the invasion of Southern France, Vice Admiral Henry K. Hewitt (center) confers with Major General Patch (to his right), Brigadier General G. P. Saville (far left), navy secretary James Forrestal (to Hewitt's left) and Rear Admiral A. G. Lemonnier (far right).

The Navy Goes Ashore

For all practical purposes, naval combat operations might have stopped in Europe had it not been for crossing Germany's River Rhine. During the winter of 1944-1945, Commander William J. Whiteside began hauling 37- and 50-foot craft overland to carry out river crossings. Each unit contained two hundred and eighteen officers and men with twenty-four LCVPs (Landing Craft, Vehicle and Personnel). During March 11-27, 1945, Boat Unit 1 ferried fourteen thousand troops and four hundred vehicles across the Rhine at Bad Neuenahr. Similar crossings occurred at Boppard, Oberwesel, Oppenheim, and Mainz. When not ferrying troops, the navy worked with army engineers laying pontoon bridges. Some tasks could not have been performed without the navy there to do them.

On May 7 representatives of the German High Command met with General Eisenhower at his headquarters at Rheims, France, and signed the instrument of surrender, a ceremony repeated the following day in Berlin. Four months later, on September 2, the war officially ended in the Far East.

The Soviet Union emerged from the war as the world's strongest land power. The United States emerged as the world's greatest sea power, with the added advantage of being the world's only nuclear power. All would change, for the Soviets had stolen from America the secrets of the atomic bomb.

ABOVE: Prior to catapult launch, two Vought OS2U Kingfisher float-planes warm up on the cruiser USS Quincy (CA-71). They will provide observation and anti-submarine reconnaissance during Operation Dragoon in Southern France.

CHAPTER 6

COLD WAR: KOREA 1950–1953

Before the rubble of World War II could be cleaned from the streets of Europe and Japan, the peace formulated between the United States, the United Kingdom, and the Soviet Union disintegrated when Josef Stalin broke his promise to leave Poland alone and to refrain from imposing communism on East Germany and the Balkan States. In early 1946, former British Prime Minister Winston Churchill came to America and warned, "An Iron Curtain has descended across the [European] continent, allowing police governments to rule Eastern Europe." Indeed, the Soviet Union resorted to treachery and went from ally to adversary. President Truman, perhaps reacting to Churchill's advice, asked for a postwar navy of 600,000 men, an army of 1.5 million, and an air force of 400,000. Congress would not support such a force. Old thinking still prevailed in the legislative body.

The navy had been upstaged at the end of the war by two atomic bombs, and for a while their primary job was to answer the call of the public to "bring the boys home." Sea power had played a major role in the defeat of Japan and Germany, yet the navy suffered more than any other service from the strategic fallout of the atom bomb. General Carl A. Spaatz, who had directed the bombing of Germany, asked, "Why should

> Our policy [is] to support the cause of freedom wherever it [is] threatened.
> *Harry S. Truman in* Memoirs*, 2:101.*

we have a Navy at all? The Russians have little or no Navy....The only reason for us to have a Navy is because someone else has a Navy and we certainly do not need to waste money on that." As far as Spaatz was concerned, all the United States needed, being the only nuclear power in the world, was an air force of long-range bombers to deliver atomic bombs. Nothing more mattered.

The Forrestal Era

Spaatz's statement annoyed Secretary of the Navy James V. Forrestal, who like Churchill distrusted the Soviet Union. During budget discussions, Congress asked Forrestal to explain his bellicose attitude toward the Soviet Union. The secretary replied, "We are going to fight any international ruffian who attempts to impose his will on the world by force. We should make that determination clear—by deeds as well as words."

For the postwar navy, Forrestal asked for four hundred ships and eight thousand aircraft—about one-third the number at war's end. Anything less, he warned, would likely "ensure a third world war." Congress ignored the warning and in 1947 reduced the navy to 319 combat ships, 1,461 combat aircraft, 491,663 naval personnel, and 108,796 marines. The timing could not have been worse. To keep the Soviets out of the Mediterranean, Forrestal needed ships. In 1948 he created a small task force that eventually became the Sixth Fleet, the first Mediterranean squadron since the nineteenth century, and he did it in time to keep communists from overthrowing Italy's government.

I cannot help but feel that if this country, in the present state of the world, goes back to bed, we don't deserve to survive.

Secretary of the Navy James V. Forrestal.

Forrestal's statements irritated congressional penny-pinchers, who preferred the less costly views of the air force and the army. In 1947 Congress passed the National Security Act, stripping the air force from the army and creating the U.S. Air Force (USAF). The act also established a new cabinet post, secretary of defense, which downgraded the authority of the secretaries of the navy and the army. To placate enormous irritation in the navy, Truman attempted to ameliorate the situation by naming Forrestal the first secretary of defense. Forrestal took the job and held it until he died in 1949. By then, the Cold War had heated up in Berlin, Greece, Turkey, and Czechoslovakia, and Mao Zedong's communists had ousted the Nationalist government of China.

Forrestal's replacement, Louis A. Johnson, believed future battles would be fought by ground troops and America's monopoly on nuclear devices delivered by USAF bombers. A lawyer-politician active in veterans' affairs, Johnson obtained the post as a reward for fund-raising activities during Truman's 1948 presidential campaign. Johnson received a rude awakening on September 23, 1949, when Truman announced that the USSR had exploded an atomic bomb. Nuclear parity delighted the North Koreans, who now felt less restrained about invading South Korea.

RIGHT: *After World War II, Secretary of the Navy Forrestal found a solution for disposing of excess ships. He sent them to Bikini Atoll, Marshall Islands, to determine the effect of an underwater atomic explosion on surface ships.*

Revolt of the Admirals

Twenty-six days after assuming office, Secretary of Defense Johnson canceled the construction of the aircraft carrier *United States* (CVA-58), although the shipyard had already laid her keel. He made the decision without consulting Admiral Louis E. Denfield, CNO, or John L. Sullivan, secretary of the navy. Both men learned of the cancellation through a press release. The action flabbergasted the navy, and six days later Sullivan resigned in protest. When other admirals learned the details, they suspected a conspiracy between Johnson and the USAF to sabotage the navy's only hope for a future. Suspicions blossomed after Denfield discovered that funds cut from the *United States* were to be used to build the USAF's B-36 intercontinental bombers.

Word soon circulated that key naval officers, in particular Denfield, were pointedly critical of Johnson's defense policy as one jeopardizing the security of the nation. The uproar led on October 2, 1949, to a congressional hearing on the armed forces, during which Admiral Arthur W. Radford spearheaded the attack on the USAF's all-or-nothing B-36 concept of future warfare. On October 17 Denfield, who had initially let his subordinates carry the ball, stepped into the fight over the objections of Johnson and Secretary of the Navy Francis P. Matthews. He called the B-36 program "a billion dollar blunder." Denfield made a point. Driven by piston engines, B-36s flying at 375mph were no match for Soviet MiG-15 jet fighters.

On November 1, Denfield lost his job for disobeying Johnson and Matthews, but the "Revolt of the Admirals" resulted in Congress preserving an important role for the navy and Marine Corps in the postwar defense muddle, and Truman's announcement that Russia had developed the A-bomb certainly helped.

TOP: After President Truman cancelled the carrier USS United States (CVA-58), CNO Admiral Louis Denfield (shown here) led the "Revolt of the Admirals." He criticized the decision before the House Naval Affairs Committee and made his point but lost his job.

ABOVE: After distinguishing himself as a carrier commander during World War II, Admiral Arthur W. Radford (1896–1973) joined the "Revolt of the Admirals" but survived the scuffle. In 1953 he became Chairman of the JCS and held the post until 1957.

The Downsized Navy

	1945	June 1950
Warships	1,200	237
Aircraft	41,000	4,300
Personnel	3,400,000	382,000
Marines	669,000	74,000

The Korean Intervention

At the end of World War II, the Soviet Union accepted the Japanese surrender of Korea above the agreed-upon but temporarily fixed 38th Parallel, and the United States accepted Japan's surrender of the lower half. The understanding that future elections were to be held to reunify Korea dissolved when the USSR dropped the "Iron Curtain" and refused to allow United Nations observers into the northern zone. On June 25, 1950, knowing that Russia now possessed the atomic bomb and aware that in 1949 American troops had evacuated South Korea, the North Korean People's Army (NKPA) plunged into South Korea with a hundred and thirty thousand men (ten divisions), Soviet artillery, a brigade of Soviet T-34 medium tanks, and a hundred and eighty Soviet Yak planes. An additional hundred thousand reserves waited at the border.

The Republic of Korea Army (ROKA)—basically a national police force—consisted of about a hundred thousand lightly armed men. The ROKA had no medium or heavy artillery, armored tanks, combat aircraft, or reserves.

Neither side had a navy, although Russia provided North Korea with a number of torpedo boats to augment their flotilla of small patrol boats. The only naval clash occurred on July 2, 1950, when three or four torpedo boats attacked the cruisers USS *Juneau* (CL-119) and HMS *Jamaica* and were sunk or put out of action.

The U.N. Security Council called an emergency meeting that the USSR boycotted. On June 27 President Truman authorized General MacArthur, supreme commander in the Far East, to use American air and naval forces to aid South Korea. MacArthur immediately dispatched two destroyers, the *Mansfield* (DD-728) and the *DeHaven* (DD-727), to evacuate seven hundred American and other foreign citizens from Inchon, South Korea. The general flew to Seoul, and on the day it fell to the North Koreans informed Truman that the ROKA was incapable of stopping the invasion. Two days later Truman authorized MacArthur to use his four infantry divisions (which had no artillery, medium tanks, or other supporting arms), the Seventh Fleet, and planes from the Far East Air Force, all of which were understrength.

The Seventh Fleet, commanded by Vice Admiral Arthur D. Struble, consisted of only the *Essex*-class carrier *Valley Forge* (CV-45), the heavy cruiser HMS *Rochester*, eight destroyers, and a collection of minesweepers and auxiliary craft. TF-96, also based in Japan and commanded by Vice Admiral C. Turner Joy, consisted of only the antiaircraft cruiser *Juneau* and four destroyers. Joy, however, soon took command of TF-77, which became the combat force of the Seventh Fleet. The problems for the navy were further complicated by Red China. MacArthur had to keep part of the Seventh Fleet in the Formosa Strait to discourage communists in China and nationalists on Taiwan from attacking each other.

ABOVE RIGHT: On June 29, 1950, the light cruiser USS Juneau (CL-119) became the first U.S. warship to fiure her guns on North Korean troops, marking the beginning of the navy's entry into the Korean War.

RIGHT: A Grumman F9F-2 Panther jet fighter taxies forward to the catapult on the flight deck of the USS Valley Forge (CV-45) in preparation for air strikes against North Korean positions along the Pusan perimeter.

RIGHT: *After completing a bridge-destroying mission in North Korea, two F4U-5 Corsairs piloted by Lieutenant John D. Ely and Lieutenant (jg) J. G. Stranlund begin circling the USS Boxer (CV-21) in preparation for landing.*

Carriers in Korea

Essex-class

Antietam (CV-36)
Bon Homme Richard (CV-31)
Boxer (CV-21)
Essex CV-9)
Kearsarge (CV-33)
Lake Champlain (CV-39)
Leyte (CV-32)
Oriskany (CV-34)
Philippine Sea (CV-47)
Princeton (CV-37)
Valley Forge (CV-45)

Light Carrier

Bataan (CVL-29)

Escort Carriers

Badoeng Strait (CVE-116)
Sicily (CVE-118)

BELOW: *Landing craft from the USS Union (AKA-106) circle in the transport area as they prepare to assemble and go ashore at Pusan. A Japanese-manned tank landing ship is to the left in the background.*

The Pusan Perimeter

During June, the NKPA penetrated deep into South Korea, pushing ROKA troops toward the port city of Pusan. On the last day of June the Seventh Fleet began piecemeal deliveries of Major General William F. Dean's 24th Infantry Division to Korea. In an effort to slow the rampaging NKPA, planes from the *Valley Forge* and the light carrier HMS *Triumph* ranged up and down the coast of Korea providing close air support while striking enemy positions and supply routes. On July 3 aircraft from *Valley Forge* bombed military installations at Pyongyang, the North Korean capital, and pilots from VF-51 splashed two Yak-9 fighters, the navy's first kills in the skies over Korea.

There were few targets for USAF strategic bombers, and air force jets stationed in Japan did not have the range for operations in Korea, so carriers flying Douglas AD Skyraiders and Grumman F9F-2 Panther jets shouldered the work. Despite the great performance of carriers during World War II, after 1945 they had become subjects of derision by the press, the USAF, and the secretary of defense as being hopelessly vulnerable to nuclear attack by land-based Soviet planes. Most of the carriers had been mothballed or scrapped. The outbreak of the Korean War proved all the naysayers wrong. The remaining three active *Essex*-class carriers were immediately deployed to the Seventh Fleet. Seven more *Essex*-class carriers would eventually be reactivated for service in Korea.

Without airfields in South Korea, Allied forces in the Pusan perimeter became entirely dependent upon carrier planes for close air support. General Dean delayed the NKPA drive for three weeks but was finally pushed back into what became the Pusan perimeter. On July 18-19 Rear Admiral James H. Doyle began landing Amphibious Group 1 at Pohang to support Dean's battered division on the shrinking perimeter. On August 3, after Marine Fighter Squadron VMF-214 arrived, pilots began operating off the escort carrier *Sicily* to provide close air support during operations at Chinju. Without aircraft carriers, there would have been no close air support or air supremacy over Korea until after the capture of Kimpo airfield near Seoul. Without the Seventh Fleet, Lieutenant General Walton H. Walker may never have put the U.S. Eighth Army on the Pusan perimeter to prevent the NKPA from pushing the defenders into the Sea of Japan.

Inchon (Operation Chromite)

While Admiral Joy's TF-77 protected both sea flanks, and carrier planes harassed NKPA operations along the Pusan perimeter, General MacArthur's staff, despite objections from the JCS and many of his commanders, planned the amphibious assault of Inchon. MacArthur wanted a second front behind enemy lines, and Inchon, in addition to being Korea's second largest port, was only fifteen miles from the ROK capital of Seoul. The city also happened to be North Korea's main artery for forwarding supplies to the NKPA divisions assaulting

ABOVE: Prior to the invasion of Inchon, Major General Oliver P. Smith (left), commanding the 1st Marine Division, and Rear Admiral James H. Doyle, commanding Amphibious Group One, meet on the cruiser USS Rochester (CA-124) to discuss last minute details.

Pusan. Of equal importance to MacArthur's planners, one of the few hard-surfaced airfields in Korea lay near Seoul at Kimpo. MacArthur's strategy was both brilliant and simple. General Walker's Eighth Army would break out of the Pusan perimeter after the assault at

Navy/Marine Combat Aircraft

Model	Engine	Speed (mph)	Range (miles)	Ceiling (feet)
Vought F4U-4*	Piston	446	1,005	41,500
Douglas AD-2	Piston	321	915	32,700
Douglas F3D	Jet	565	1,540	38,200
Grumman AF-2*	Piston	317	1,500	32,500
Grumman F6F-K*	Piston	375	1,500	39,900
Grumman F7F-3N	Piston	447	1,750	40,600
Grumman F9F-2	Jet	575	1,353	44,600
Grumman TBM*	Piston	267	1,130	23,400
McDonnell F2H-2	Jet	575	1,475	44,800

*Denotes World War II models

…amphibious operations are a thing of the past. We'll never have any more amphibious operations.
Statement of Secretary of Defense Louis Johnson quoted in Robert D. Heinl, Victory at High Tide, 6-7.

Inchon and crush the North Koreans in the jaws of a vise.

MacArthur's masterstroke was not without problems, and the amphibious phase was indeed a gamble. Huge tides at Inchon not only created unusually strong currents but also limited the period during which a landing could be made to two brief intervals of 33-foot tides during one or two days a month. LSTs drew twenty-nine feet, other landing craft twenty-three feet, leaving small margin for error. Fortifications guarded the entrance to the city, which could only be approached through twisting and treacherous Flying Fish channel, which was flanked by mud flats that could ground landing craft on their way to shore. There were no sandy beaches. High sea walls encased the city, and men equipped with ladders would have to scale them while under fire. MacArthur hoped to capitalize on the likelihood that the NKPA would not expect an assault on Inchon. One freighter properly sunk could have blocked the channel and crippled the Inchon operation.

MacArthur chose September 15 as D-Day because of tidal conditions and brought Major General Oliver P. Smith's 1st Marine Division hurriedly across the

RIGHT: Besides being 150 miles behind enemy lines, Inchon rated as one of the worst places in the world to launch an amphibious assault. The navy told General MacArthur they could do it, the marines agreed to lead it, and the dual combination made it work.

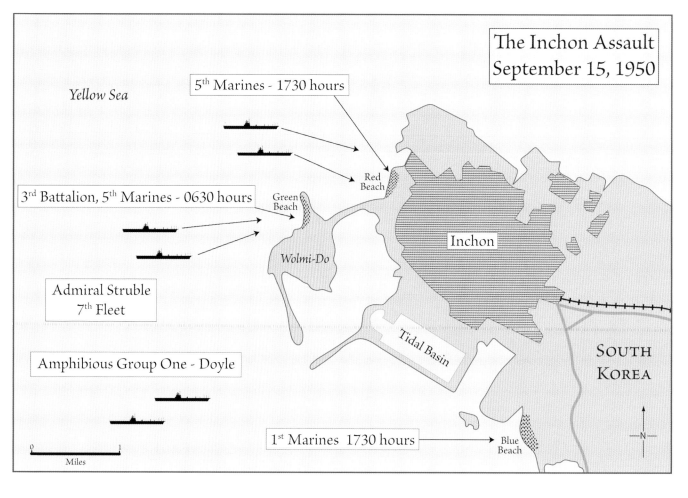

The Inchon Assault September 15, 1950

Yellow Sea

5th Marines - 1730 hours

3rd Battalion, 5th Marines - 0630 hours

Green Beach

Red Beach

Admiral Struble 7th Fleet

Wolmi-Do

Inchon

Amphibious Group One - Doyle

Tidal Basin

1st Marines 1730 hours

Blue Beach

SOUTH KOREA

0   1
Miles

N

Pacific to lead the assault. On September 10, Admiral Joy's carrier planes from TF-77 began the softening-up process while Admiral Doyle's TF-90 amphibious force headed into the Yellow Sea. After navy cutbacks, assembling two hundred and thirty ships in a month was no small accomplishment. When on September 3 and 13, respectively, typhoons Jane with 110mph winds and Kezia with 60mph winds struck the invasion fleet, the navy still adhered to MacArthur's deadlines.

Shortly before dawn on September 15, the convoy settled into position off Inchon Narrows. Four cruisers and six destroyers of the Gunfire Support Group moved inshore and bombarded enemy positions on Wolmi-do, a fortified island protecting the inner harbor. At 6:33 A.M. the 5th Marines went ashore and twenty-two minutes later raised the American flag on

Radio Hill. By noon, and at the cost of only seventeen wounded, the marines secured Wolmi-do and opened the way to Inchon.

At 2:30 P.M. the heavy work began when the Gunfire Support Group opened on Inchon. At 4:45 the first wave of landing craft cut loose from transports, and at 5:31 the first marines climbed ladders and poured over the seawall against light resistance. Many landing craft in the second wave grounded, but eight LSTs loaded with jeeps, tanks, and trucks made it ashore. On September 17 the 7th Infantry Division began landing. By then the marines had moved inland and captured Kimpo Airfield.

General Walker's Eighth Army had broken out of the Pusan perimeter the previous day and drove north, scattering elements of the shocked NKPA all over the countryside. On September 26 Walker's army made contact with Major General Edward M. Almond's X Army Corps near Osan, and on the following day the 5th Marines raised the American flag over the Capitol building at Seoul. The eleven-day offensive netted a hundred and twenty-five thousand North Korean prisoners.

ABOVE: With a stream of rockets streaking overhead, landing craft transporting the first wave of men from the 1st Marine Division head for the already pockmarked island of Wolmi-do, the capture of which opened the way to Inchon.

LEFT: When Rear Admiral Doyle sent the marines ashore at Inchon, he made sure that the scaling ladders would be long enough to stretch from the bottom of the landing craft to the top of the seawall.

The Navy and the Marines have never shone more brightly.

General MacArthur on the capture of Inchon, Kimpo Airfield, and Seoul.

The Inchon-Seoul campaign gave MacArthur excessive self-confidence, and he tended to dismiss caution from Washington about his plans to unify Korea. He had beaten the NKPA so badly that he believed the war had been won, leaving one more operation to mop up North Korea.

Wonsan (Operation Tailboard)

After Inchon, MacArthur obtained agreement from the United Nations and President Truman to invade North Korea and once again unify the country, despite repeated warnings that doing so could result in Chinese intervention. While Walker's Eighth Army moved up the western side of Korea, MacArthur planned another amphibious landing at Wonsan, a hundred and ten miles north of the 38th Parallel on the eastern side of Korea's peninsula. A city of seventy-five thousand people, Wonsan was also Korea's main port on the Sea of Japan; it also had a major refinery and a hard-surfaced airfield.

RIGHT: After minesweepers opened a way through Wonsan's mine-infested harbor, landing craft began transporting the 1st Marine Division ashore. Marines found the town already occupied by South Korean troops.

Once again, Doyle's TF-90 provided the amphibious force and Almond's X Corps, which included Smith's 1st Marine Division, provided the infantry assault force. Smith did not get along with Almond, mainly because Almond did not understand marine doctrine. Nor did Smith agree with MacArthur's push to the Yalu River on the Manchurian border, because he questioned the wisdom of a campaign during Korea's bitterly cold winters, especially with both wings of the army separated.

The Wonsan operation clearly tested the patience of the navy. Admiral Joy argued that the infantry could march overland and reach Wonsan quicker "and with much less effort than it would take to get the Corps around…by sea." Walker protested against taking troops off by sea when they could be used during the march to Wonsan to mop up NKPA positions in the interior. Almond insisted upon a sea expedition as being "cheaper." Because Almond did not report to Walker, which was unfortunate, MacArthur approved the plan.

On October 15 the 1st Marine Division, led by Doyle's amphibious force command flagship *Mount McKinley* (AGC-7), departed from Inchon with 30,184 troops for the 830-mile voyage to Wonsan. Arriving five days later, Doyle learned that the harbor had been salted with several thousand Soviet magnetic and contact mines, and that the minesweepers *Pirate* and *Pledge* had been sunk.

While other minesweepers continued clearing Wonsan's harbor, Doyle ordered what the marines called "Operation Yo-Yo." The convoy steamed north then south and five days later returned to Wonsan. When Almond's X Corps landed at Wonsan on October 25, two ROKA divisions had already captured the city two weeks earlier. Air maintenance crews had arrived on October 12, and Bob Hope's entertainers began performing their first show the day before the X Corps returned from "Operation Yo-Yo," thereby vali-

LEFT: After finding Wonsan's harbor seeded with more than 2,000 mines, a navy underwater demolition team (UDT) discuss plans for cutting through the field so that landing craft can transport marines ashore.

ABOVE: During sweeping operations in Wonsan harbor, the Korean minesweeper YMS-516 (formerly the USS YMS-148) is blown up after striking a mine. The elaborate Soviet-laid minefield delayed U.S. landings for more than a week.

dating Joy's argument against Almond's useless amphibious operation.

Because ROKA divisions had also captured Pyongyang on October 19, the X Corps moved north instead of west. The 1st Marine Division marched up the coast to Hungnam and from there took the road to the Chosin (Changjin) Reservoir. On November 27, 120,000 Chinese troops began isolating the 1st Marine

Division on the western side of the reservoir. East of the reservoir, Chinese divisions attacked the 3rd and 7th infantry divisions. MacArthur ordered the evacuation of the entire area, including Walker's Eighth Army on the western side of the Korean peninsula.

The Hungnam Evacuation

In sub-zero weather on November 28, the 1st Marine Division held off an attack by eight Chinese divisions and for twelve days slugged their way south against heavy snows and overwhelming odds to the port of Hungnam. Joy's TF-77 stood off shore, using planes from the *Philippine Sea, Leyte, Princeton*, and *Valley Forge*, and the escort carriers *Sicily* and *Badoeng Strait* to pummel Chinese troop movements. Despite terrible weather, other planes managed to airdrop supplies to the retreating forces. Joy also sent a squadron under the command of Rear Admiral Lyman A. Thackery to Korea's west coast, along with British, Australian, and Canadian ships, to cover the retreat of Walker's Eighth Army. The light carrier *Bataan*, ferrying USAF planes to Japan, flew them off, took on Corsairs, and on December 15 joined Thackery's squadron off Korea's west coast.

On December 4 near Hagaru-ri, the Chinese shot down Ensign Jesse Brown's F4U Corsair, which had sortied from the carrier *Leyte*. After making a forced landing, Brown became pinned in the cockpit. Lieutenant (j.g.) Thomas J. Hudner purposely crash-landed his plane to save Brown, who happened to be the first African-American naval aviator. Brown soon died, but Hudner survived. Rescued by a helicopter, Hudner received the Medal of Honor for his efforts to save Brown.

On December 10, while Joy's carrier planes struck enemy positions and Rear Admiral Roscoe H. Hillenkoetter's gunfire support group protected the defensive perimeter around Hungnam, Doyle's TF-90 began embarking ground troops and tons of equipment. During the retreat from the Chosin Reservoir, the 1st

Marine Division left nothing of value behind. By December 24 TF-90 had embarked 105,000 troops, 17,500 tanks and vehicles, 350,000 tons of cargo, and 91,000 Korean civilians. As the task force pulled away from Hungnam, navy underwater demolition teams blew up the waterfront, toppling cranes, warehouses, piers, and port facilities, leaving nothing behind but twisted rubble. Although the troops would not be home for Christmas, as MacArthur had promised, they were nevertheless out of harm's way.

Carrier Air Operations

By January 15, 1951, Chinese forces in Korea numbered five hundred thousand. They pushed MacArthur's army below the 38th Parallel and recaptured Seoul. Against the advice of Joy, who believed his planes could serve best by providing close air support, MacArthur directed TF-77 to strike the railway and bridge network along North Korea's east coast.

ABOVE: During the evacuation from Hungnam, North Korean refugees prepare to board an LST while other less fortunate civilians (left) transfer their scant belongings from an ox cart to a fishing boat.

LEFT: During a White House ceremony, President Truman decorates Lieutenant (jg) Hudner with the Medal of Honor. Hudner received the award for his heroism while trying to save squadronmate Ensign Jesse Brown by crash-landing his own Corsair in the rescue attempt.

RIGHT: The task of blowing up bridges crossing the Yalu River were left to carrier-based AD-1 Skyraiders because the USAF's strategic bombers could neither hit the bridges nor avoid crossing the boundary into Manchurian air space.

Supplies continued to reach Chinese forces until one day in March fliers from *Princeton* discovered a partly concealed and untouched 600-foot bridge with tunnels at both ends. Rear Admiral Ralph A. Ofstie ordered a strike and eight Skyraiders from *Princeton*, led by Commander Harold G. Carlson, "dropped one span…damaged a second, and twisted two others" out of alignment. *Princeton*'s crew called the area "Carlson's Canyon," and Hollywood producers turned the episode into "The Bridges of Toko-Ri."

Vice Admiral Charles Turner Joy (1895–1956)

Charles Turner Joy was born on February 17, 1895, in St. Louis, Missouri, and he grew up always wanting to be a navy man. He accepted an appointment to the U.S. Naval Academy in 1912, graduating four years later. He understood the Far East, having served for nineteen years on the navy's Yangtze Patrol. He also understood carrier operations, having served as a staff officer on the USS *Lexington* during World War II. In 1944-1945, as rear admiral with the U.S. Pacific Fleet, he performed with skill and valor during amphibious operations in the Marianas, Philippines, Iwo Jima, and Okinawa.

After World War II, Joy remained in the Far East, using naval forces on the Yangtze River and along the Chinese coast to support Chiang Kai-shek. Promoted to vice admiral in August 1949, Joy became commander of naval forces in the Far East and a year later used his surface and air units to hold back the NKPA at Pusan and discourage Chinese and Soviet military action in the Yellow Sea. General MacArthur could not have succeeded at Inchon without Joy's carriers, cruisers, destroyers, and amphibious ships; and two hundred thousand troops and civilians would have been stranded at Hungnam had Joy not provided the means to embark them with all of their equipment and supplies during the harsh Korean winter.

Admiral Joy frequently disagreed with General Almond, who commanded the X Army Corps, and his opinions were usually correct. Almond, however, was a long-standing and personal friend of MacArthur.

In 1952 Admiral Charles Turner Joy, commander U.S. Naval Forces, Far East, served as the United Nations delegate to the Korean Armistice Conference at Panmunjon, a village between the lines where he appeared on May 12 to hold a press conference.

In 1951 Joy also became the senior U.N. delegate when cease-fire negotiations began with China and North Korea. He lost patience because the U.N. constantly changed its policy positions. Exasperated by the lack of progress, he asked to be replaced. In May 1952 Joy became the superintendent of the Naval Academy and died four years later of cancer.

Joy took a personal interest in finding ways to plug the tunnels and keep the bridge out of commission. For several months, two carrier air groups spent all their time blasting the span and tracks leading to and from it. The Chinese finally shifted their supply lines to western Korea, where the USAF took over.

However, Carlson was not quite finished with his work. During the 1951 battles along the 38th Parallel, the Chinese controlled the water from the Hwachon reservoir, opening sluice gates to drive back advances of U.N. troops and closing the gates to facilitate their own attacks. Soon after Lieutenant General Matthew B. Ridgway replaced MacArthur on April 11, 1951, he ordered the dam destroyed. When B-29s failed to hit the dam, Ridgway called on the navy. Rear Admiral George Henderson, commanding *Princeton*, sent a squadron of Skyraiders armed with 2,000-pound bombs, but the mission failed. Carlson said he could blow the dam with aerial torpedoes—a weapon seldom used during the Korean War. With his squadron of AD Skyraiders, Carlson's aircraft ran a gauntlet of antiaircraft fire, knocked out the gates, and flooded the Han and Pukhan River valleys.

Operation Strangle

On June 5, 1951, General Ridgway launched Operation Strangle in an effort to interdict the flow of supplies to Communist troops on the front lines. Ridgway concentrated on eight supply routes having roads, bridges, tunnels, and rail lines. He divided Korea into three sectors with carrier aircraft from TF-77 assigned to two routes in central Korea. The USAF covered three routes in western Korea and the First Marine Aircraft Wing covered three routes in eastern Korea. The operation, which lasted through December, enjoyed moderate success. TF-77 spent the entire summer and fall, day and night, bombing truck routes, country roads, bridges, and railroads. The Chinese formed highly effective teams of manual labor to repair the damage or create new routes around bomb-cratered areas. Navy pilots argued that much of the effort was a waste of time, and Ridgway, being of the same mind, suspended Strangle in December. Korean prisoners, however, admitted that a major August offensive had been cancelled because forty thousand trucks had been destroyed. Strangle also brought about the first serious peace talks.

ABOVE LEFT: Shown sitting proudly in the cockpit of his F9F Cougar on November 11, 1950, Lt. Cdr. W. T. Amen was the first navy pilot to shoot down a MiG-15 jet fighter.

ABOVE: During ground operations along the DMZ in mid-1952, the battleship USS Iowa (BB-61) provides heavy fire support to U.N. troops with salvos from her 16-inch guns.

BELOW: After serving a tour of duty off the eastern coast of Korea, the USS Antietam (CV-36) returned stateside for modifications. In January 1953 the ship went back to sea as the navy's first aircraft carrier with an angled flight deck.

In late October, during the second phase of Operation Strangle, Ridgway learned that communist commissars and party officials planned to meet at Kapsan. Admiral John Perry, commanding TF-77, ordered aerial photographs taken of the area. On the morning of the meeting, eight Skyraiders flew off the *Essex* and headed for Kapsan. Each plane carried two 1,000-pound bombs, eight 250-pound bombs, and napalm. At 9:13 A.M., just as the gathering took seats at the table, Skyraiders swooped over a 6,000-foot range, dropped into the valley, and destroyed the compound, killing 509 high-level communist party members.

Perry proved to be an excellent innovator. He tinkered with ways to save the lives of his pilots, while meeting the demands of the war, and devised the navy's first "smart bombs." Perry obtained six World War II F6F-K Grumman Hellcats and fitted them with remote guidance systems. During August-September 1952, he had the unmanned planes loaded with high explosives and catapulted into the air. Technicians guided the planes to predetermined enemy targets. Photographic evidence collected the following day showed the experiment actually worked.

Operations resolved themselves into a day-to-day routine where stamina replaced glamor and persistence was pitted against oriental perseverance.
From The Sea War in Korea, *71, by Malcolm W. Cagle and Frank A. Manson.*

By then, the Korean War had settled into a political stalemate, though TF-77 continued to strike supply lines and enjoy an occasional dogfight with Soviet MiG-15s. During the autumn of 1952, aerial combat increased between Panthers and MiGs flown by Russian pilots out of Vladivostok. After several skirmishes in the air, observers admitted that the MiGs were better planes than Panthers, but Americans were better pilots. After losing several MiGs to navy fliers, Russia's aerial interference from Vladivostok stopped.

The Awakening

By 1952, President Truman recognized that the USAF had hoodwinked him and his secretary of defense into believing that all future wars would depend upon nuclear weapons delivered by long-range bombers. He lobbied Congress for a five-year, $50 billion program to upgrade conventional forces. The navy's portion financed 173 new ships, refitted 291 existing ships, provided a second aircraft carrier, and funded a nuclear submarine. But this did not slow down the nuclear arms race with the Soviet Union or suspend work on the hydrogen bomb, which debuted in 1953; the same year General Eisenhower became president.

Wars stimulate technology, and the Korean War gave the navy a big boost as well as the addition of modern ships. New Grumman F9F-6 Panther models called Cougars appeared with swept wings. Flattops began carrying HO3S-1 Sikorsky helicopters for rescue and minesweeping operations. Midway through the war the

navy added F2H Banshee jets, which became excellent escort fighters during bombing missions. The Grumman F7F-3N and the F4U-5N became the navy's night heckler. Although carrier night-fighting had been developed during World War II, it never became a big factor in Korea. *Princeton*, designated for Operation "No Doze," became the only carrier with aircraft flying night missions. Night jets were too fast to knock down enemy planes, so Corsairs did the work. Lieutenant Guy P. Bordelon shot down five planes in three night actions and became the first and only navy ace of the war.

One night-fighting weapon made a difference, the 2.75-inch folding-fin aircraft rocket, nicknamed "Mickey Mouse." Designed as an air-to-air weapon, it became a popular night interdiction weapon late in the war. The rockets came in pods of seven. Skyraiders carried six pods, flares, and 250- and 500-pound

Using [Mickey Mouse rockets] was like going after a bug with a flyswatter instead of trying to stab him with a pencil.

From The Sea War in Korea, *267, by Cagle and Manson.*

bombs. Pilots fired a pod in a ripple, with split-second pauses between each rocket.

With the introduction of jet aircraft and new weaponry, technology changed so rapidly that no ship under construction ever went into commission as originally designed. Had it not been for the Korean War, one might wonder whether the navy would have been able to withstand the attacks by Congress to diminish it.

The Navy's Pride in Performance

Fifteen American carriers and five British carriers served in the Korean War, refuting the USAF's claims that flattops were extinct. The navy flew 167,552 sorties, the marines 107,000 sorties, most of which were from carriers. Carrier planes flew a third of all operations in Korea, dropping 120,000 tons of bombs. The navy claimed sixteen kills in the air and thirty-six aircraft destroyed on the ground. A few navy pilots flew North American F-86 Sabres, but Panthers and Banshees remained the carrier pilots' first choice. The Korean War muffled the claims of the USAF, whose B-29s delivered the most ineffective bombing of the war.

At 10:00 A.M. on July 27, 1953, U.N. and communist negotiators at Panmunjon signed the formal cease-fire agreement, reestablishing the 38th Parallel as the dividing line.

In February 1953 the navy had 84,124 men in Korea. Of 2,243 combat casualties, only 458 were killed or died of wounds, and 209 became prisoners or were missing in action (MIA). The navy had been a principal handicap to communist success in Korea. After the armistice, most of the navy went home, leaving the peacekeeping effort to the army.

North Korea Today

Wars of unconditional surrender ended with World War II and the formation of the United Nations, an organization designed to prevent wars and foster permanent peace. Many still question whether President Truman and the U.N. made the right decision by pulling back to the 38th Parallel and negotiating a settlement instead of fighting for the reunification of Korea.

North Korea is still a rogue nation and a threat to world peace. The NKPA in 2005 had an active military force of 1.2 million men, a reserve force of five million more, and more than a hundred thousand special forces troops. Ground equipment consisted of 3,800 main battle tanks, 2,270 armored personnel carriers, and 11,200 artillery pieces. The NKPA navy consisted of 48,000 personnel, 430 combat vessels, 40 submarines, and 340 support ships. The air force contained 103,000 personnel, 850 combat aircraft, and 820 support aircraft and helicopters. There were 13,000 hardened artillery sites, nuclear weapons, and the world's third largest stockpile of chemical and biological weapons.

Looking back fifty-plus years, and following North Korea's testing of a nuclear weapon in October 2006, one might ask whether the U.N. decision to leave Korea divided was the correct one to make.

ABOVE: On January 12, 1954, President Eisenhower stands with three men to whom he has just presented Medals of Honor. Left to right are 1st Lieutenant Edward R. Showalter, Jr., PFC Ernest E. West, and Hospital Corpsman Third Class William R. Charette.

LEFT: Medal of Honor recipient Hospital Corpsman William Charette selects the unknown soldier of World War II (right) during ceremonies on the USS Canberra (CAG-2). The other two unknowns, one from World War II, the other from Korea, are buried at sea.

COLD WAR: VIETNAM 1961–1975

The Vietnam conflict began on the day the war with Japan ended. Ho Chi Minh's followers seized Japan's abandoned weaponry, and in mid-August 1945 Vietminh forces under Vo Nguyen Giap struck Ha Tinh province and other key locations. After ousting the emperor, Ho issued an imperial rescript to the country in an effort to unite the nation under his leadership. American operatives in Vietnam reported that Ho's party, despite allusions to democracy, was dominated by "a 100 percent communist party," and that Ho sought support from the United States and the United Nations to insure the exclusion of the French and the Chinese. On September 2, 1945, the same day Japan signed the official surrender agreement, Ho issued a

"Declaration of Independence" modeled after the American document, and established himself as president of Vietnam.

Despite warnings from allies, the new French government decided to recapture Vietnam and retain it as a colony. To rebuild its navy, France borrowed from the United States the light carrier USS *Langley* (CVL-27), renamed *LaFayette*, and the *Belleau Wood* (CVL-24), renamed *Bois Belleau*. On March 16, 1947, surplus Douglas SBD dive-bombers flown by French pilots provided air cover for troops landing's on Vietnam's coast. Ten days later two hundred SBDs dropped sixty-five tons of bombs on Minh bases near Hanoi and started the Vietnam (Indo-China) War. French President Charles de Gaulle requested better aircraft, and the U.S. Department of Defense sold France a carrier-load of F6F Hellcat fighters and SB2C Helldivers. Requests from France continued, and three years later the carrier USS *Saipan* (CVL-48) arrived off Danang, and marine pilots flew twenty-five AU-1 Corsairs ashore.

As French forces increased, Vietminh resistance stiffened. A crisis developed in November 1953 when General Henri Navarre, commanding French forces, dropped thousands of parachutists into the remote northern outpost of Dienbienphu. Vietminh supplied with Chinese artillery quickly surrounded the valley base. Soviet 75mm antiaircraft guns shot down 47 and damaged 167 French planes that were attempting to provide air support. Navarre asked the U.S. Navy for help, but Admiral Robert B. Carney, CNO, wanted nothing to do with Vietnam.

BELOW: During the Indo-China War in 1953, the United States leased the carrier Belleau Wood *(CVL-24), renamed* Bois Belleau, *to France. Before leaving the Norfolk Naval Station, she loaded up with Hellcats and Helldivers.*

The Geneva Period (1954-1965)

With the Korean War settled and navy cutbacks on the chopping block, Carney approached the JCS and suggested retaining the *Essex* (CVA-9), the *Wasp* (CVA-18), and a squadron of destroyers at Subic Bay under Rear Admiral Robert E. Blick, Jr., to aid, if necessary, the removal of French forces from Vietnam. The JCS agreed and augmented Blick's force with the *Boxer* (CV-21) and four more destroyers. In 1954 Blick took the squadron into the South China Sea for readiness maneuvers. Although Carney continued to strengthen the Seventh Fleet, he lobbied against any participation in the Indo-China War. President Eisenhower agreed with Carney's position and refused to engage naval forces in supportive air strikes. On May 7 Dienbienphu fell to the Vietminh.

On July 20 France and the Vietminh concluded an accord at Geneva, Switzerland, that divided Vietnam into two countries: the Democratic Republic of Vietnam (North Vietnam) and the Republic of Vietnam (South Vietnam), separated by a demilitarized zone (DMZ) along the 17th Parallel. The agreement provided for the Vietnamese to live wherever they wanted, and the navy transported 293,002 civilians and 17,846 military personnel from North Vietnam to South Vietnam. Among the latter came insurgents who joined with southern communists to become the Viet Cong (VC). They had the full support of Ho Chi Minh, Red China, and the Soviets, and they wasted no time creating civil strife. As a consequence, an American-French mission remained behind to help President Ngo Dinh Diem build a nation and a military force to defend South Vietnam.

For the next ten years the Tokyo-based Seventh Fleet maintained a presence in the South China Sea. One group, formed around the *Lexington* (CVA-16), patrolled Vietnamese waters, while a second group, formed around the *Shangri-La* (CVA-38), patrolled the Straits of Formosa to discourage China from attacking Taiwan. During the same period, President Eisenhower

ABOVE: As aid to French forces fighting Ho's Viet Minh communist army, the USS Saipan (CVL-48) arrived off Tourane, Vietnam, on April 25, 1953, with 25 AU-1 Corsairs. Marine pilots promptly flew the planes ashore.

LEFT: During Operation Passage to Freedom in August 1954, the USS Montague (APA-98) lowers a ladder to a French LSM in Haiphong's harbor to embark hundreds of refugees seeking a better life in Saigon.

ABOVE: On August 4, 1964, the destroyer USS Turner Joy (DD-951) joined the destroyer USS Maddox (DD-731) in the search for North Vietnamese-manned, Soviet-made P-4 gunboats that created the controversial Tonkin Gulf incident.

I am trying to keep us from having the same kind of experience as the French during their catastrophic Indo-China War when they won many [battles] but lost the campaign.

Vice Admiral Frederick N. Kivette, quoted in The United States Navy and the Vietnam Conflict, *vol. 2, p. 36, by Edward J. Marolda and Oscar P. Fitzgerald.*

increased the number of military advisors in Vietnam.

In March 1961, after he assumed the presidency, John F. Kennedy became immediately concerned about the instability in South Vietnam. He sent more ships to Vice Admiral Frederick N. Kivette, Seventh Fleet commander, who reformed TF-77 under Rear Admiral Frank B. Miller. Kennedy was assassinated before he could dictate military policy in Vietnam, and those decisions devolved upon Lyndon B. Johnson, Kennedy's vice president.

The Gulf of Tonkin Incident

On the afternoon of August 2, 1964, while patrolling the Tonkin Gulf in international waters thirty miles off the coast of North Vietnam, Captain Herbert L. Ogier of the destroyer USS *Maddox* (DD-731) reported an unprovoked attack by three North Vietnamese Soviet-made P-4 torpedo boats. Ogier opened fire and radioed the carrier *Ticonderoga* (CVA-14) for air support. Captain D. W. Cooper launched four F-8E Crusaders, all-weather fighter/interceptors armed with an arsenal of general-purpose rockets. Using UHF/ADF radar, the pilots flew to the scene of the attack and reported sinking one boat.

Two days later at 9:30 P.M., the *Maddox* and *Turner Joy* (DD-951), patrolling together, picked up radar blips in the Gulf of Tonkin, which they assumed were North Vietnamese torpedo boats. Both destroyers opened in the direction of the radar contacts, and claimed to have sunk two torpedo boats. Crusader pilots arrived on the scene and found nothing. Both destroyer skippers later admitted that the supposed contacts were probably only radar blips.

Johnson, having assumed the presidency, ordered retaliatory strikes against North Vietnam. On August 5 A-1H Skyraiders, A-4 Skyhawks, and F-4 Phantoms from the *Constellation* (CVA-64) and the *Ticonderoga* flew sixty-four sorties against petroleum storage facili-

ABOVE: After the Gulf of Tonkin incident, President Johnson authorized a retaliatory strike on North Vietnamese patrol boats. A Douglas A-1 Skyraider attached to the catapult cable on the USS Constellation (CVA-64) prepares to make that strike.

ties and naval bases along a hundred-mile stretch of the North Vietnamese coast. Although the four-hour strike damaged or destroyed twenty-nine patrol boats and 90 percent of the petroleum facilities in the strike zones, enemy antiaircraft fire killed Lieutenant (j.g.) Richard A. Slather and knocked down Lieutenant (j.g.) Everett Alvarez, who became the first navy POW and remained incarcerated until February 1973.

Political Indecisiveness

Johnson used the Tonkin Gulf incident as grounds for waging war on North Vietnam. On August 7, 1964, Congress passed the Tonkin Gulf Resolution, giving the president virtually unlimited authority to conduct war in Vietnam. For six months Admiral Miller's TF-77 stood off the coast of Vietnam waiting for instructions while Johnson and Secretary of Defense Robert McNamara wrestled indecisively with possible political fallout from initiating an unrestricted bombing campaign as opposed to a restricted bombing campaign. Meanwhile, TF-77 aircraft carriers rotated and new flattops arrived off the Vietnam coast.

On February 7, 1965, the VC gave Johnson an opening by attacking the barracks at the Pleiku Airbase, killing eight American servicemen and wounding a hundred and twenty-six. Johnson immediately authorized Flaming Dart I, and eighty-three planes from the carriers *Coral Sea* (CVA-43), *Hancock* (CVA-19), and *Ranger* (CVA-61) flew 182 sorties against North Vietnamese military installations. Three days later VC countered by blowing up an enlisted men's barracks at Qui Nhon. Johnson replied by authorizing Flaming Dart II, and ninety-nine aircraft from the three carriers clobbered military installations near Chan Hoa.

Johnson and McNamara could not have picked a worse time of the year to begin air strikes. Monsoon weather, torrential rains, low clouds, and poor visibility hid targets and screened enemy missile sites. Carrier commanders further fumed because McNamara's staff

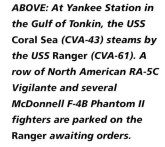

ABOVE: At Yankee Station in the Gulf of Tonkin, the USS Coral Sea (CVA-43) steams by the USS Ranger (CVA-61). A row of North American RA-5C Vigilante and several McDonnell F-4B Phantom II fighters are parked on the Ranger awaiting orders.

LEFT: Lieutenant Rene Leeds from Fighter Squadron 21 (VF-21), flying an F-4B Phantom, drops his payload on a Viet Cong concentration in South Vietnam. Leeds flew more than 100 missions during his tour in Vietnam.

LEFT: During a break in the weather in October 1965, an A-4 Skyhawk makes a strafing run in North Vietnam against a train importing military supplies from Red China.

decided what routes to fly, what ordnance to use, what aircraft to deploy, and what hour of the day to strike, all without regard for the weather or the disposition of enemy antiaircraft. During bad weather, when navy pilots could not locate their Washington-assigned targets, they dropped their payloads in the South China Sea before returning to the carriers. Infrequent clear and sunny days passed without any sorties because meteorologists in Washington were of no help in scheduling McNamara's air strikes. Miller did what he could to protect his pilots from Washington micromanagement, but executive directives for political purposes led to preventable losses.

Rolling Thunder

On March 2, 1965, Johnson authorized Rolling Thunder, a sustained bombing campaign developed around a strategic theory concocted by McNamara's so-called "whiz kids" that a progressively escalated bombing of North Korea would eventually touch the enemy's "ouch level" and terminate Hanoi's support of the Viet Cong. To add emphasis to the theory, Johnson authorized the landing of the 9th Marine Expeditionary Brigade near the DMZ at Danang, thereby committing the first combat ground troops to South Vietnam. Over time, "meaningless" best described the president's policy for conducting warfare.

Rolling Thunder, which kept navy planes occupied day and night, might have been effective had Johnson not imposed restrictions on which targets could be bombed and which could not. He placed supply depots in Cambodia off limits, forbade the pursuit of the enemy into Laos and Cambodia, banned napalm, made Hanoi an enemy sanctuary, and ordered that Haiphong, North Vietnam's key seaport, not be bombed, blockaded, or mined for fear of killing a

RIGHT: An A-4 Skyhawk from the carrier USS Oriskany (CVA-34) fires a cluster of 2.75-inch rockets at a Viet Cong stronghold in South Vietnam. The versatile Skyhawk was capable of delivering bombs, rockets, and missiles.

BELOW RIGHT: During operations at Yankee Station in the Gulf of Tonkin, the ordnance crew on the USS Oriskany (CVA-34) prepare to deliver M-117 500-pound and 1,000-pound bombs to A-4 Skyhawks preparing for a mission.

We will not be defeated. We will not grow tired. We will not withdraw, either openly or under the cloak of a meaningless agreement...and we will remain ready...for unconditional discussion.
Lyndon B. Johnson's commitment to South Vietnam quoted in "Task Force 77 in Action off Vietnam," Proceedings, *no. 831, 71, by Malcolm W. Cagle.*

Russian or Chinese advisor. Navy pilots could attack only *moving* military trucks, but not until after they departed from Haiphong and disappeared into the jungle. No one in Washington explained how pilots flying at 1,000mph at two thousand feet could distinguish a military truck from a civilian vehicle. General Giap responded by moving his trucks at night.

On December 24, 1965, Johnson ordered the second bombing halt in the war and waited for the enemy to request peace talks. On January 31, 1966, after nothing happened, he escalated the air war against North Vietnam, still seeking the elusive "ouch factor" promoted by the secretary of defense.

Yankee Station—Dixie Station

Admiral Ulysses S. G. Sharp, Commander U.S. Pacific Fleet, became sharply critical when he discovered that Washington was routing USAF strikes and TF-77 air strikes against the same target at the same time without notifying either party of orders given to the other.

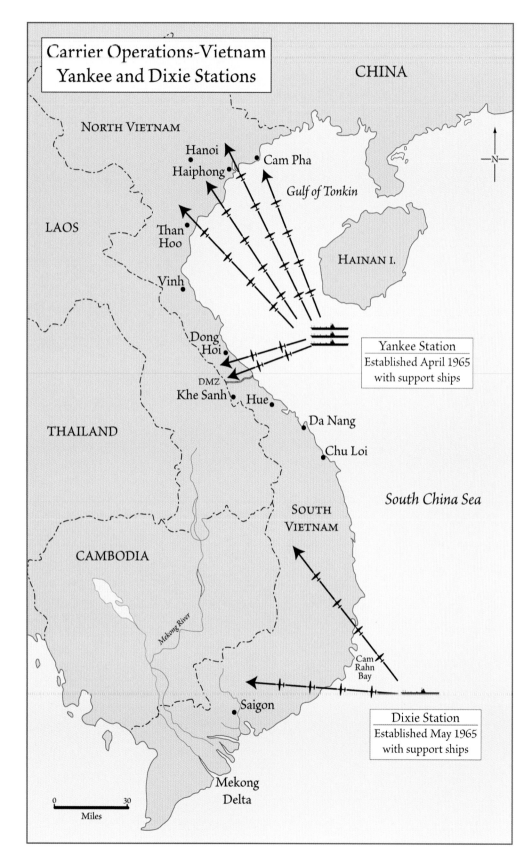

Carrier Operations-Vietnam Yankee and Dixie Stations

CHINA

NORTH VIETNAM

Hanoi
Haiphong
Cam Pha
Gulf of Tonkin
HAINAN I.

LAOS

Than Hoo

Vinh

Dong Hoi

Yankee Station
Established April 1965
with support ships

DMZ
Khe Sanh
Hue

THAILAND

Da Nang

Chu Loi

South China Sea

SOUTH VIETNAM

CAMBODIA

Mekong River

Cam Rahn Bay

Saigon

Dixie Station
Established May 1965
with support ships

Mekong Delta

0 ——— 30
Miles

LEFT: Long before the USAF brought planes into Vietnam, the navy's aircraft carrier pilots carried the load. Yankee Station became the roving area in the Gulf of Tonkin, and Dixie Station in the South China Sea. There were no better pilots than those on carriers.

ABOVE: During operations underway in the Gulf of Tonkin, a phone talker radios information to crewmen fueling aircraft during flight preparations on the nuclear-powered attack aircraft carrier USS Enterprise (CVAN-65).

McNamara's "whiz kids" decided to divide North Korea into two sectors and established a geographical point in the upper South China Sea as the operational sector for the navy and called it Yankee Station. Although the purpose was to provide air coverage by three carriers over coastal targets in North Vietnam, TF-77 continued to be called upon for air strikes in South Vietnam.

As Johnson committed more troops to Vietnam, the North Vietnamese increased support of the VC. As a consequence, aircraft from *Coral Sea, Midway* (CVA-41), and *Oriskany* (CVA-34) became involved in ground support operations off Cam Rahn Bay because of the scarcity of airfields in South Vietnam. McNamara then authorized the establishment of Dixie Station, which was to be covered by a single carrier group but often contained two and sometimes three flattops. Dixie Station remained in operation for fifteen months, until air bases could be built ashore. During the Vietnam

War, seventeen different carriers participated in operations out of Yankee Station and Dixie Station.

Soviet SAM Sites

On March 17, 1965, Rear Admiral Edward C. Outlaw had relieved Miller as commander of TF-77 and soon encountered a new problem. A photoreconnaissance mission flown by an RF-8 Crusader from *Coral Sea* showed surface-to-air missile (SAM) sites under construction around Haiphong and Hanoi. Outlaw flew to Saigon to plan a joint strike with the USAF. Such strikes required approval from Washington, and after several weeks' delay McNamara's staff disapproved the proposal. Outlaw resentfully wrote, "Such a refusal was beyond my comprehension."

SAMs changed the tactics of war. Pilots had to fly higher, which meant more bomb-misses, or fly lower, which meant more damage from visually controlled Soviet weapons. On the night of August 11-12, 1965, a new era of navy warfare began. SAMs struck two A-4E Skyhawks flying reconnaissance at 9,000 feet sixty miles south of Hanoi. During the next five years, Soviet SA-2 SAM sites shot down a hundred and fifteen American planes. Outlaw later argued that all the SAM sites "could have been destroyed at minimum risk before they became operational." McNamara allowed planes to destroy just two SAM sites and refused to allow pilots to strike any SAM installations where Soviet MiGs were based. McNamara eventually allowed more SAM sites to be struck, but by then the Soviets had developed a system for quickly packing up the

launchers and repositioning them elsewhere.

On August 12, 1966, Outlaw declared war on SAM sites and launched Operation Iron Hand, an anti-SAM campaign developed around the navy's new Shrike missile, which homed on a SAM battery's radar guidance system. Two months passed before the Shrikes' homing system worked properly. An A-6 Intruder and four A-4E Skyhawks from the *Independence* (CVA-62) knocked out the first SAM site sixty miles north of Hanoi without suffering a loss.

During SAM site reconnaissance missions, TF-77 pilots reported seventy-five MiG-17 and MiG-21 Fishbed fighters and eight Il-28 Beagle light bombers in North Korea. Rear Admiral James R. Reedy, TF-77's new commander, applied to Washington for permission to strike the planes on the ground. McNamara vetoed the request, leaving navy pilots to fight it out in the sky.

ABOVE: Lieutenant (jg) Denny Earl, with both legs shattered by North Vietnamese antiaircraft fire, returns to Yankee Station and successfully guides his A-4 Skyhawk into the USS Oriskany's nylon emergency barrier.

We were restrained to carrying out a campaign which seemed designed *not* to win.
Admiral Outlaw, quoted in "Task Force 77 in Action off Vietnam," Proceedings, *75, by Cagle.*

Search and Rescue (SAR)

One of the tactical successes of the Vietnam War occurred during TF-77's operations at Yankee Station. Admiral Reedy and his staff developed an SAR capability for rescuing pilots not only in the water but also deep in enemy territory. Some downed pilots landed in the sea, others in the jungle. No pilot wanted to be captured and sent to a POW camp to be tortured or starved to death, and helicopters made it possible to recover flyers wherever they landed. Besides saving lives, Reedy believed that effective SAR operations would improve the flagging morale of pilots, who every day climbed into cockpits to fly politically restrained missions that prevented them from winning the war. When pilots knew they had a good chance of being rescued it improved their outlook when slipping into the cockpit, especially when flying every day.

The SAR system in 1965 involved a pair of UH-2A/B Seasprite helicopters from the *Ranger* working together with a destroyer. Because the unarmored helicopters carried only one .30-caliber machine gun mounted in the cabin, a pair of heavily armed, slow-flying A-1 Skyraiders provided protective cover. The first recorded rescue occurred in North Vietnam on September 20 when Lieutenant (j.g.) John R. Harris's Skyhawk from *Independence* went down twenty miles east of Hanoi. A UH-1B rescued Harris and flew him to safety on the *Galveston* (CLG-3), a guided-missile light cruiser.

In 1966, on the recommendation by Reedy, the first SH-3 Sea King helicopters arrived at Yankee Station. Known as "Big Mothers," they came armed with two M60 machine guns. Prior to each air strike in North

The USS *Enterprise* (CVAN-65)

On December 2, 1965, after serving in the Mediterranean, the first nuclear-powered carrier, USS *Enterprise*, launched a hundred and eighteen sorties against targets in South Vietnam. At 35 knots and 85,830 tons, she was the fastest and largest carrier afloat. Commissioned on November 25, 1961, she was 1,123 feet long with an extreme width of 252 feet, a 4.5-acre deck, and a crew of 4,600 officers and men. Powered by eight nuclear reactors, she could stay at sea for three years without refueling. The new *Enterprise* carried a maximum of a hundred aircraft, and with four catapults she could launch four planes a minute. Secretary of the Navy John B. Connally. Jr., predicted she would "reign a long, long time as Queen of the Seas." At a cost of $445 million, she was also the most expensive ship ever built at the time. Because of her cost, Congress voted to forego another nuclear carrier until she proved herself. With her came Admiral Miller on a second tour as commander of TF-77. One of his jobs was to put her through a battery of combat exercises.

Enterprise's extra length and angled deck provided her with the capacity to carry the navy's latest jets. The first North American AJ-3/RA-5 Vigilante twinjet bombers and the first McDonnell Aircraft F4H Phantom II fighters found homes on the *Enterprise*. New instrumentation on Vigilantes provided a quantum leap in reconnaissance and electronic countermeasure support against a Soviet air defense system that had become increasingly lethal. The new Phantom, capable of Mach-2+ speeds, became TF-77s all-purpose MiG killer.

Although Miller had persistently warned Washington that half of the enemy's cargo moved in sampans and barges along inland waterways, two years passed before McNamara allowed the navy to mine rivers—but not the port of Haiphong. Planes from *Enterprise* and *Kitty Hawk* sowed the first minefields in the mouths of five rivers. The Johnson-McNamara policy of applying military pressure in gradual doses had not slowed the war or forced North Vietnam to the peace table, nor did planting a few mines in rivers.

The *Enterprise*'s operational capabilities, however, exceeded original estimates during the first week in the South China Sea and solidified what the navy already knew about nuclear-powered ships, yet still had to prove to Congress. *Enterprise*'s first tour lasted six months. During that time she launched 13,202 combat sorties and delivered 8,000 tons of ordnance on Washington-designated targets.

***ABOVE:** Operating out of Yankee Station, the nuclear-powered USS* Enterprise *(CVAN-65) cruises off the shore of North Vietnam to recover incoming aircraft on her angled deck. A squadron of A-4 Skyhawks are parked on her bow.*

Carriers In the Vietnam War

Attack Carriers
America (CVA-66)
Constellation (CVA-64)
Enterprise (CVAN-65)
Forrestal (CVA-59)
Independence (CVA-62)
Kitty Hawk (CVA-63)
Ranger (CVA-61)
Saratoga (CVA-60)

Essex-class Carriers
Bon Homme Richard (CV-31)
Hancock (CV-19)
Oriskany (CVA-34)
Ticonderoga (CVA-14)

Antisubmarine Carriers
Intrepid (CVS-11)
Shangri-La (CVS-38)

Tours lasted six to nine months, and some carriers served several tours.

Midway-class Carriers
Coral Sea (CVB-43)
Franklin D. Roosevelt (CVB-42)
Midway (CVB-41)

ABOVE: After steaming 105,000 miles during an 11-month deployment, the carrier USS Coral Sea (CVA-43) heads for home. Carrier Air Wing 15 flew more than 160 missions and dropped more than 6,000 tons of ordnance on enemy targets.

LEFT: Somewhere in the South China Sea, aircraft sit idle on the deck of the carrier USS Hancock (CVA-19) while fuel and supplies are high-lined from the USS Sacramento (AOE-1) and airlifted by a CH-46 Sea Knight.

Rescue over North Vietnam

Lieutenant (jg) Clyde E. Lassen and his HC-7 co-pilot made a daring night rescue of two downed aviators on June 19, 1968, while flying a UH-2 Seasprite helicopter. Here Lassen poses (far left) with the HC-7 search and rescue crew.

After midnight on June 19, 1968, a Soviet SAM struck an F-4 Phantom II fighter on a mission about twenty miles south of Hanoi. Lieutenant Commander John W. Holtzclaw and Lieutenant Commander John A. Burns from the USS *America* (CVA-66) ejected and parachuted into a rice paddy between two densely populated towns.

Lieutenant (j.g.) Clyde E. Lassen received Holtzclaw's call to SAR and gathered together his crew. Flying a UH-2A Seasprite, Lassen lifted off the deck of the guided-missile frigate USS *Preble* (DLG-15) and headed for the airmen's signals, which emanated three miles from the crash site. In difficult terrain during a dark overcast night, Lassen touched down, only to be assaulted by small arms and automatic weapons fire. He knew the two pilots were in tall, thick woods and lifted off, waiting for other TF-77 aircraft to arrive and illuminate the area with flares. The flares burned out as Lassen was trying to drop into a small opening, and the helo grazed a tree. Lassen righted the Seasprite but struck another tree. Although the helicopter developed vibration, Lassen remained overhead, waiting for more planes to arrive with flares while his crew fired back at flashes coming from the ground.

Lassen told the two downed pilots to find an opening, which they did, but when the helicopter descended, the enemy again opened with heavy ground fire. SAMs also began whizzing by. Lassen went aloft a third time and finally put the helo down by the edge of a clearing. With North Vietnamese converging from every direction, Lassen and his co-pilot pulled the downed flyers on board while his crew returned fire from a pair of .30-caliber machine guns. Now aloft but short of fuel, the Seasprite ran into heavy flak and automatic fire before reaching the Gulf of Tonkin. An hour later Lassen landed on the *Jouett* (DLG-29) with only five minutes of fuel left.

For his intrepidity and conspicuous gallantry, Lassen was awarded the Medal of Honor.

Vietnam, one or more Sea Kings would be dispatched to a combat SAR station closest to the assigned targets. Whenever an actual rescue began, the navy dispatched four Skyraiders to protect the helicopters while keeping A-4s or A-7s within hailing distance if needed.

During the first two years of the war, 269 navy and air force pilots and crewmen were shot down or forced to abandon their aircraft over North Vietnam. Of those, 103 were recovered, 75 were killed, and 46 became POWs. The fate of the others could never be determined.

Guided Missile Ships

As weaponry changed, the big guns of battleships and cruisers could not compete with the pinpoint accuracy of guided missiles. Changes began in 1953 when the battleship *Mississippi* (AG-128, formerly BB-41) made the first shipboard launching of a Terrier surface-to-air missile. The experiment led in 1955 to the creation of a Special Projects Office under Rear Admiral William F. Raborn, Jr., to direct the development of a shipboard launching system for ballistic missiles. One of the projects included the development of the compact, solid-fuel Polaris missile. The submarine *George Washington* (SSBN-598), commissioned December 31, 1959, became the navy's prototype for accommodating A-1 Polaris missile-launching tubes and made the first successful launch on July 20, 1960.

ABOVE: On September 16, 1960, the Charles F. Adams (DDG-2) becomes the lead ship of a new class of 4,500-ton general-purpose "keel up" missile destroyers. The Adams also becomes the first of twenty-three ships equipped with Tartar missiles.

ABOVE: The USS George Washington (SSBN-598) became the first submarine to fire a Polaris A-1 missile from beneath the surface. The submarine's skipper then fired a second, reporting that both came "from out of the deep to target—perfect."

Carrier Aircraft

Type	Manufacturer	Drive	Speed
Attack Aircraft			
A-1 Skyraider	Douglas	Prop	365mph
A-3 Skywarrior	Douglas	Jet	630mph
A-4 Skyhawk	Douglas	Jet	664mph
A-6 Intruder	Grumman	Jet	Mach-.95
A-7 Corsair II	Vought	Jet	Mach-1
Fighter Aircraft			
F-4 Phantom II	McDonnell Douglas	Jet	Mach-2.6
F-8 Crusader	Vought	Jet	Mach-2
Reconnaissance Aircraft			
RA-3B	North American	Jet	Mach 2
RA-5 Vigilante	North American	Jet	Mach 2.1
Early Warning/Air Control Aircraft			
E-2A Hawkeye	Grumman	TurboJet	297mph
EA-6 Prowler	Grumman	Jet	659mph
Helicopters			
SH-3 Sea King	Sikorsky	Rotary	166mph
UH-1 Huey	Bell	Rotary	127mph
UH-1B Seawolf	Bell	Rotary	127mph
UH-2 Seasprite	Bell	Rotary	127mph

LEFT: An A-7 Corsair II armed with 250-pound bombs is pulled down the deck by a catapult bridle cable in preparation for takeoff from the carrier USS Ranger (CVA-61).

LEFT: During operations in February 1968, Lieutenant (jg) J. Quaintance of VF-154 flies an F-4B Phantom from the USS Ranger (CVA-61) over the DMZ and drops his payload of bombs on enemy artillery harassing marine operations.

LEFT: The pilot of a returning F8U Crusader from VF-62 swings around the carrier USS Shangri-La (CVA-38) and queues up behind other aircraft before descending for the final landing approach.

Raborn did not stop with submarines and Polaris missiles. In 1958, the *Galveston* became the first light cruiser to be equipped with Talos antiaircraft missiles. On September 10, 1960, the *Charles F. Adams* (DDG-2) became the first of twenty-three 4,500-ton general-purpose destroyers equipped with Tartar missiles. A year later the navy commissioned the first nuclear-powered guided-missile cruiser, the 17,100-ton (fully loaded) *Long Beach* (CGN-9), which on May 13, 1964, joined an all nuclear-powered task group consisting of the *Enterprise* and the first 8,580-ton (fully loaded) guided-missile frigate *Bainbridge* (DLGN-25).

Conventionally powered guided missile frigates (DL/DLG) began reporting for duty off North Vietnam in the mid-1960s. They rated between a light cruiser and

LEFT: On June 18, 1964, America's first three nuclear-powered ships cruise together. The USS Enterprise (CVAN-65) (left), her flight deck displaying Einstein's theory of relativity ($E=mc^2$), is accompanied by the cruiser Long Beach (CGN-9) (center) and the destroyer Bainbridge (DLGN-25).

destroyer in size, carrying a cruiser's missile armament on a destroyer's hull. Guided missile frigates, like the *Preble* and the *Jouett,* also carried helicopters for reconnaissance, Special Forces (SEAL) missions, and SAR operations. Over time, frigates would carry up to eight Tomahawk, eight Harpoon, and a hundred and twenty Terrier SAM guided missiles, along with conventional firepower and six 12.75-inch MK 32 torpedoes.

U.S. Navy SEALs

In January 1962 the navy commissioned the first Sea-Air-Land (SEAL) teams from the existing combat demolition units and underwater demolition teams (UDTs). The group had already earned a distinguished record in Europe and the Pacific during World War II and again during the Korean War. SEALs achieved the next level of fitness and capability, becoming expert in unconventional warfare, counter-guerrilla warfare, intelligence gathering raids, and clandestine special operations deep within the boundaries of the enemy.

Two SEAL teams were authorized, one for the Atlantic and one for the Pacific. Each consisted of only two hundred specially trained officers and men. Every SEAL spent twenty-five weeks in a basic UDT course, three weeks training in an army airborne school, and special training in small arms use and hand-to-hand combat.

SEALs often worked with two other navy units, the Special Boat Squadrons (SBSs) and the Swimmer Delivery Vessel Teams (SDVs), but in Vietnam they would use river patrol boats (PBRs), fast patrol craft (PCF), mechanized landing craft (LCM), specially designed SEAL assault boats, or helicopters. SEALS could be inserted anywhere, complete their mission, and be extracted from a combat zone without ever being detected.

Despite their small numbers, SEALS were everywhere in Southeast Asia. Between 1962 and 1964 they trained South Vietnamese commandos. In 1964 and 1965 they became hunter-killer teams, seldom less than three or more than seven men in a team. By mid-1966, they were assaulting VC villages and killing or capturing VC leaders. By 1968 they were deep in VC territory rescuing prisoners of war held in the Mekong Delta. During the Vietnam War, forty-nine SEALS died in action. None was ever captured, but three of their members received the Medal of Honor.

I felt that a properly oriented bombing effort could either bring the enemy to the conference table or cause the insurgency to wither from shock. The alternative would be a long and costly war....
Admiral Sharp quoted in Vietnam: The War in the Air, *171, by Gene Gurney.*

The POL Campaign

North Vietnam possessed good petroleum, oil, and lubricants (POL) facilities, which General Giap used advantageously in waging war. Most of the oil came from Red China, and Admiral Sharp persistently argued that air strikes could cripple the industry and hamstring the army. The North Vietnamese already understood that Johnson opposed bombing Hanoi and Haiphong, so General Giap kept most of his POL stocks in the bomb-free sanctuaries created by Johnson.

Finally on June 16, 1966, Sharp got the green light to commence a restricted bombing campaign against POL facilities closer to Hanoi and Haiphong. Tankers in Haiphong harbor could not be attacked unless they flew the North Vietnamese flag, which was asking a lot of A-4 Skyhawk pilots swooping over the harbor at 650mph. Using bombs and Mighty Mouse rockets, twenty-eight aircraft from *Ranger* turned the POL complex at Haiphong into huge fireballs. On July 23 Skyhawks hit the POL storage at Vinh and put it out of business. By Christmas the campaign had wrecked all the above ground POL storage sites, including the largest facility near Hanoi. Most of the oil barges and tank cars had also been destroyed. North Vietnam resorted to storing oil in drums and hiding them in caves. Soviet deliveries began coming out of China in drums instead of tankers. For the first time, North Vietnam's public began shouting to government officials, "Stop the bombing!"

Admiral U. S. Grant Sharp (1906–2001)

LEFT: Admiral U. S. Grant Sharp, commander-in-chief in the Pacific, doubted the wisdom of going to war in Vietnam. He remained constantly frustrated by President Lyndon B. Johnson's strategy and tactics for fighting the enemy.

Born in Montana, Ulysses Simpson Grant Sharp was named for the famous Civil War general and eighteenth president of the United States, who had married his father's aunt. Sharp, however, chose the navy instead of the army. In 1927 he graduated from the U.S. Naval Academy and in 1950 from the Naval War College. During World War II he received two Silver Stars while commanding the destroyer *Boyd* in the Pacific. During the Korean War he commanded a destroyer squadron and helped to plan MacArthur's masterful amphibious landing at Inchon. In the early 1960s he served as deputy CNO for policy and planning and in 1963 as commander of the U.S. Seventh Fleet. In 1964 he became commander-in-chief of the Pacific Command and held the post until he retired from active duty in 1968 as a four-star admiral. His Pacific Command covered nearly half the globe and included some four hundred and fifty ships and more than a million men.

Sharp disagreed with President Johnson and Secretary of Defense McNamara on North Vietnamese policy. He believed that once Johnson made the decision to go to war, the United States should provide an immediate and massive military response. The Johnson administration opted for a gradual response. Sharp became involved in the decision-making process after the Gulf of Tonkin incident when he recommended immediate punitive air strikes against North Vietnam, to which Johnson agreed. Johnson then changed his mind. Sharp tried to explain to his baffled operational commanders that while Rolling Thunder's restricted bombing campaign did "not seek to inflict maximum damage to the enemy," it was to be "a precise application of military pressure for the purpose of halting aggression in South Vietnam." Sharp had difficulty making sense out of the policies of Johnson and McNamara, but he was obliged to support them.

Sharp persisted in making recommendations to step up the bombing campaign, on many occasions going directly to Washington to expand targeting. He firmly believed the war could be won. He lobbied for the POL campaign to deny the enemy petroleum, oil, and lubricants, and he tried to get Washington to agree to a campaign to shut off the supply of arms deliveries from Red China and the USSR. He wanted to destroy North Vietnam's resources, which by 1967 American air power could have accomplished. Johnson and McNamara remained firm on bombing restrictions, which led to America's longest, strangest, and most unpopular war.

RIGHT: Aircraft from the USS Oriskany plaster Haiphong's petroleum terminal. President Johnson rarely permitted strikes on oil centers and strategic targets close to major cities, such as Haiphong and Hanoi.

FAR RIGHT: After aircraft from the USS Oriskany (CVA-34) blew up a POL-laden barge circulating through the islands east of Haiphong, an A-1 Skyraider pilot flew over the burning mass to witness the damage.

Early in 1967 Sharp went to Washington to report the enormous success of the POL operation and to obtain approval for stepping up the bombing of power transmission stations, transportation support facilities, ammunition depots, and MiG airfields in North Vietnam. Months passed before Johnson allowed McNamara to pick a few new targets, but the president quashed Sharp's plans for an accelerated bombing campaign. He insisted upon a ten-mile no-bombing circle around Hanoi, which doomed any chance of bringing the war to a quick conclusion.

Had Washington fully understood the navy's arsenal of new weapons, the TV-guided Walleye air-to-surface glide bomb could have surgically disposed of targets in downtown Hanoi with minimum collateral damage. Instead, the first strikes from aircraft carriers were against bridges, barracks, and railroad sidings. Eventually, approval was given for aircraft from the *Bon Homme Richard* to bomb the Hanoi Thermal Power Plant and on May 19, 1967, it was blown up. On July 21 another squadron from the *Richard* took out POL facilities at Ta Xa. Despite the ability of Walleyes to destroy with reasonable precision any target in North Vietnam, McNamara's "whiz kids" still called the shots from Washington. When Soviets lodged complaints about being attacked, Johnson became rattled and put some strategic targets back on the no-bombing list.

Riverine Operations

The Mekong River flowed through Laos and Cambodia and formed the Mekong Delta south of Saigon. From 1962 to 1966, the VC controlled most of the northern half of the delta. Many of the VC's objectives during the 1968 Tet offensive involved the delta, where the enemy established control over more than five hundred strategic villages. In December 1965 the U.S. Navy River Patrol Force (TF-116) launched Operation Game Warden. At first, TF-116 consisted of only four large patrol landing craft (LCPLs). The first patrol boats did not arrive until April 1966.

In the Mekong's sixteen hundred miles of navigable

RIGHT: After the president put POL (petroleum, oil, and lubricants) targets back on the bombing list, planes from the USS Bon Homme Richard (CV-31) clobbered the My Xa petroleum center fifteen miles northwest of Haiphong.

FAR LEFT: While working the dangerous shallows in the estuaries of the Mekong Delta, three men probe along shore in a navy skimmer boat while reconnoitering enemy activity in the brush.

LEFT: A navy Assault Support Patrol Boat (ASPB) patrols a river in the Mekong Delta as part of a joint army/navy mobile riverine force operating in the Viet Cong-saturated Rung Sat Special Zone.

waterways, there were also twenty-five hundred miles of canals. TF-116 soon became linked with Operation Market Time (TF-115), which involved the navy's surveillance and control of South Vietnam's twelve-hundred-mile coastline. While Market Time operated out of Dixie Station, TF-115 patrolled the coastal areas and TF-116 worked the rivers, the Mekong Delta, and the VC-infested Rung Sat Zone south of Saigon.

Captain Wade C. Wells's TF-117 came into being as the Riverine Assault Force. A typical river assault squadron consisted of four hundred men with three command-and-communications boats, five monitors, twenty-six armored troop carriers (ATCs), sixteen assault patrol boats, one refueler, a team of SEALs, and other resources. Nor was it uncommon to find OV-10A Bronco twin-prop aircraft armed with Zuni rockets attached to the River Patrol Force to strike VC boats attempting to evade patrols by slipping into Cambodia.

Fire on the *Forrestal*

Secretary of the Navy Louis Johnson cancelled the supercarrier *United States* on April 23, 1949, and upset every admiral in the navy. Six years passed before the lead ship of the new *Forrestal*-class of six supercarriers went into commission. At 78,000 tons displacement, she was the largest carrier ever built at that time. Four shaft-geared steam turbines drove her at thirty-three knots. She carried up to ninety aircraft, 2,790 sailors and 2,150 aircrew, and was armed with three octuple Sea Sparrow SAM launchers.

On July 25, 1967, the *Forrestal* arrived at Yankee Station for her first Vietnam tour of duty. Four days later, while preparing to launch her second strike of the day, a Zuni rocket ignited, shot across the carrier's flight deck, and smashed into a fully armed and fueled Skyhawk, which blew up and triggered catastrophic explosions. Fires engulfed the ship's stern, spreading below and setting off bombs and ammunition. Nearby ships rushed to aid the firefighting effort. Sailors risked their lives removing bombs from burning aircraft, pitching the ordnance into the sea. During the twelve-hour conflagration, a 134 crewmen were killed and sixty-two injured; twenty-one aircraft were destroyed, and forty-three planes suffered damage. The fire on the *Forrestal* marked the navy's costliest day in the Vietnam War.

ABOVE: As the USS Forrestal (CVA-59) prepared to launch her second strike, a Zuni rocket ignited, shot across the deck, and detonated munitions, killing 134 men and wounding 62. Determined efforts by the crew saved the navy's first supercarrier.

Combined, Game Warden and Market Garden were more than a navy operation because they included marine, army infantry, and coast guard elements. Although several units operated on the Mekong watershed, ships of TF-117 also worked out of Da Nang, escorting amphibious craft up the Perfume and Cua Viet

Rivers, which were infested with guerrillas. During 1968 members of a single unit earned one Medal of Honor, six Navy Crosses, and five hundred Purple Hearts.

The capital ships for TF-117 operations were shallow-draft monitors looking much like ugly ironclads from the Civil War era. Fitted with either a 105mm howitzer or 81mm mortar, two 22mm and three .30-caliber machine guns, and two 40mm high-velocity grenade launchers, monitors became the battleships of the rivers. Some carried two army M10-8 flamethrowers. Like Civil War monitors, they were slow, the top speed being eight knots. Their purpose was to escort amphibious craft up waterways and blast guerrilla hideaways concealed in the jungle.

Monitors escorted ATCs to hot spots in the IV Corps sector south of Saigon. ATCs carried their own batteries, usually two 20mm, plus two to six .30-caliber and two .50-caliber machine guns. ATCs were also fitted with one 40mm high-velocity grenade launcher, two 40mm low-velocity grenade launchers, and a landing platform so UH-1D Huey's could evacuate the wounded. On occasion, sailors could be observed car-

rying bows and arrows; a handy weapon for flinging a burning wad into a bamboo hut.

TF-117 also operated the speedy, steel-hulled assault support patrol boats (ASPBs) used by TF-116 in Operation Game Warden. Converted from LCMs (Landing Craft, Medium), ASPBs were powered by three gas turbines that drove three water jets at speeds up to forty knots. The boats carried a lightweight 105mm howitzer and two 20mm cannon mounted in a tank-like turret. A small remote forward mount contained two 20mm cannon and a 40mm grenade launcher.

ASPBs were usually commanded by a petty officer with a crew of four or five, some having been yeomen before the new crop of WAVES became available. (On March 7, 1967, the navy increased the number of WAVES by 20 percent to six hundred officers and six thousand enlisted women.) Twelve-hour patrols took ASPB units up the steamy, winding rivers where they spent endless hours inspecting junks and sampans for contraband. Men suffered from boredom, mosquitoes, fatigue, dysentery, humidity, torrential downpours, ambushes, booby traps, and carefully camouflaged floating mines.

Fast Patrol Craft (PCF), though not originally intended for riverine operations, proved valuable in larger waterways. Originally designed by the Sewart Seacraft Company for transporting crews back and forth from offshore oil platforms, the diesel-powered, dual-propeller-driven, aluminum-hulled craft became the navy's "Swift" boats. Two designs emerged, the MK 1 and the little-different MK II. Both models cruised at twenty-five knots and carried a .50-caliber machine gun mounted over an 81mm mortar aft and twin .50-caliber machine guns mounted in a turret atop the pilothouse.

Throughout the Vietnam War, the navy continued to experiment with different types of riverine craft because of shallow areas in the Mekong Delta. Jet-driven PBRs came with only a nine-inch draft and could operate at thirty knots. The experimental patrol air

cushion vehicle (PACV) resembled commercial hover-craft ferries used to cross the English Channel. When airborne, it cleared the water by four feet, traveled at seventy knots, and carried two .50-caliber machine guns in the pilothouse. Later in the war, as riverine operations were turned over to the South Vietnamese, the navy began shedding the more conventional river patrol boats.

An Ignominious Withdrawal

No person who fought in the Vietnam War departed from it filled with pride. Instead, the veterans felt misused and abused. It had been a war poorly conducted by a president who paid for his mistakes by voluntarily declining to run for a second term of office. In 1969 Richard M. Nixon became president because he promised to bring the men home and turn the fighting over to the South Vietnamese.

The process began on June 8, 1969, Not until April 1, 1972, were all navy personnel removed from Vietnam. The Seventh Fleet remained offshore shelling harbors and sending aircraft on missions over North Vietnam. After both parties signed a peace accord on January 27, 1973, the navy remained behind to sweep mines from coastal North Vietnam.

Along with the navy, a few marine units also remained behind. On April 12, 1975, marine helicopters removed embassy personnel from the communist-besieged capital of Cambodia. Seventeen days later navy and marine helicopters evacuated nine thousand civilian and military personnel from Saigon, among them 989 marines who had been inserted to cover the operation. On April 30 the final flight took off from the roof of the American embassy in Saigon as North Vietnamese tanks rolled into the compound.

The United States got most of her men back but left Southeast Asia in the hands of the communists. The navy performed its role and met every expectation of the government, but nobody came home pleased about the outcome.

LEFT: *During operations in the South China Sea. sailors from the amphibious cargo ship* USS *Durham (LKA-114) load refugees into small boats, where they will be transferred to landing craft and shuttled to the freighter* Transcolorado.

BELOW: *The peace agreement signed on January 27, 1973, provided for the exchange of prisoners of war. A few days later the first American POWs stepped off a camouflaged North Vietnam bus and lined up at Hanoi's Gia Lam Airport for release.*

The Navy in Vietnam (1965–1973)

	Maximum deployed	Combat casualties	Killed	Wounded	Prisoners or Missing	Non-battle deaths
Navy	37,011	6,443	1,477	4,178	788	880
Marines	86,727	64,486	12,953	51,389	144	1,631

CHAPTER 8

COLD WAR AND TERRORIST THREATS 1960–2006

ABOVE: On June 29, 1974, during CNO change of command ceremonies at the U.S. Naval Academy, senior attendees include (right to left) Admiral James L. Holloway, III, incoming CNO; Admiral Elmo R. Zumwalt, outgoing CNO; Admiral Thomas H. Moorer, Chairman, JCS; Secretary of Defense James R. Schlesinger; and Vice Admiral William P. Mack, Naval Academy Superintendent.

Although the Korean War dominated the 1950s, and the Vietnam War took center stage during the 1960s. The Cold War expanded across Europe and Asia, into the Mediterranean, and made lodgments in Africa and the Americas. Had it not been for the Cold War, the USAF may have succeeded in its efforts to reduce the navy to a collection of obsolete ships with World War II technology. Instead, the spread of communism made the navy and its marines the most powerful and flexible fighting force on earth. During the mid-1950s, President Eisenhower promised to aid any country threatened by communists, and he backed up the promise, often with only the navy. On July 15, 1958, when Syrian-backed Muslims attempted to overthrow the president of Lebanon, Admiral J. L Holloway, Jr., put

three marine battalions from the Sixth Fleet ashore at Beirut as a warning to pro-Soviet and anti-Western influences that had taken over Iraq.

Six weeks later, Eisenhower ordered six carriers from the Seventh Fleet to Matsu and Quemoy to prevent Red China from seizing the tiny island outposts from the Nationalist Chinese. The standoff lasted until December, when Red China withdrew the threat.

Eisenhower's second term ended in January 1961, and he left office after signing a budget proposal for 1962 that included a navy of 817 ships and 625,000 personnel, and a Marine Corps of three divisions, three air wings, and 175,000. Moscow naturally took keen interest in what John F. Kennedy, the incoming president, might do and seemed determined to find out.

When running for office, Kennedy had blamed Eisenhower for allowing a "missile gap" to occur between the United States and the USSR, but the Soviets discounted the charge as political rhetoric, and for good reason. Eisenhower's administration had provided for the *Nautilus* (SSN-571), the first nuclear-powered subma-

> ...when you have anything to do, the time to do it is right now. If you've got power, use it and use it fast, and the time to make a decision is as soon as the problem presents itself.
> *Admiral Arleigh A. Burke, CNO, 1955-1961.*

rine; the *George Washington* (SSN-598), the first ballistic-missile submarine; the *Enterprise* (CVAN-65), the first nuclear-powered aircraft carrier; the *Bainbridge* (DLGN-25), the first nuclear-powered guided-missile frigate; the *Long Beach* (CGN-9), the first nuclear-powered guided-missile cruiser; and the *Kitty Hawk* (CVA-63), the first missile-armed aircraft carrier. Eisenhower's administration also paved the way for a host of new missiles, including the solid-fuel Polaris; the navy's first nuclear power school; and Vanguard I, the navy's first satellite.

In 1960, had it not been for nuclear-propulsion developed by navy scientist Hyman Rickover, Commander Edward L. Beach would not have been able to circle the earth underwater in the USS *Triton* (SSN-586), the first submarine to do so. The voyage took twelve weeks.

By then, Rickover was old enough to retire, but his career was only beginning. Promoted to rear admiral, he forced through the development of the navy's

ABOVE: USS Nautilus **(SSN 571), the navy's first nuclear-powered ship, began its first trial run from Groton, Connecticut, January 17, 1955. Skipper was Commander Dennis Wilkinson.**

ABOVE: In 1960 the USS Triton **(SSN-586), a nuclear-powered submarine and part of the navy's modernization program, became the first ship to circumnavigate the earth submerged, logging 41,519 miles in 84 days.**

Admiral Hyman George Rickover (1900–1986)

Hyman Rickover, born in Russia and raised in Chicago, developed an interest in submarines that made him one of the most influential and brilliant scientists in the navy. Having graduated from the U.S. Naval Academy in 1922, Rickover continued studying and in 1929 graduated from Columbia University with an M.S. in electrical engineering. Later, he attended submarine school at New London, Connecticut, served on three submarines, and also saw duty on the battleship *New Mexico* (BB-40). The navy recognized rare genius in the irascible engineer and during World War II made him head of the electrical section of the Bureau of Ships.

In 1946 Rickover received instruction in nuclear physics and engineering at Oak Ridge, Tennessee. There he became immersed in the technology of the Manhattan Project and the team of scientists who created the atomic bombs dropped on Japan. When he returned to the Bureau of Ships in September 1947, he had already formed his own ideas about converting nuclear energy to propel ships. He took charge of the program, formed a nuclear development team of deeply devoted followers, and energetically assumed the task of building a nuclear reactor for ship propulsion. On January 17, 1955, the USS *Nautilus* (SSN-571), the world's first nuclear-powered submarine, got underway with Captain Rickover on the bridge. In characteristic style, he sent a short message to Washington, "Underway on nuclear power." Rickover then went to work on designing the propulsion system for *Enterprise* (CVAN-65), the first nuclear-powered aircraft carrier.

ABOVE: In September 1947 Rear Admiral Hyman Rickover took charge of the U.S. Navy's nuclear propulsion program. A man of brilliant intellect, he retired in 1981.

RIGHT: An American reconnaissance plane flying over Cuba's Port Casilda on October 14, 1962, photographed the Soviet ship *Volgoles* pulling into the wharf to have six Russian-made missile transporters unloaded.

6 MISSILE TRANSPORTERS

TRUCK

> The cleverest, the most cunning and the rudest man in the whole United States Navy.
>
> *Quoted by a Rickover characterizer in Stephen Howarth,* To Shining Sea, *494.*

nuclear fleet. In between, he worked with the Atomic Energy Commission and was instrumental in developing the first full-scale commercial nuclear power plant in the United States at Shippingport, Pennsylvania. For almost forty years he served as head of the navy's nuclear program. On November 19, 1973, Rickover received his fourth star upon mandatory retirement age, but Congress passed an act exempting him from retirement. By the time the "father" of America's nuclear navy retired in 1982 he had configured nuclear cores to last the life of a ship—thirty years. Even those who disdained Rickover for his abusive arrogance could not deny his great contribution to the navy. In 1983

Rickover received his second congressional gold medal, becoming the only person other than President Zachary Taylor to be awarded the honor twice.

The Cuban Missile Crisis

At the outset of his administration, Kennedy failed to back the strong position he had taken against the Soviets during his presidential campaign. The weakness of his resolve became manifest on April 17-20, 1961, when fourteen hundred Cuban exiles trained by American personnel attempted to overthrow dictator Fidel Castro during the Bay of Pigs fiasco. Kennedy allowed the entire force to be slaughtered as they entered the harbor because he refused to allow the carrier *Essex* (CVA-9) and five destroyers positioned offshore to interfere since it might "worsen the situation." In addition to damaging American prestige, doing nothing merely gave Castro an excuse to invite protection from the Soviets, which resulted in the 1962 Cuban Missile Crisis.

On October 14, 1962, an American U-2 reconnaissance plane returned to base with photographs showing the first of forty-two Soviet missile sites under construction at San Cristobal, Cuba, a hundred miles west of Havana. Two days later, new photographs showed Soviet Il-28 bombers being assembled on Cuban airfields. Kennedy spent six days deciding what to do. The JCS recommended surgical strikes, but Kennedy's military advisors worried that some sites might be missed.

Since the United States and Cuba were not at war, Kennedy could not legally declare a blockade. Instead, he imposed a new gimmick and on October 22 announced a maritime quarantine to block the entry of Soviet offensive weapons into Cuba. To carry out the quarantine, the navy organized TF-136 under Second Fleet commander Vice Admiral Alfred G. Ward, who pulled together 183 ships, including the carrier *Essex*, two heavy cruisers, several squadrons of destroyers, and support ships. Rear Admiral John T. Hayward's Carrier Division Two, organized around the *Enterprise*, and Rear Admiral Robert J. Stroh's Carrier Division Six, organized around the carrier *Independence* (CVA-62), stood by to intervene, but only if necessary.

On October 24, air reconnaissance reported twenty-five Soviet ships approaching Cuba. Submarines stopped all the ships before they reached the quarantine line, and several hours later all but one tanker reversed course. The navy allowed this ship to pass because she carried only oil.

Kennedy's bluff worked. On October 26 Soviet Premier Nikita Khrushchev phoned the White House to state that the Kremlin had merely placed missiles in Cuba to deter an American invasion and promised to remove them if the United States would pledge to lift the quarantine and never attack Cuba. Kennedy accepted Khrushchev's terms. The navy lifted the quarantine and the Soviets removed the missiles. Because of this agreement, Cuba became a communist satellite, and Fidel Castro remained in power.

VOLGOLES ENR USSR 9 NOVEMBER

The Navy in Space

The navy produced some of the most remarkable men in American history, and not all of them spent their careers at sea. On May 5, 1961, Commander Alan B. Shepard, Jr., lifted off from Cape Canaveral, Florida, in the Mercury capsule Freedom 7 on a sub-orbital flight and reached the altitude of 116.5 miles. On his return a helicopter from the carrier *Lake Champlain* (CVS-39) plucked the first man in space from the Atlantic 302 miles downrange. Ten years later, during January 31 and February 9, 1971, Shepard joined the Apollo XIV mission and became the seventh man to walk on the lunar surface, earning the rank of rear admiral.

Other navy astronauts soon followed. On May 24, 1962, Lieutenant Commander M. Scott Carpenter emulated Lieutenant Colonel John H. Glenn's example and made three orbits in the Aurora 7. Next came the two-man Gemini space capsule called Molly Brown, which on March 23, 1965, completed three orbits with Commander John Young and Lieutenant Colonel Virgil

ABOVE: After the Soviets agreed to remove their missiles from Cuba, the navy radar picket ship Vesole *(DDR-878) and an overhead P2V Neptune patrol plane followed the* Volgoles, *still laden with missile transporters, to sea.*

Grissom at the helm. On October 3 Commander Walter W. Schirra completed an orbital flight of 160,000 miles in ten hours and forty-six minutes. Then on December 4, 1965, Commander James A. Lovell, Jr., partnering in Gemini VII with Lieutenant Colonel Frank Borman, USAF, established a new record by remaining in orbit for fourteen days. On Borman's eleventh day in orbit, Captain Schirra in Gemini VIII made the first manned vehicle rendezvous in space with Gemini VII. On June 3, 1966, as the Gemini program neared the completion of its mission, Lieutenant Commander Eugene A. Cernan became the second American to walk in space.

Gemini XII made the program's last space flight on November 15, 1966, with navy Captain James A. Lovell on board, giving way to the Apollo program. But disaster struck during a training session on January 27, 1967, when a fire on Apollo 1 took the lives of three astronauts, including Lieutenant Commander Roger B. Chaffee. The accident slowed the program, but two years later the main event began.

On July 20, 1969, Apollo 11 landed on the moon. Former navy fighter pilot Neil A. Armstrong exited from the spacecraft and became the first man to walk on the lunar surface. Armstrong successfully launched from the moon and returned to earth, where he rendezvoused at sea with the carrier *Hornet* (CVS-12). On November 14 Apollo 12 took three navy men on a second moon shot—Commander Charles Conrad, Commander Richard Gordon, and Lieutenant Commander Alan Bean. When they returned, President Nixon promoted each of them to the rank of captain.

Navy personnel, who for nearly two centuries had made their careers on the seven seas, could now place a claim on outer space.

The *Pueblo* Affair

On January 23, 1968, seven days before North Vietnam launched the Tet offensive, North Korea took advantage of Soviet-supplied intelligence and seized the USS

Admiral Elmo Russell "Bud" Zumwalt (1920–2000)

Fifty-year-old Elmo Zumwalt emerged from the mess of the Vietnam War years to become the youngest full admiral and CNO in the navy's history. Probably the best-known admiral since Nimitz and Halsey, Zumwalt readily admitted, "I have a wonderful list of friends and a wonderful list of enemies, and am very proud of both lists." He aggressively changed the navy by liberalizing it, especially with regard to equal opportunity for minorities, and he put women sailors and officers on an equal basis with men. Even some dissident "old salts" later looked back on Zumwalt's practices as CNO and admitted that he probably saved the navy.

Born in San Francisco, Zumwalt graduated from the U.S. Naval Academy in 1942 and served on cruisers and destroyers in the Pacific during World War II. During the Korean War he served on the battleship *Wisconsin* (BB-64), after which he attended the Naval War College. Later, in 1968-1970, he commanded navy operations at Vietnam.

Zumwalt had his own philosophy about the navy, and the experience of Vietnam helped shaped that philosophy. In his view, the navy failed to keep pace with America's changing social culture. He observed the abiding reluctance of senior conservative officers to change with the times, and in Zumwalt's view that same conservatism was sucking the initiative out of the navy's young officers and career enlisted men and women. To bring the navy into the modern age, he believed that to achieve unconventional changes required unconventional methods of implementation.

Zumwalt opened lines of communication with the entire navy by adopting what sailors called "Z-Grams." One of his earlier missives pointedly said, "There is no black Navy, no white Navy—just one navy, the United States Navy."

He discontinued the practice of having certain policies communicated by senior officers through the chain of command—where his instructions might be reinterpreted to suit an individual commander—and "Z-Grammed" those policies directly to the entire navy. While senior officers grumbled about Z-Grams undermining their authority, the results had an amazingly positive effect on everyone else. Zumwalt wiped away many of the long-standing "chicken" regulations that for decades had been holding back a smooth-sailing navy like old barnacles. Zumwalt wasted little time letting everyone know that he meant business by allowing his hair, sideburns, and bushy eyebrows grow and letting sailors wear beards and their own hairstyles. In 1971, despite the malaise of the Vietnam War when every soldier and sailor wanted to go home, first term reenlistments doubled in the navy. On May 28, 1980, through the efforts of Admiral Zumwalt, the U.S. Naval Academy for the first time graduated and commissioned fifty-five women out of a class of 770.

ABOVE: Admiral Elmo R. Zumwalt served as Chief of Naval Operations (CNO) from July 1, 1970, to July 1, 1974. Coming into office during the Vietnam War, his opponents called him an "instigator of permissiveness," but he proved to be the right man at the right time.

Pueblo (AGER-2), a navy electronic intelligence ship. Because of cutbacks, every combat ship in the Seventh Fleet was serving elsewhere when Commander Lloyd M. Bucher accidentally strayed into North Korea's territorial waters. It was a baffling affair that took months to unravel. Bucher's two .50-caliber machine guns had frozen fast under their tarpaulins, one of his crew was mortally wounded, and Bucher and two other men had been hit. Having no air or naval forces available to come to his rescue, Bucher simply surrendered and followed his captors into Wonsan harbor. Because the sensitive intelligence-gathering electronics on the ship was not destroyed, it fell into Soviet hands.

During the investigation, Secretary of the Navy Paul R. Ignatius learned that Bucher had radioed for help when the *Pueblo* was first threatened. No ships or aircraft came because they were all out of range. The USS

LEFT: The environmental research ship USS Pueblo (AGER-2), loaded with sensitive electronic instrumentation, is underway off the coast of California. Lieutenant Commander Lloyd M. Bucher took her to Korea and ended up in an international incident dubbed "The Pueblo Affair."

Enterprise eventually appeared offshore, but President Johnson authorized no punitive strikes.

Ignatius soon learned that the incident occurred because of poor command procedures, stemming in part from the involvement of too many federal agencies directing the *Pueblo*'s covert operations. Though Bucher remained accountable for the ship, no control-

ABOVE: Lt. Commander Lloyd M. Bucher, skipper of the USS Pueblo (AGER-2), surrendered to North Korean patrol boats.

BELOW: The navy's second nuclear-powered carrier Nimitz (CVAN-68) went into commission on May 3, 1975. Designed to carry 100 aircraft and helicopters, Nimitz became the lead ship in a class of flattops that forms the bulk of today's carrier fleet.

ling authority would accept responsibility for sending the ship into North Korean waters.

Eleven months later the United States issued an apology to North Korea—which it later retracted—for the sole purpose of recovering the eighty-two-man crew. After the men returned home, a court of inquiry recommended that Bucher be tried for failing to fight the ship and allowing sensitive electronic equipment to fall into the hands of the enemy. Ignatius overruled the recommendation, saying the men had "suffered enough."

A Decade of Neglected Preparedness

While the United States threw money at prosecuting the Vietnam War, the USSR took advantage of America's preoccupation with an unpopular war and began expanding the Soviet Navy. By the time that Zumwalt turned the office of CNO over to Admiral James L. Holloway, Jr., in July 1, 1974, Soviet warships outnumbered the U.S. Fleet. The presence of the Soviet Navy in the Mediterranean had prevented the Sixth Fleet from mixing into the Arab-Israeli War of 1967, the Jordanian crisis of 1970, and the Yom Kippur War

Comparison of Naval Strength—1978	United States	Soviet Union
Carriers	21	3
Nuclear submarines	68	84
Other submarines	51	210
Ballistic nuclear ships	41	58
Other combat ships	36	91
Other types of ships	219	394
Totals	436	840

of October 1973. During the latter conflict, Zumwalt had strengthened the Mediterranean Fleet to sixty-five ships, only to be challenged by a force of ninety-eight Soviet ships. The confrontation triggered a worldwide alert, the first since the Cuban crisis, and it occurred during President Nixon's troubling Watergate scandal. Zumwalt later admitted that the United States "lacked either the military strength or the stable domestic leadership—one or the other might have been enough—to have supported the Israelis."

The problem festered, partly within the navy and partly within the government. Carrier admirals greatly influenced naval expenditures. They wanted larger ships, like the 81,600-ton carrier *Nimitz* (CVAN-68), which went into commission on May 3, 1975. Other officers pointed to the development of cruise missiles, nuclear-tipped weapons, and highly sophisticated torpedoes, arguing against large surface vessels because of their vulnerability to nuclear attack. They lobbied for the construction of more submarines and antisubmarine ships. Seventy-six-year-old Admiral Rickover stepped into the debate demanding that all future ships be nuclear-powered, despite higher cost and the consequence of being forced to build fewer ships. He later appeared before a congressional committee and told them that he would rather command the Soviet submarine fleet because if it came to war he would have a better chance of winning. Congressional inquiries

Operation Blue Light

In April 1980 President Carter made a stab at preserving American respectability in the world by approving Operation Blue Light—the rescue of embassy hostages held in Tehran. For more than five months, the navy had positioned twenty-seven ships in the Arabian Sea waiting for instructions.

The operation required six air force C-130 transports to fly from Egypt and rendezvous with eight RH-53D helicopters launched from the USS *Nimitz*. Each air group would carry Special Forces commandos and meet at Desert One, a remote staging point two hundred miles from Tehran.

By 1980, every asset in the navy suffered from disrepair. On the way to Desert One, two helicopters suffered mechanical problems and turned back. The engine on a third helicopter seized up while landing in a whirl of sand. Because the rescue effort required a minimum of six helicopters, mission commander Colonel Charles Beckwith cancelled the mission. On departure, the engine of a fourth helicopter clogged with sand; it collided with a C-130 transport, and created a fiery holocaust that killed five aircrew and three marines.

The embarrassing attempt further damaged the diminished esteem of the United States and encouraged the Soviet Union and their friends in the Middle East to take reckless chances. The bungled mission contributed to Jimmy Carter's defeat in the 1980 presidential election. The unfortunate experience also led to a valuable observation. Helicopters could not operate effectively in desert conditions without major design changes, and ten years later the United States would need aircraft and vehicles that could.

LEFT: Navy RH-53D Sea Stallion helicopters line up on the deck of the USS Nimitz *(CVAN-68) on April 24, 1980, to participate in the ill-fated joint services commando operation to rescue American hostages held in Tehran.*

BELOW: One of the worst commando operations of the Cold War occurred on April 24, 1980, when a joint hostage rescue operation commanded by the army disastrously fell apart at Desert One, 200 miles from Tehran, because of accidents and equipment failure.

ABOVE: Six of the navy's Sea Stallions en route from the Nimitz *the the rendezvous at Desert One. The hostage rescue attempt was more than just a public relations disaster: eight men died and two aircraft were lost.*

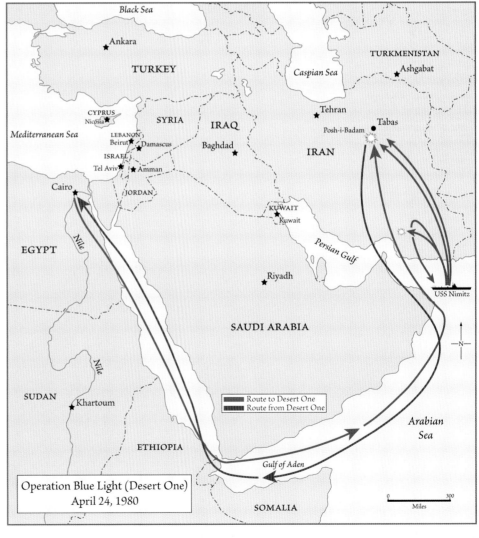

Operation Blue Light (Desert One)
April 24, 1980

Route to Desert One
Route from Desert One

merely slowed down the process of getting ships built.

On August 8, 1974, President Nixon resigned over the Watergate scandal, and Gerald Ford took over the reigns of government. Neither Ford nor Georgia Democrat Jimmy Carter, who won the presidency in 1976, did anything to strengthen the navy. Though Carter had served as a naval officer during World War II, he seemed oblivious to the growing gap in power between the navy and its Soviet counterpart.

Having entered upon another era of progressive reductions under the Carter administration, senior naval officers became apathetically discouraged. Harold Brown, Carter's shortsighted secretary of defense, redefined the navy's role as mainly protectors of "the sea lanes of communication between the United States and Europe." Admiral Holloway warned that if Brown's limited view of the world prevailed, the United States would by the turn of the century be unable to protect its international interests or its sea-lanes. The Carter administration appeared to ignore the growth of terrorism in the Middle East and the importance of having a naval presence. Iran revolted against the shah, and the Soviet Union threatened to invade Afghanistan. Preoccupied by problems in Iran, three months passed before

Carter became involved with Afghanistan. The Kremlin sneered at an eleventh hour warning from Carter and in December 1979 invaded Afghanistan.

Previously, on November 4, after many months of harassing Americans in Iran, Muslims stormed the U.S. embassy in Tehran and took sixty-six hostages, including three navy personnel. It was by any other definition an act of war. In 2005, some of the hostages identified Mahmoud Ahmadinejad, the newly elected president of Iran, as one of the leaders of the raid. The successful hostage-taking incident merely encouraged Muslims in Islamabad (Pakistan) and Tripoli (Libya) to raid other U.S. embassies. Carter dispatched a carrier group to the Arabian Sea without clearly explaining the task. The Iranians, perhaps understanding Carter better than he understood himself, ignored the show of force and held the hostages for four hundred and forty-four days. Iran released the detainees on January 20, 1981, the day Ronald Reagan took office.

Resurrection

Although Jimmy Carter had tried to cut funding for almost everything, Congress balked, and four years of bickering over the status of the navy looked pathetically silly to most Americans. After Iranian militants broke into the U.S. embassy in Tehran, Carter finally agreed to approve a previously cancelled carrier. Voters removed Carter from office, saving the nation and the navy from further embarrassment. After fifteen years of confusion and cutbacks, incoming president Ronald Reagan named Casper M. Weinberger secretary of defense and John F. Lehman, Jr., secretary of the navy. To anyone questioning what an aging, ex-movie star might understand about navy affairs, Reagan provided a quick answer by following Weinberger's advice and adding $9.5 billion to Carter's naval budget for 1981-1982.

Fielding questions from the press, Lehman replied that by 1990 the service would provide "outright maritime superiority over any power…which might attempt

BELOW: At the Long Beach Naval Shipyard in California, on December 28, 1982, CNO Admiral James D. Watkins, Secretary of the Navy John F. Lehman, Jr., and President Ronald Reagan stand left to right during the re-commissioning ceremony for the battleship USS New Jersey (BB-62).

to prevent our free use of the seas and the maintenance of our vital interests worldwide." He envisioned a navy of fifteen carrier battle groups, a hundred nuclear attack submarines, and four surface battle groups, which included the reactivation of the World War II battle-ships *New Jersey* (BB-62) and *Iowa* (BB-61) and the Korean War vintage carrier *Oriskany* (CVA-34). Senior naval officers lobbied for new battleships, but Lehman replied that the country could not wait. In 1982, when the *New Jersey* was recommissioned, she had been updated with the latest weaponry, including sixteen Harpoon missiles with ranges of fifty to sixty miles and thirty-two Tomahawk cruise missiles with ranges up to five hundred miles. As the range of nuclear-tipped Tom-ahawks increased to fifteen hundred miles, the navy refitted every active battleship to carry the improved weapon. The resurrection of the navy had begun.

Resurgence

Reagan wasted no time demonstrating that the United States would not be intimidated by the Soviet Union. On August 19, 1981, when Soviet-backed Colonel

Moammar al-Qaddafi declared the entire Gulf of Sidra as Libyan territorial waters, Reagan sent a carrier group from the Sixth Fleet to test Qaddafi's so-called "Line of Death." When two Libyan-piloted Su-22 Fitter fighters approached, a pair of F-14 Tomcats from the USS *Nimitz* (CVN-68) shot them down. Qaddafi retired to his tent to consider his options.

In 1982 fighting erupted in Lebanon between the Israeli Army and the Palestine Liberation Organization (PLO). Lebanon had become a haven for Soviet-backed Syrian intervention. Elements from the Sixth Fleet interceded and evacuated twelve thousand Palestinians over a ten-day period, and twelve hundred marines from the Sixth Fleet remained in Beirut as part of a multinational peacekeeping force.

The situation continued to worsen. On April 18, 1983, terrorists exploded a truck bomb outside the U.S. embassy in Beirut, killing sixty-one people, among them one marine and seventeen American civilians. More terrorist acts followed. At 6:25 A.M., October 23, a Mercedes truck loaded with two thousand pounds of high explosives crashed through barricades

ABOVE LEFT: Smoke and flames eject from the 16-inch guns on the USS New Jersey (BB-62) as a broadside is fired against Syrian artillery positions lodged in the hills above Beirut, December 9, 1983.

ABOVE RIGHT: On December 8, 1983 off the coast of Lebanon, the USS Independence (CV-62) circulates with a deck-load of aircraft parked on the bow while supporting marines serving as members of a multi-national peacekeeping force ashore.

Operation Urgent Fury—Grenada

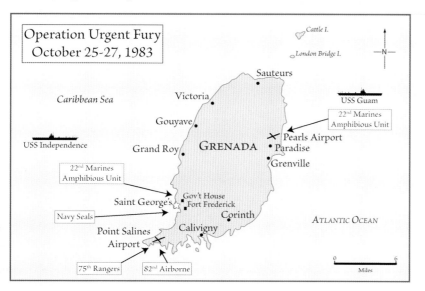

ABOVE: Marines were en route to Beirut when Cuban-led insurrectionists fomented a coup on Grenada. Navy amphibious assault ships reversed course and landed the 22nd Marine Amphibious Unit and SEALs on Grenada instead of Lebanon.

On October 19 1983, a Marxists military coup overthrew Grenada's government and imprisoned General Sir Paul Scoon, the commonwealth's governor. A former British colony, the 133-square-mile island of Grenada lay in the eastern Caribbean about sixteen hundred miles from Florida. Had it been possible to fortify it, the remote island would have provided the Soviets with military advantages similar to those avoided during the Cuban crisis of 1962. Soviet aid had already provided communists on Grenada with a naval base, military facilities, weapons storage capabilities, and a partially built military airfield. One thousand Americans lived on the island, mostly students attending St. George's University Medical School.

With cooperation from the Organization of Eastern Caribbean States, Reagan diverted to Grenada a task force of twelve ships and nineteen hundred marines en route to Lebanon and issued orders to Vice Admiral Joseph Metcalf, Jr., to occupy the island. Early in the morning of October 25, Metcalf put SEALs ashore to infiltrate the capital of St. George's, rescue Governor Scoon, and secure the Government House. At 5:36 A.M. helicopters from the USS *Guam* (LPH-9) landed four hundred men from the 22nd

Marine Amphibious Unit on Pearls Airport, Grenada's only operational airfield. Thirty minutes later C-5A and C-130 transport planes from Barbados dropped army Rangers on the unfinished nine-thousand-foot airstrip being built by Cubans on Point Salinas. By 8:50 A.M. American forces secured every objective but the Government House, where SEALs had been surrounded and pinned-down by Cuban forces.

On the morning of October 26, marines secured Government House and, on the following day, the entire island. During the operation eighteen Americans were killed and a hundred and sixteen wounded. While mopping-up the island, marines found unmistakable evidence of a major communist military buildup, which included the presence of forty-nine Russian, twenty-four North Korean, and thirteen Eastern European diplomats and advisors. The American force rounded up 638 Cuban prisoners, cleaned out warehouses filled with Soviet arms, and uncovered documents revealing plans to garrison the island with 6,800 Cuban troops.

The navy's timely action stifled communist operations in the Caribbean and disrupted Soviet plans to expand operations in Central America.

outside the headquarters building of the 24th Marine Amphibious Unit, killing 241 marines and wounding seventy. Lehman beefed up the Sixth Fleet with more ships, including the carriers *Independence* and *John F. Kennedy* (CV-67) and the battleship *New Jersey*. On December 4, after Syrian antiaircraft shot down two navy reconnaissance planes with Soviet-supplied surface-to-air missiles twenty miles east of Beirut, A-6 Intruders and A-7 Corsairs from the *Independence* and the *Kennedy* retaliated and bombed six Syrian positions in the mountains. Ten days later the *New Jersey* lobbed 16-inch shells, the first fired from her guns since 1969, into Syrian positions.

While the Sixth Fleet countered Soviet-backed terrorism in the Middle East, Cuban and Nicaraguan communists, supplied with Soviet arms, attempted to incite a Marxist revolution in the small Central American country of El Salvador. Navy SEALs went ashore during 1983 on a covert mission and remained there for more than a year while two carrier groups exercised offshore. Reagan believed the best way to prevent wars was to impede them before they escalated, and it came as no surprise when he reacted to reports of communist activity in Grenada.

Action in the Gulf of Sidra

In 1981, after navy Tomcats shot down two Libyan fighters off the Gulf of Sidra, Qaddafi began brokering widespread terrorism. In one incident on December 27, 1985, he sent terrorists to open fire on passengers in Rome and Vienna's airports, while Libya financed other attacks. The center of gravity shifted to Qaddafi and in January 1986 Vice Admiral Frank B. Kelso, commanding two battle groups, moved the carriers *Saratoga* (CV-60) and *Coral Sea* (CV-43) into position off the Gulf of Sidra. Qaddafi announced that any American ship or airplane entering the "Line of Death," being international waters within the Gulf of Sidra, would be destroyed. A cat-and-mouse game began when Libyan

FAR LEFT: An F/A-18 Hornet armed with AIM-9 Sidewinder missiles on the wingtips lands aboard the carrier USS Coral Sea (CV 43) on March 18, 1986, during flight operations off the coast of Libya.

LEFT: A Soviet built Libyan guided missile corvette burns in the Gulf of Sidra after a clash with aircraft from the USS Nimitz (CVN-68). The carrier was part of Sixth Fleet operations off Muammar Qadaffi's so-called "Line of Death."

MiG-25 Foxbats feigned attacks but always skedaddled before engaging navy combat air patrols.

The carrier *America* (CV-66) joined the squadron and for several weeks the minuet continued. On March 24 the missile cruiser *Ticonderoga* (CG-47) crossed the "Line of Death," followed by carrier aircraft, which evaded five SAMs fired from Libyan shore batteries. Kelso retaliated. A-6E Intruders from the *America* sank a Libyan missile patrol boat, and A-7E Corsairs from *Saratoga* wiped out land-based SAM sites and two Libyan missile corvettes. Ten days later Qaddafi responded, his terrorists blowing up passenger jet TWA flight 847 and a Berlin discotheque jammed with American servicemen.

Reagan ran out of patience with Qaddafi's insolence and ordered an air strike. On April 10 dozens of carrier planes struck Benghazi's Benina airfield, military barracks, terrorist training camps at Sidi Bilal, and Tripoli's military airbase. The night attack came as a complete surprise to Qaddafi and the rest of the world. Aircraft clobbered every assigned target, while the navy lost one plane because of mechanical failure. The attack wounded Qaddafi and unfortunately killed one of the colonel's adopted children. Libyan-sponsored terrorism subsided, but Reagan sagely cautioned, "We must be careful that we do not appear as terrorist ourselves."

The Budget-cutters

During his first term, Reagan rebuilt the navy, but during his second term naval expenditures became the target of congressional budget-cutters. When in 1985 Congress passed the Gramm-Rudman Bill in an effort to balance the national budget, one naval expert groaned, "If Gramm-Rudman stays in force for the full five years, the U.S. Navy will suffer its greatest defeat since Pearl Harbor." The focus of the bill was to kill expenditures for big-ticket items, such as nuclear-powered carriers and *Ohio*-class submarines. The legislation infuriated Secretary of the Navy Lehman, and on April 11, 1987, he resigned. Marine veteran James H. Webb filled the post for less than a year, resigning because Secretary of Defense Frank C. Carlucci settled for the existing 509-ship navy instead of the proposed 600-ship navy.

While navy men fumed at the cost-cutters, a long, bloody war between Iraq and Iran threatened to disrupt the flow of oil from the Persian Gulf. Both belligerents preyed on unguarded vessels flying neutral flags. The navy sent ships to the gulf to escort tankers through the war zone.

Reagan allowed Kuwaiti ships to fly the American flag and, because Kuwait supported Iraq, the president inadvertently involved the navy in Iraq's war with Iran. This did not prevent Iraqi pilots from firing Exocet

RIGHT: On May 17, 1987, while on picket duty in the Persian Gulf eighty miles northeast of Bahrain, 37 crewmen were killed on the USS Stark (FFG-31) when two Exocet missiles launched by an Iraqi F.1 Mirage ripped into the port side of the frigate.

FAR RIGHT: On July 24, 1987, during the Iran-Iraq War, the American-flagged Kuwaiti tanker SS Bridgeton struck a floating Soviet contact mine in the Persian Gulf that ripped a 30-by-45-foot hole in the ship's hull. There were no casualties, and the ship made a Kuwaiti port safely.

RIGHT: On April 18, 1988, during Operation Preying Mantis, the guided-missile destroyer Lynde McCormick (DDG-8) and the destroyer Merrill (DD-976) attack Iranian oil platforms in the Persian Gulf being used as command and control centers against Kuwaiti super tankers.

missiles at the frigate USS *Stark* (FFG-31), killing thirty-seven Americans, or Iranian mines from blowing a hole in the supertanker *Bridgeton*, which was flying the Stars and Stripes. On April 14, 1988, another Iranian mine struck the frigate *Samuel B. Roberts* (FFG-58), and this time the navy took revenge on a number of old oil platforms used by Iranians to conduct operations against neutral shipping.

War in the Middle East caused concern, but not enough to justify beefing-up the navy, especially when in 1987 General Secretary Mikhail Gorbachev admitted that the USSR was being driven into national bankruptcy caused by military competition with the United States. Reagan's mainly bloodless war with the Soviet Union cost a great deal of money, but a hot war would have cost immensely more. On December 8, 1987,

Reagan signed a treaty with Gorbachev as the first step in reducing the stockpile of nuclear weapons, and the forty-year Cold War ended with the gradual dissolution of the Soviet Union. When Reagan left office in January 1989, he turned a safer world over to his successor, George H. W. Bush. Even the eight-year Iran-Iraq war had ended, initiating a new chance for peace throughout the world.

Ignoring instability in the Middle East, cost-cutters in Congress resumed their work with vigor and began contemplating ways to spend money saved from navy appropriations on pet domestic projects.

In 1990, CNO Admiral Carlisle A. H. Trost stepped into the dispute and outlined the new role of the navy: first, to control the sea and deny the same privilege to opponents during a time of war; second, to project power ashore using aircraft, naval gunfire, missiles, and marine forces; third, to provide strategic sealift for joint operations ashore; and fourth, to provide a nuclear deterrent. Trost's tenets blended perfectly with the four central elements of national strategy, those being strategic deterrence, forward presence, crisis response, and force reconstitution. Trost's lucid perception of the 21st century navy compares in stature with Alfred Thayer Mahan's 1890 view of the 20th century navy. Much had changed during the hundred years that separated the two men, but each concisely articulated the role of the navy at a time when it needed to be redefined.

When a crisis confronts the nation, the first question often asked by policymakers is: 'What naval forces are available and how fast can they be on station.'
Admiral Carlisle A. H. Trost, May 1990.

Instead of slashing the navy's $100 billion budget, Congress retained all but a very small part of it and increased the fleet to 546 ships.

Operation Desert Shield

Admiral Trost emphasized the importance of maintaining close alliances with countries crucial to the interests of the United States. The oil-rich Middle East fell into that category, and since 1949 countries like Saudi Arabia and tiny Kuwait had come to depend upon the United States for naval protection. In 1990, Admiral Trost, President Bush, and Secretary of Defense Richard Cheney did not anticipate a new war in the Middle East, but on August 2 Iraqi dictator Saddam Hussein sent divisions from the fourth largest army in the world into Kuwait. Elements of the navy were already in the Persian Gulf when President Bush and the United Nations began building a thirty-three-nation Coalition. The action did not curb Hussein, who on August 8 formally annexed Kuwait. Urged by the United States, the U.N. authorized trade sanctions against Iraq, and the navy deployed a naval blockade, thereby severing Saddam Hussein's economic lifeline.

On August 6, 1990, Bush authorized Operation Desert Shield, the buildup of forces in Saudi Arabia to oust the Iraqi army from Kuwait if Hussein refused to withdraw peacefully. The following day Secretary of State James Baker opened discussions with Iraqi minister Tariq Aziz to explain exactly what would happen if Iraqi forces did not withdraw. During the talks, carrier

LEFT: In preparation for Desert Storm, the aircraft carrier USS John F. Kennedy (CV-67) gets in line in the Great Bitter Lake to transit through the Suez Canal. Directly behind her is the nuclear-powered guided-missile cruiser USS Mississippi (CGN-40).

battle groups formed around the *Saratoga* (CV-60), and the *John F. Kennedy* (CV-67) departed from the East Coast for the Red Sea packed with aircraft, bombs, and guided missiles. A few weeks later carrier groups organized around the *Theodore Roosevelt* (CVN-71) and the *America* got underway from Norfolk, Virginia, for the Red Sea. The *Midway* (CV-41) and *Ranger* (CV-61) relieved the *Independence* in the Gulf of Oman at the eastern end of the Persian Gulf.

BELOW: On September 15, 1990, fresh from indicting drug-smuggling traffic at sea, the nuclear-powered guided-missile cruiser USS Mississippi (CGN-40) gets underway in the Suez Canal in support of Operation Desert Storm.

FAR RIGHT: On December 1, 1990, the hospital ships USNS Comfort (T-AH-20), left, and USNS Hope (T-AH-19) steam into the Persian Gulf during operation Desert Shield in preparation for Desert Storm.

RIGHT: The guided-missile destroyer USS MacDonough (DDG-39), left, the command ship USS La Salle (AGF-3), center, and the aviation logistics ship USNS Curtiss (T-AVB-4) tie up together in the Persian Gulf, December 1, 1990.

BELOW: The vehicle cargo ship 2nd Lt. John P. Bobo (T-AK-3008) offloads cargo in Saudi Arabia on December 13, 1990, during Operation Desert Shield. The cargo ship is part of the navy's Maritime Pre-positioning Squadron 1.

Desert Shield became a navy operation. Over a period of thirteen days, after Bush received permission from King Fahd Al-Saud to land troops in Saudi Arabia, ships transferred 45,000 marines with tanks, ammunition, heavy equipment, and supplies to defend the Saudi borders. From Camp Lejune, North Carolina, the 4th Marine Expeditionary Brigade embarked in thirteen amphibious vessels. The Military Sealift Command activated eight fast cargo ships and dispatched nineteen prepositioning ships to carry munitions and supplies for the joint services, and a navy field hospital. Eight cargo ships picked up the 24th Army Infantry Division (Mechanized) at Savannah, Georgia, along with M1 Abrams battle tanks to lead the ground attack during what was to become Operation Desert Storm.

On August 22 the navy called up its "selected reserves" and thousands of men and women, many in specialist roles, packed their gear and began trundling off to debarkation centers for assignments in the Gulf. Nor did the navy overlook the coast guard, calling it into service for the first time since World War II.

By October, as land forces reached their peak, a hundred thousand sailors, coast guard personnel, and marines were either in the area of the Persian Gulf or on the way. More than 240 ships responded to the call, the largest number of U.S. warships assembled in a single theater since World War II. In the fastest sealift in history, the navy transported 18.3 billion pounds of equipment and supplies to sustain forces on the ground.

By January 15, 1991, Coalition forces were all in place for Desert Storm. The delay could be partly attributed to a feuding Congress. After much debate, on January 12 the House voted 250-183, the quarreling Senate 52-47, and President Bush received congressional approval for launching Operation Desert Storm.

Operation Desert Storm

The AirLand Battle doctrine, conceived after the Vietnam War, had really never been tried against a foe. While designed for fighting a war against the Soviet Union and Warsaw Pact armored divisions in Europe, the doctrine was about to get its first trial against Iraq. For AirLand Battle enthusiasts, and for those who still pondered Trost's axioms for a navy finely tuned for attack-defense situations, Desert Shield/Desert Storm unfolded in near textbook fashion. At "H-hour" on January 17, 1991, Desert Storm erupted with a shattering attack on Iraq's air defenses and command and control centers. In the Persian Gulf, Red Sea, and the eastern Mediterranean, two battleships, the *Missouri* (BB-63) and the *Wisconsin* (BB-64), nine cruisers, five destroyers, and two nuclear-powered submarines launched the first Tomahawk II Land Attack Missiles

The AirLand Battle Doctrine

AirLand Battle doctrine is based on securing or retaining the initiative and exercising it aggressively to defeat the enemy. Destruction of the opposing force is achieved by throwing the enemy off balance with powerful initial blows from unexpected directions and then following up rapidly to prevent his recovery. [Combined forces] will attack the enemy in depth with fire and maneuver and synchronize all efforts to attain the objective. They will maintain the agility necessary to shift forces and fire to the points of enemy weakness. Our operations must be rapid, unpredictable, violent and disorienting to the enemy.
Richard A. Schwartz, Encyclopedia of the Persian Gulf War, 15.

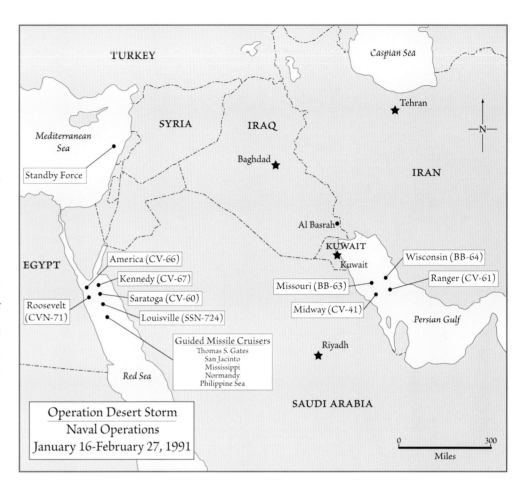

Operation Desert Storm
Naval Operations
January 16-February 27, 1991

(TLAMs). It probably came as quite a shock to Red Sea fishermen when the first fiery Tomahawk, launched by the submerged *Louisville* (SSN-724), spurted from the Red Sea. Two battleships, firing their 16-inch guns in combat for the first time since the Korean War, hurled a million pounds of ordnance, including 112 2,700-pound shells, on Iraqi positions.

A carefully crafted joint strategic air campaign with precision-guided projectiles followed, demonstrating a revolution in the art of warfare for which the Iraqis were unprepared. At H-Hour the Iraqi air force consisted of 730 planes, but only sixty French-built Mirage F-1s and some one hundred and fifty Soviet-built MiGs were state of the art. During the first day's action, four navy Hornets on a bombing mission intercepted two Iraqi MiG-21 fighters at seven miles. Switching their F/A-18 strike-fighters from bombing profile to

ABOVE: During Desert Storm, the U.S. Navy occupied every stretch of saltwater in range of Iraq. When operations began on January 17, 1991, nine navy ships in the Persian Gulf and Red Sea launched 122 Tomahawk cruise missiles at Iraqi targets.

Navy Missiles

The most common types of ship-launched missiles fall into seven categories.

The AGM-84D Harpoon is the navy's primary anti-ship missile. Capable of being launched from aircraft, submarines, or surface ships, the weapon has a range of sixty nautical miles and carries a 488-pound warhead that can take out "over-the-horizon" targets.

The RIM-116A Rolling Airframe Missile (RAM) is an infrared-guided missile used against enemy antiship ordnance by amphibious ships, cruisers, and destroyers. The missile travels at supersonic speeds and carries a conventional 25-pound explosive warhead.

The RIM-7M Sea Sparrow is a surface-to-air radar-guided antimissile and aircraft weapon with a 90-pound fragmentation warhead that travels at 2,660 knots.

The SM-2 Standard missile is carried on Ticonderoga-class cruisers and Arleigh Burke-class destroyers. Radar-guided, the Standard can be fired from a MK 41 Vertical Launch System (VLS) or the MK 26 Guided Missile Launcher system (GMLS), travel two hundred miles, and detonate on contact with the target.

The Tomahawk is the navy's primary long-range cruise missile and can be launched from surface ships or submarines. With a range of a thousand miles, Tomahawks travel at five hundred knots and can be programmed to follow an evasion path. Using Global Positioning System (GPS) technology, Tomahawks carry cameras to survey the battlefield so that they can be shifted in mid-flight to fifteen alternative targets.

The Trident fleet ballistic missile with a nuclear warhead is a three-stage missile with a range of more than 4,600 miles. It can develop speeds of more than 11,000 knots and carry Multiple Independently Targetable Re-entry Vehicles (MIRVs) for warheads.

The Vertical Launch Antisubmarine Rocket (VLA), which is also carried on cruisers and destroyers, is a three-stage missile that can carry a 98-pound warhead or launch a MK 46 MOD 5 torpedo.

(1): On January 1, 1991, a Harpoon missile launcher canister is lowered into place on board the guided-missile destroyer USS Arleigh Burke (DDG-51). The destroyer will see action during Desert Storm. (2): An all-weather, high-firepower RIM-116 Rolling Airframe Missile (RAM) is launched from the carrier USS Dwight D. Eisenhower (CVN-69) during an exercise to test the ship's self-defense combat system. (3): A RIM-7 Sea Sparrow missile is fired from the Mark 25 basic point defense missile system launcher during a live-fire exercise on the amphibious assault ship USS Nassau (LHA-4), May 2, 1984. (4): A Tomahawk cruise missile is launched from the nuclear-powered attack submarine USS La Jolla (SSN-701) on the Pacific Missile Test Center Range. Tomahawks continue to be improved with longer ranges and improved targeting capabilities. (5): A vertical launch ASROC (VLA) missile is fired during tests at the Naval Weapons Center at China Lake, California. (6): A UGM-96 Trident missile streaks into the air during the 20th demonstration and shakedown launch of the nuclear powered strategic missile submarine USS Mariano G. Vallejo (SSBN-658). (7): On February 24, 2005, a navy Standard Missile 3 (SM3) is launched from a Mark 41 vehicle launch system (VLS) on the Aegis guided-missile cruiser USS Lake Erie (CG-70) to intercept a short-range ballistic missile target.

air-to-air, the pilots downed both MiGs using Sidewinder missiles, producing the navy's only air-to-air kills during the campaign.

Most of Iraq's aircraft never got off the ground. Those that did, including 122 MiGs, took refuge in Iran. Iraqi pilots had used Exocet missiles during the eight-year war with Iran, and their retreat from the skies came as some relief to Coalition ships in the Persian Gulf. Lieutenant Commander Michael S. Speicher was the only navy pilot killed in the

operation, when a SAM from the *Saratoga* accidentally struck his Hornet.

Fighter-attack planes and helicopters from six aircraft carriers and several amphibious ships joined USAF, marine, and Coalition air groups in striking 160 sites throughout Iraq. Targets included airfields; surface-to-air missile sites; command and communication centers; chemical, biological, and nuclear facilities; bridges; oil refineries; and launchers for Soviet-made Scud-B surface-to-surface missiles. Navy EA-6B Prowlers (defense suppression aircraft) loaded with powerful electronic countermeasure equipment jammed every enemy air defense system or communication post still capable of operating. When Prowlers detected enemy signals, navy tactical aircraft used high-speed antiradiation missiles (HARMs) to destroy the sites. The navy also used the first stand-off land-attack missile (SLAM), a variant of the Harpoon, which allowed carrier pilots to hit high-value targets from

more than fifty miles away. Even SH-60 Seahawk helicopters from the guided-missile frigate *Nicholas* (FFG-47) got into the act, firing precision–guided missiles at two Iraqi observation posts positioned on Dorrah oil-field platforms.

General H. Norman Schwarzkopf, supreme commander of Coalition forces, oversaw the air campaign from his headquarters command post in the fortified basement of the Saudi Ministry of Defense and Aviation at Riyadh. Of the 1,800 aircraft involved in Operation Instant Thunder, 450 came from the six carriers, and more than 300 came from other navy ships in the Persian Gulf and the land-based 3rd Marine Air Wing. Schwarzkopf followed the AirLand Battle doctrine when he outlined the air mission in four phases: first, to gain air superiority by destroying Iraq's strategic capabilities (which Coalition pilots accomplished in seven days); second, to knock out the enemy's air defenses in the Kuwaiti area; third, to attack the Iraqi army in Kuwait while maintaining the first two objectives; fourth, to give air support to ground operations.

During Operation Desert Storm, navy and marine

FAR LEFT TOP: In January 1991, a BMG-109 Tomahawk land-attack missile heads towards an Iraqi target after being launched from the battleship USS Wisconsin (BB-64) during Operation Desert Storm.

ABOVE: F/A-18C Hornets from Strike Fighter Squadron 74 (VFA-74) fly over the carrier USS Saratoga (CV-60) as she turns to starboard during Desert Shield operations in the Persian Gulf, November 4, 1990.

FAR LEFT BOTTOM: On February 6, 1991, a Mark 7 16-inch/50 caliber gun is fired from the battleship USS Missouri (BB-63) as night shelling of Iraqi targets begins along the northern Kuwaiti coast during Operation Desert Storm.

RIGHT: During Desert storm, aviation ordnancemen deliver Mark 20 Rockeye II cluster bombs to three Attack Squadron 35 (VA-35) A-6E Intruders positioned on the deck of the USS Saratoga (CV-60). Parked nearby is an EA-6B Prowler.

FAR RIGHT: During a flyover, an F-14A Tomcat from Fighter Squadron 84 (VF-84) used a Tactical Air Reconnaissance Pod System (TARPS) to photograph two reinforced concrete aircraft hangars bombed at Ahmed Al Jaber Airport during Operation Desret Storm.

RIGHT: During Desert Storm, an HH-60H Seahawk from Helicopter Search and Rescue Squadron/Special Warfare Support Squadron 4 (HCS-4) takes off in the sand for its first search and rescue operation behind enemy lines.

RIGHT: An F-14A Tomcat overflies the USS America (CV-66) on returning to the carrier after completing its mission. Under the Tomcat's fuselage are one AIM-7 Sparrow and two AIM-54 Phoenix missiles; under the wings are AIM-9 Sidewinders and more Sparrows.

pilots flew more than thirty thousand sorties. Fighting against such advanced technology must have been a dizzying experience for Iraqi forces. Three weeks into the air campaign, Hornets and Intruders using Harpoon missiles and Skipper and Rockeye bombs sank or disabled most of Iraq's missile gunboats, minesweepers, and Silkworm antiship missile sites.

On February 23, 1991, as the ground war got underway, navy planes shifted from hitting mainly stationary targets to striking roving targets, such as tanks and truck convoys. The navy's newer aircraft, such as the F/A-18D night attack Hornets, prevented the enemy from moving men and material at night. F-14 Tomcats equipped with Phoenix missiles and tactical air reconnaissance pod systems (TARPS) flew real time and near-real-time missions over tactical areas in support of the ground offensive. Even UAVs (unmanned aerial vehicles) made an appearance; no Coalition troops were handy when one Iraqi unit attempted to surrender to a UAV circling overhead.

The hundred-hour ground war might have ended sooner had Saddam Hussein realized that his vaunted Republican Guard had been cut to pieces and driven out of Kuwait early on day three. The victory cost the navy six killed, twelve wounded, and six planes. The Iraqi navy had been eliminated; the enemy air force was crippled; some 4,200 tanks, armored vehicles, and artillery pieces were destroyed; and more than a hundred thousand Iraqi troops were killed, wounded, or captured. What Hussein once called the "Mother of All Battles" ended in a whimper.

A Decade of Brush Fires

The Persian Gulf War convinced Congress that the last world threat had been abolished and by 1995 the navy could be reduced from 540 ships to 451. Desert Storm would become the last major navy operation of the twentieth century, but despite the dissolution of the Warsaw Pact on March 31, 1991, the world continued to be a dangerous place filled with brush fires.

With the final collapse of the USSR in December 1991, the scene quickly shifted to Serbia-dominated Yugoslavia, where Croatia, Slovenia, Bosnia-Herzegovina, and Macedonia followed the pattern of the Soviet breakup and opted for independence. The struggle developed into a three-way war among Serbians, Bosnians, and Croats. In January 1992 a U.N. peacekeeping force entered the area after recognizing Slovenia, Croatia, and Bosnia as independent states, but Bosnian Serb irregulars launched a barbaric "ethnic cleansing" campaign against Muslims and Croats. President Bush sent a carrier group into the Adriatic Sea to provide air cover for USAF transports flying supplies into the contested area.

The situation in Bosnia escalated, and in 1993 incoming President William J. Clinton upped the ante and committed the navy, the marines, and other services to a limited peacekeeping role that lasted until December 1995. Secretary of Defense William Perry stationed one battle carrier group in the Adriatic to provide a mobile base for navy pilots flying air cover and reconnaissance missions. With the *Abraham Lincoln* (CVN-72) and *Independence* still deployed against Hussein's calumniations in Iraq, the Bosnian problem fell mostly on pilots from the *Theodore Roosevelt* or the *America*. Limited intervention in the area continued until 2001, when President George W. Bush took over the presidency and scaled back operations after more than a hundred thousand sorties had been flown.

On August 18, 1992, during the Serbian disturbance, the United States also became involved in sending aid to Somalia, on the coast of East Africa. On December 9, after tribal warlords prevented food from

ABOVE: On the USS America *(CV-66) during December 1993, an S-3 Viking from Air Anti-Submarine Warfare Squadron 32 is being prepared for takeoff during Operation Deny Flight over Bosnia. Parked on the edge of the flight deck are three F-14 Tomcats and one F/A-18 Hornet.*

BELOW: The USS Theodore Roosevelt *(CVN-71), the navy's fifth* Nimitz-*class nuclear-powered aircraft carrier, returns from a tour of duty in the Red Sea with her deck-load of aircraft.*

Clan activity intensified, the muddling U.N. effort collapsed, and marines began losing their lives. On February 27, 1995, the navy sent in the Marine Amphibious Group from the *Essex* (LHD-2) to form a perimeter through which U.N. peacekeepers could withdraw.

ABOVE: On January 17, 1993, an air cushion landing craft (LCAC-6) creates a cloud of sand in Somalia as it heads for the water during Operation Restore Hope's multinational relief effort.

FAR RIGHT: At 2:55 P.M., June 25, 1996, terrorists blew up a fuel truck outside the northern fence of the Khobar Towers complex near King Abdul Aziz Air Base in Saudi Arabia, killing 19 and wounding 260 U.S. servicemen.

RIGHT: On October 29, 2000, the crew of the USS Cole (DDG-67) uses the navy tug USNS Catawba to escort their damaged destroyer to a staging point in Yemen's harbor before being transferred to a Norwegian ship for repair.

getting to Somalia's starving population, the navy sent SEALs ashore at Mogadishu, followed by marines in rubber boats. The so-called secret landing was met on the beach by the glare of video lights and photoflashes from the news media. The food distribution mission somewhat improved, and the two warlords occupying Mogadishu signed a truce. In May 1993 President Clinton turned the project into a nation-building enterprise with American forces providing cover for U.N. peacekeepers. Clinton acceded too much authority to the U.N., which resulted in a lack of direction; a lack of military and political insight; and no guidance.

A New Wave of Terrorism

During the 1990s a new terrorist regime emerged through the organizing efforts of Saudi multi-millionaire Osama bin Laden, who after being ousted from his native country established the worldwide al-Qaeda terrorist network in Afghanistan. He understood that, in order to control the Middle East, it was important to drive Westerners out of the oil-rich areas, and built a quasi-military organization to cleanse the Middle East of Jews and Christians by declaring a holy war. The Clinton administration took little notice of the warning because the president sought a "peace dividend" from the Persian Gulf War.

Bin Laden forged ahead with his plans and funded a terrorist group who in 1993 exploded a bomb under New York's World Trade Center but failed to destroy it. In 1995 al-Qaeda terrorists bombed a U.S. military building in Riyadh, Saudi Arabia, and in 1996 struck the Khobar Towers building in Dhahran, in Saudi's Eastern Province, killing nineteen American flyers. When interviewed by ABC News in 1998, bin Laden said, "We do not differentiate between those dressed in

Navy Strength:	2000
Total ships	318
Ships deployed	100
Submarines deployed	11
Personnel deployed	46,249
Total operational aircraft	4,108
Total naval personnel	
Active duty	373,193
Officers	53,550
Enlisted	315,471
Midshipmen	4,172
Ready Reserve	183,942
Employed civilians	184,044

military uniforms and civilians: they are all targets."

Weeks later al-Qaeda terrorists bombed the U.S. embassies in Nairobi (Kenya) and Dar es Salaam (Tanzania), killing and injuring 5,036 people, including Americans. Then in October 2000, during the last months of Clinton's second term, al-Qaeda operatives attempted to sink the USS *Cole* (DDG-67) while she refueled at a Yemeni port.

By the time Clinton left office in January 2001, he had cut the navy back from 546 ships to 318, partly on the advice of Secretary of State Madeline Albright, who told then-Chairman of the Joint Chiefs of Staff General

Colin Powell, "What's the point of having this superb military you are always talking about if you can't use it."

The War on Terror

On September 11, 2001, eight months into the administration of President George W. Bush, al-Qaeda terrorists struck the United States with enormous impact. In coordinated attacks, two airliners taken over by terrorists destroyed both towers of the World Trade Center in New York, another jumbo jet slammed into the Pentagon building and damaged the Navy Command Center, and a fourth airliner crashed in Pennsylvania. In all, 2,793, including nineteen hijackers, died, and a further twenty-four people were reported missing, presumed dead. Within hours, the navy dispatched the hospital ship *Comfort* (T-AH-20) from Baltimore to aid the injured in Manhattan.

Bush reacted swiftly. He declared war on terrorism and authorized immediate retaliatory operations against bin Laden and the controlling Taliban government in Afghanistan. The aircraft carriers *Enterprise* and *Carl Vinson* (CVN-70) steamed immediately for the Arabian Sea. On the night of October 7 carrier aircraft launched the first surgical strikes. Hornets and Tomcats targeted Taliban-controlled airfields, air defense sites, command-and-control centers, al-Qaeda training camps, and the Kandahar residential compound of Taliban leader Mullah Mohammad Omar. By mid-December, the two

ABOVE: In January 2002, during a sensitive mission in the Zhawar Kili area of eastern Afghanistan, navy SEALs found valuable intelligence information, including this Osama bin Laden propaganda poster.

LEFT: During the terrorist attack on 9/11, a jetliner crashed into the west wall of the Pentagon in Washington, D.C. On October 11 soldiers from the 3rd U.S. Infantry Regiment begin removing the huge flag put there after the catastrophe.

FAR LEFT: On September 15, 2001, four days after the smoke cleared from the terrorist bombing of the World Trade Center, New York, rescue and recovery efforts continue in an attempt to locate victims of the atrocity. Nearly 3,000 people were killed in the attack.

Landing Platform Helicopter Carriers

In 1962 the navy, working with the Marine Corps, authorized the first Marine Expeditionary Units (MEUs) as part of the Cold War's "Flexible Response" program. Over time, the marine units became "Special Operations Capable" and were designated MEU/SOC amphibious ready teams.

In 1961 the navy commissioned the first Landing Platform Helicopter Carrier, the USS *Iwo Jima* (LPH-2), which became the cornerstone of the MEUs' rapid deployment force. The *Iwo Jima* was the first amphibious ship deployed in the Persian Gulf during Operation Desert Shield and Desert Storm and participated in marine landings and mine countermeasure operations.

As soon as President Bush made the decision to strike the Taliban in Afghanistan, the *Peleliu* (LHA-5) and the *Bataan* (LHD-5) arrived in the Arabian Sea with the 15th and 26th MEU/SOCs, each carrying fifteen hundred marines and an air wing of AH-1W Super Cobras, CH-53E Super Stallion helicopters, and up to twenty-four McDonnell Douglas AV-8 Harrier jets. Joined by the *Bon Homme Richard* (LHD-6) during operations against the Taliban in the mountainous Torabora region, Harrier

LEFT: On June 21, 1997, an AV-8B Harrier jump jet from Marine Attack Squadron 214 (VMA-214) takes off from the deck of the amphibious assault ship USS Peleliu *(LHA-5).*

pilots flew four hundred sorties, dropping GBU-12 500-pound and MK-82 bombs on specified targets, while on November 24 marines from the *Peleliu* and *Bataan* landed by helicopter in southern Afghanistan and secured the Kandahar airfield.

Landing Platform Helicopter Carriers, which also carried Harrier attack planes, added a new dimension to naval operations by providing MEU/SOC battalions with the capability of arriving at any hotspot in the world in about forty-eight hours.

carrier groups had flown more than six thousand missions without losing a plane. On October 9, with most of the known SAM sites destroyed, daylight raids began.

On October 7 other navy ships got into the act. The Aegis cruiser *Philippine Sea* (CG-58) and the Aegis destroyers *John Paul Jones* (DDG-53) and *McFaul* (DDG-74) launched Tomahawk cruise missiles at new targets. On October 12 the carrier *Kitty Hawk* arrived and added her planes to the strikes. The three carriers remained in the Arabian Sea until December 15, when the *John C. Stennis* (CVN-74) arrived to relieve the *Carl Vinson*. By then, the *Vinson's* airwing had flown 4,200 sorties and dropped two million pounds of ordnance. In a matter of weeks the Taliban regime and its forty-thousand-man army collapsed.

Operation Iraqi Freedom

For navy pilots, operations in Afghanistan became a dress rehearsal for the coming war with Iraq. In Desert Storm, many aircraft were assigned to the same target. In Afghanistan, a navy pilot on average struck two or more targets per flight. When pilots launched their ordnance, it was often against targets they could not see because remote fire-direction air controllers picked most of the targets and controlled the firing.

At 5:34 A.M. on March 20, 2003, Baghdad time, U.S. and Coalition forces began conducting air operations against Iraq. The objective: to remove Saddam Hussein's regime from power in an effort to bring stability to the Middle East and expand the war against terrorism.

Without carriers in the area, it is difficult to see how success would have been achieved.

Dr. Milan Vego, "What Can We Learn from Enduring Freedom," Proceedings, *128 (July 2002), 5.*

During months of negotiation between the United States and the U.N., Hussein transferred most of his chemical and biological weapons by jumbo jet to Syria.

The air strikes, though reminiscent of Desert Storm, were far more accurate and caused less collateral damage. The opening attack consisted of forty Tomahawk cruise missiles and aircraft strikes from the carriers *Abraham Lincoln, Constellation* (CVA-64), *Harry S. Truman* (CVN-75), and *Kitty Hawk* on communications sites, SAM missile installations, early-warning radar defense systems, and elements of Iraqi's leadership. F/A-18 Hornets from the *Constellation* and the *Abraham Lincoln* took out targets around Basra to pave the way for amphibious landings by the I Marine Expeditionary Force and the British Royal Marines. Two Amphibious Readiness Groups in the USS *Tarawa* (LHA-1) and the *Nassau* (LHA-4) waited offshore in preparation for the Basra assault. Two Amphibious Task Forces also waited offshore, one organized around the *Saipan* (LHA-2) and the other around the *Boxer* (LHD-6). All four units carried helicopters and AV-8B Harriers, and as the opening day progressed all four combat units went ashore near the mouth of the Tigris River. By the time the *Theodore Roosevelt* arrived on March 22, coalition forces had already flown six thousand sorties, neutralized Iraqi's control and intelligence centers, and degraded the much-heralded Republican Guard's ability to coordinate efforts on the ground.

When on March 25-26 a two-day sandstorm interrupted ground operations, F/A-18Cs from the *Constellation* knocked out three naval targets near Basra. While working with Super Hornets, one S-3B Viking, the navy's first jet-powered antisubmarine warfare plane, destroyed a fourth target with an AGM-65E laser-guided missile, marking the first time in thirty years that a navy S-3B had become involved in an overland strike.

In late March, navy jets and helicopters switched from striking high-value targets, which by then had been mostly destroyed, to providing close air support against Republican Guard units defending Baghdad and Saddam

Hussein International Airport. Afterwards, when marine units moved out of Baghdad and headed toward Hussein's hometown near Tikrit, carrier planes covered the advance. Tikrit fell two days later. By then, the war with Iraq had withered to sporadic fire in a few principal cities.

Carriers remained on duty off Iraq, with pilots perpetually ready to fly on call against mercenaries and insurgents opposed to democracy. After freeing Iraq, the navy remained on duty, rotating ships on a regular basis. The *George Washington* (CVN-73), after serving her tour of duty in the Persian Gulf, returned to Norfolk, Virginia, on July 26, 2004. During her six-month deployment she covered 51,000 nautical miles. Her Carrier Air Wing 7 flew 7,592 sorties, dropped eighty-two tons of ordnance, and never lost a plane.

The navy has come a long way since the first biplanes flew off the USS *Langley* (CV-1) in 1922. Carriers, submarines, ships, aircraft, and technology are still combining to make the future navy even more capable and effective in the years to come.

ABOVE: On February 20, 1998, during Operation Southern Watch, an F-14B Tomcat from Fighter Squadron 102 takes off from the USS George Washington (CVN-73) in the Persian Gulf. Two F/A-18C Hornets are parked in the foreground.

CHAPTER 9
INTO THE FUTURE

When Admiral Michael G. Mullen became Chief of Naval Operations on July 22, 2005, one of his first tasks was to look at the navy of today and decide how to configure the navy of tomorrow. Former CNO Vern Clark (2000-2005) had already begun the process when he handed the office over to Mullen. When compiling a $132 billion budget for 2006 and a $127 billion budget for 2007, Mullen considered the most important factors as being: (1) to sustain combat readiness; (2) build a fleet for the future, and (3), develop 21st century leaders. Mullen not only wants the right combat capabilities—speed, agility, persistence, and dominance—for the right cost, he also wants the navy to "better compete for the talent our country produces and create the conditions in which the full potential of every man and woman serving our Navy can be achieved."

> We have amazing talent in the navy, and we need to continually look for ways to send that talent to challenging, meaningful, joint duty. It's a joint world out there, and it's getting more joint every day. The war on terror proves that.
> *Admiral Michael G. Mullen, CNO.*

The Navy Organization

ABOVE: On Memorial Day 2006, Chairman of the Joint Chiefs of Staff General Peter Pace, USMC, addresses the audience at Arlington Memorial Cemetery. Sitting to Pace's right are President George W. Bush and then-Secretary of Defense Donald H. Rumsfeld.

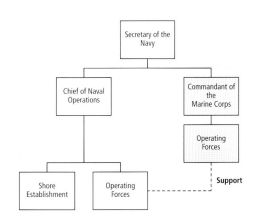

Secretary of the Navy → Chief of Naval Operations, Commandant of the Marine Corps → Operating Forces → Shore Establishment, Operating Forces — Support

ABOVE: The crew of sailors assigned to the new Arleigh Burke-class destroyer USS Halsey (DDG-97)—named for World War II Fleet Admiral William F. "Bull" Halsey, Jr—stand at attention during the commissioning ceremony at San Diego, California, July 30, 2005.

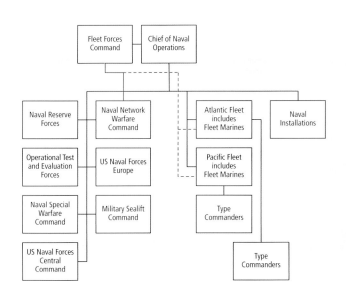

Fleet Forces Command, Chief of Naval Operations — Naval Reserve Forces, Naval Network Warfare Command, Atlantic Fleet includes Fleet Marines, Naval Installations, Operational Test and Evaluation Forces, US Naval Forces Europe, Pacific Fleet includes Fleet Marines, Naval Special Warfare Command, Military Sealift Command, Type Commanders, US Naval Forces Central Command, Type Commanders

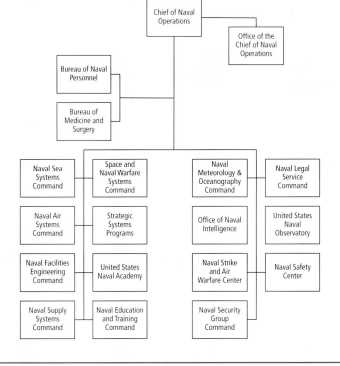

LEFT: Two navy Special Warfare Combatant-Craft crews (SWCC) assigned to Special Boat Team-22 (SBT-22) demonstrate the new Special Operations Craft-Riverine (SOC-R) during training at John C. Stennis Space Center in Mississippi, April 21, 2004.

LEFT: The high aerial view of Virginia's Norfolk Navy Station, shown September 1995, looks east, toward the Hampton Roads Bridge Tunnel. The station, among the oldest in the United States, is an immense modern naval industrial complex serving both navy surface and air commands.

Chief of Naval Operations — Office of the Chief of Naval Operations; Bureau of Naval Personnel; Bureau of Medicine and Surgery; Naval Sea Systems Command; Space and Naval Warfare Systems Command; Naval Meteorology & Oceanography Command; Naval Legal Service Command; Naval Air Systems Command; Strategic Systems Programs; Office of Naval Intelligence; United States Naval Observatory; Naval Facilities Engineering Command; United States Naval Academy; Naval Strike and Air Warfare Center; Naval Safety Center; Naval Supply Systems Command; Naval Education and Training Command; Naval Security Group Command

"Zulu" time is actually Greenwich Mean Time (GMT), or time on the prime (zero) meridian in Greenwich, England. The practice traces back to the early 18th century when mariners needed a starting point to determine longitude. Establishing the prime meridian led to the development of chronometers (highly accurate clocks) and time zones. The U.S. time zones in navy vernacular are Eastern ["R"—Romeo]; Central ["S"—Sierra]; Mountain ["T"—Tango]; Pacific ["U"—Uniform]; Alaska ["V"—Victor]; and Hawaii ["W"—Whiskey].

Because the Earth does not rotate at a constant rate, the navy has adopted a new timescale for Zulu—Coordinated Universal Time (UTC)—in place of GMT.

ABOVE: On August 16, 2006, sailors crowd the rails as the dock landing ship USS Germantown (LSD-42) arrives at the San Diego Naval Station, California, after returning from a six-month deployment in support of maritime security operations in the war against terror.

The Navy's Vision

Americans secure at home and abroad; sea and air lanes open and free for peaceful, productive movement of international commerce; enduring national and international naval relationships that remain strong and true; steadily deepening cooperation among maritime forces of emerging partner nations; and a combat-ready Navy—forward-deployed, rotational and surge capable—large enough, agile enough, and lethal enough to deter any threat and defeat any foe in support of Joint Force.

Admiral Michael G. Mullen, CNO, March 1, 2006.

The building blocks for the navy of tomorrow begin with the navy of today. The three main building blocks of the Fleet Forces Command involve the Carrier Strike Force, the Carrier Air Wing, and the Expeditionary Strike Group of the Atlantic Fleet, Pacific Fleet, and the Naval Network Warfare Command. Each strike group has its own unique structure, but the mix of combat ships is flexible depending upon the nature of the mission. Navy personnel represent a fourth building block, which consists of 354,703 men and women on active duty (officers: 53,463; enlisted: 296,944; midshipmen: 4,296), and 131,600 in the ready reserve. The current deployable battle force consists of 281 ships and more than 4,000 aircraft. Missing entirely from the arsenal of combat ships are battleships. The last two battleships to see action were the *Missouri* (BB-63) and the *Wisconsin* (BB-64), during Desert Storm. Both of them are now museums.

The Carrier Strike Group

The navy is the first to admit that there is no firm composition of a strike group. They are formed and disestablished on an as-needed basis, and one strike group may be much different from another. They are all composed of similar types of ships. A typical carrier strike group consists of a *Nimitz*-class carrier and at least a *Ticonderoga*-class guided missile cruiser; two *Arleigh Burke*-class destroyers; a *Los Angeles*-class attack submarine, and a *Supply*-class replenishment ship.

Nimitz-class carriers

There are nine *Nimitz*-class carriers in commission, ranging from the USS *Nimitz* (CVN-68) to the USS *Ronald Reagan* (CVN-76). A tenth carrier is under construction, the *George H. W. Bush* (CVN-77), which might well become the last of the class. Two more carriers are in the schedule with hull numbers CVN-78, planned for construction in 2007, and CVN-79, planned for construction to begin in 2012. Because the construction cycle takes from six to seven years, CVN-78 will not go into commission until 2014, if ever. Both may be cancelled, giving way to the new CVNX.

Part of the reason for long delays in building new carriers is that they are lasting much longer. The *Enterprise* (CVN-65) and the *Kitty Hawk* (CV-63), both commissioned in 1961, and the *John F. Kennedy*, commissioned in 1968, are all still in service. By the time CVN-78 goes into commission, the *Enterprise* will be more than fifty years old. Other factors in the decrease of large attack carriers is the cost, which is approaching $10 billion each; the development of the Expeditionary Strike Force, which carry AV-8B Harrier aircraft for close air support and precision bombing; and the Aegis missile cruisers, destroyers, and frigates that can strike targets hundreds of miles away without the aid of aircraft. With battleships already phased out of the fleet, aircraft carriers may be next.

Nimitz-class carriers, however, will be around for

decades to come and remain the centerpiece of the Carrier Strike Force. The typical *Nimitz*-class carrier is powered by two nuclear reactors driving four shafts at thirty-plus knots. The ship displaces 97,000 tons, is 1,092 feet long, and carries eighty-five aircraft, a bank of Sea Sparrow launchers, and a battery of 20mm Phalanx mounts. The complement includes a ship's crew of 3,200 and an air wing of 2,480.

Ticonderoga-class Cruisers

Augmenting the Carrier Strike Group is at least one guided missile cruiser of the *Ticonderoga*-class. Cruisers do not come cheap, about $1 billion each. They are not exclusively tied to carriers and operate with expeditionary strike forces, in a Battle Force mode, and sometimes independently. There are currently twenty-four Aegis guided missile cruisers in commission. They are not nuclear powered, depending on four General Elec-

ABOVE: On February 15, 2006, the Ticonderoga-class guided missile (Aegis) cruiser USS Lake Champlain (CG-57) is underway in the Indian Ocean off the starboard beam of the aircraft carrier USS Ronald Reagan (CVN-76).

RIGHT: The Ticonderoga-class guided missile cruiser (Aegis) USS Vella Gulf (CG-72) is caught on camera executing a high-speed turn while on maneuvers in the Mediterranean Sea, February 3, 2004.

BELOW LEFT: On May 25, 2006, the Aegis cruiser USS Lake Erie (CG-20) launches an SM 2 surface-to-air fleet defense missile off the island of Kauai, Hawaii, during a demonstration of the first sea-based intercept of a ballistic missile in its terminal phase.

BELOW RIGHT: On March 21, 2002, the aircraft carrier USS Kitty Hawk (CV-63) fires a RIM-116A Rolling Airframe Missile (RAM) during a test of the ship's newly installed missile launching system. The RAM is a lightweight, high-firepower, anti-ship, all-weather, self-defense system against anti-ship missiles.

tric LM 2500 gas turbine engines for propulsion. At 567 feet, they are half the length of a fast carrier, but have the same thirty-plus-knot speed. The typical cruiser carries two SH-2 Seasprite or two SH-60 Seahawk helicopters, and a crew of 24 officers and 340 enlisted personnel. Their missile systems depend on their vintage. The *Ticonderoga*, which was commissioned January 22, 1983, is now decommissioned because missiles have changed. Today's cruisers with the Aegis combat system, such as the *Vella Gulf* (CG-72) and the *Port Royal* (CG-73), carry a mix of Standard missiles (SM); vertical launch ASROC (VLA) missiles; Tomahawk cruise missiles; six MK 46 torpedoes; two MK 45 5-inch/.54-caliber guns, and two SH-2 close-in-weapons systems.

Arleigh Burke-class Destroyers

Every Carrier Strike Group contains two or more guided missile destroyers. The destroyers can operate at thirty-plus knots, independently or as part of a carrier battle group, surface action group, amphibious ready group, or with an underway replenishment

Aegis Weapons System

Aegis has become a common term to mean a surface-launched missile system with a variety of lower- and upper-tier missiles applied against enemy ships, aircraft, antiaircraft, and short- and medium-range missiles. The system works in all weather conditions and in chaff and jamming environments, enabling fighter aircraft to concentrate on the outer air battle.

The Aegis system is based on an automatic detect and track, multifunction phased-array radar (AN/SPY-1), which performs search, tracking, and guidance functions on as many as a hundred targets simultaneously. The system was originally designed for destroyers and later expanded to include cruisers, frigates, and other ships. Included among the guided missiles controlled by Aegis weapons systems are AGM-84D Harpoons; the RIM-116A Rolling Airframe Missile (RAM); the Standard Missile 2 (SM-2), including the SM-2 Block III medium range missile and the Block IV Extended-Range missile; Tomahawk cruise missiles; and others.

group. For their size, about 505 feet in length and 8,400 to 9,200 tons displacement, they have almost the same firepower as a cruiser and nearly the same size crew (23 officers and 300 enlisted). In addition to two SH-60 Seahawk helicopters, the weapons system includes Standard, Harpoon, vertical launch ASROC, and Tomahawk missiles, and six MK 46 torpedoes. There are fifty-five *Arleigh Burke*-class destroyers in commission, and they are spread about between carrier strike groups, expeditionary strike groups, and a wide variety of other missions. The USS *Cole* (DDG-67) made international news when Muslim militants blew a hole in her side while she attempted to refuel in a Yemeni port.

Attack Submarines

The navy's attack submarines are still evolving. There are actually three active classes, the *Virginia*-class being the most recent and the only class currently under construction. The *Virginia* (SSN-774) went into service on October 23, 2004, with the *Texas* (SSN-775) and *Hawaii* (SSN-776) following in 2006 and 2007. Three more are planned for the future. In between the older *Los Angeles*-class and the *Virginia*-class, the navy squeezed in the *Seawolf*-class, which consisted of the *Seawolf* (SSN-21), the *Connecticut* (SSN-22), and the *Jimmy Carter* (SSN-23). Of fifty-one nuclear submarines serving today, the *Los Angeles*-class remain the most numerous and the most widely deployed. *Virginia*- and *Seawolf*-class submarines generate a speed of twenty-five-plus knots, with the *Los Angeles*-class slightly slower. All classes have one reactor and one shaft. With some slight variations, most active nuclear submarines carry Tomahawk missiles, MK 48 torpedoes, and four to eight torpedo tubes.

Technical superiority over numerical superiority is the driving impetus in American submarine development. Because Third World nations are acquiring more modern, state-of-the-art non-nuclear submarines, the

ABOVE: *Underway on June 23, 2005, the* Arleigh Burke-*class guided missile destroyers USS* Fitzgerald (DDG-62) *(foreground) and USS* John Paul Jones (DDG-53) *prepare to fire their 5-inch/.54 caliber guns during a ship sinking exercise in the Coral Sea.*

LEFT: *On the quarter stern portside of the* Los Angeles-*class attack submarine USS* Dallas (SSN-700), *sailors exit the dry deck shelter while the boat gets underway after a brief port visit at Souda Bay, Crete, July 19, 2004.*

navy is countering this threat with new nuclear attack submarines. Other missions range from intelligence collection and Special Forces delivery to antiship and strike warfare. Enemy submarines, as in World War II, continue to be a threat to aircraft carriers, which is one of the reasons why attack submarines remain a component of the Carrier Strike Group.

Supply-class Replenishment Ship

Fast Combat Support Ships (T-AOE) became necessary as attack carriers became faster and capable of remaining at sea for longer periods of time. There are only four active ships, the oldest being the USNS *Supply* (T-AOE-6) and the newest being the USNS *Bridge* (T-AOE-10). The ships displace 48,800 tons and can make twenty-five knots fully loaded with 177,000 barrels of oil, 2,150 tons of ammunition, 500 tons of dry stores, and 250 tons of refrigerated stores. A shuttle service of smaller oilers and supply ships make it possible for T-AOE ships to remain with the Carrier Strike Group in the combat area. Today, all the *Supply*-class replenishment ships have been transferred to the Military Sealift Command and are manned by a hundred and sixty civilians and twenty-nine naval personnel. The ships also operate two CH-46E Sea Knight or SH-60 Seahawk helicopters.

The Carrier Air Wing

The typical air wing aboard a *Nimitz*-class aircraft carrier consists of three F/A-18 Hornet squadrons, one F-14 Tomcat squadron, one E-2C Hawkeye squadron, one S-3 squadron, one squadron of SH-60 Seahawk helicopters, and an EA-6B Prowler squadron.

The single-seat McDonnell Douglas F/A-18 Hornet became the navy's first all-weather fighter and attack aircraft and made its initial appearance during the 1980s. The newest model, the F/A-18E/F Super Hornet, is capable of a full spectrum of missions, including air superiority, fighter escort, reconnaissance, aerial refueling, close air support, air defense suppression, and day/night precision strike.

The new Super Hornets achieve maximum connectivity with warfighters on the ground, at sea, and in the air, and Block II aircraft have seamlessly integrated the most advanced radar and communication systems ever designed for aircraft. The older dual-seat D models are still used for attack, tactical air control, forward air control, and reconnaissance missions.

The newer E model single-seat Super Hornets first saw action onboard the USS *Abraham Lincoln* (CVN-72) on November 6, 2002, against Iraq. The dual-seat F model made its combat debut about the same time. Super Hornets cost a hefty $57 million: at 60.3 feet in length, almost a million dollars a foot. They fly at Mach 1.8+, have a ceiling over fifty thousand feet, and have a range of 1,660 nautical miles. Their maximum takeoff weight of 66,000 pounds includes a mix of Sidewinder, Sparrow, Harpoon, Harm, SLAM, and Maverick missiles; Joint Stand-Off Weapons (JSOW); Joint Direct Attack Munitions (JDAM); a Data Link Pod; Paveway Laser Guided Bombs; one M61 Vulcan 20mm cannon; and capabilities for carrying various general purpose bombs, mines, and rockets.

The two-man, twinjet Grumman F-14 Tomcat served as part of Fighter Squadron 103 (VF-103) aboard USS *Saratoga* (CVA-60) during the Persian Gulf War. Tomcats generate a maximum speed of 1,241mph and are the navy's standard carrier-based interceptor. Over the long history of Tomcats, dating back to the Vietnam War, many variants have emerged. The standard armament consists of one M61 Vulcan 20mm cannon; two AIM-9, four AIM-7 Sparrows, and four AIM-54 Phoenix air-to-air missiles; and a 14,500-pound bomb load.

The Northrop Grumman E-2C Hawkeye is the carrier air wing's all-weather, tactical battle management airborne early warning, command and control aircraft. It is a five-crewmember, twin-engine, high-wing turbo-prop aircraft with a twenty-four-foot diameter radar rotodome attached to the upper fuselage. The Hawkeyes evolved from the E-1 Tracers used in Vietnam to the

E-2Cs used during Operation Iraqi Freedom. At $80 million, Hawkeyes are expensive, but their electronics combine with shipboard Aegis weapon systems to form the cornerstone for the future sea-based Theater Ballistic Missile Defense (TBMD) System. The newest advanced variant, scheduled for introduction to the fleet in 2011, will enhance Theater Air and Missile Defense (TAMD) operations with advance warning of approaching enemy surface units, cruise missiles, or aircraft. The new E-2Cs provide enhanced vector interceptors for strike aircraft to attack select targets or intercept incoming aircraft or missiles. Along with overall battle management, E-2Cs also provide area surveillance, search and rescue, and air traffic control.

The $27 million Lockheed S-3B Viking is an all-weather, carrier-based jet aircraft that provides protection against hostile submarines and surface combatants while simultaneously serving as the Carrier Strike Group's overhead/mission tanker. The jet flies at 450 knots and performs many other missions, including

ABOVE: An E-2C Hawkeye on the aircraft carrier USS Theodore Roosevelt (CVN-71) is taxied into position on the flight deck, July 27, 2006. Hawkeyes are an integral part of surveillance and reconnaissance operations in the navy's fleet response plan.

ABOVE: Two navy S-3B Viking jets assigned to Carrier Air Wing 5 (CVW-5), Sea Control Squadron 21 (VS-21), head for home after completing routine Carrier Strike Group operations near the island of Okinawa, Japan, August 6, 2004.

TOP RIGHT: A navy EA-6B Prowler from Electronic Attack Squadron 139 (VAQ-139) flies over the Naval Air Station at Whidbey Island in Washington, May 19, 2004. The Prowler's primary mission is to protect ships and aircraft by jamming hostile radars and communications.

ABOVE RIGHT: On July 27, 2005, while operating out of the Naval Air Station at Atsugi, Japan, an SH-60F Seahawk from Helicopter Anti-Submarine Squadron 14 (HS-14) prepares to land aboard the aircraft carrier USS Kitty Hawk (CV-63).

day/night surveillance, electronic countermeasures, command/control/communications warfare, targeting, and search and rescue. Manned by a crew of two to four, the Viking also carries an impressive array of airborne weaponry, including 3,958 pounds of AGM-84 Harpoon, AGM-65 Maverick, and AGM-84 SLAM missiles, along with torpedoes and bombs.

The 500-knot, twinjet Northrop Grumman EA-6B Prowler provides carrier strike aircraft, ground troops, and ships with a protective umbrella by jamming enemy radar, electronic data links, and communications. The Prowler has been around since May 1968, but today has

become a long-range, all-weather electronic warfare suppression aircraft with a pilot and three electronic countermeasure officers. Two significant upgrades being carried out are the Improved Capability (ICAP III) and the Multifunctional Information Distribution System (MIDS). ICAP III provides an accurate threat emitter geo-locator and a selective reactive jamming capability against modern threat systems, while MIDS gives the Prowler the ability to receive and utilize data via the Link 16 tactical data link. In addition to obtaining tactical electronic intelligence in the combat area, the Prowler is also armed with Harm missiles.

Every navy helicopter is in perpetual transition, and by 2015 the only models in the navy will likely be the vastly improved MH-60S and the MH-60R. Meanwhile, the Sikorsky SH-60F Seahawk 180-knot, twin-engine helicopter provides the Carrier Strike Group with antisubmarine warfare, search and rescue, drug interdiction, antiship warfare, cargo lift, and special operations capabilities. It is crewed by three or four personnel, has a range of 380 nautical miles, and a sling load capacity of 9,000 pounds. The navy's SH-60B Seahawk is an airborne platform used on cruisers, destroyers, and frigates. It deploys sonobuoys (sonic detectors) and torpedoes in an antisubmarine role. The sonobuoys also extend the range of the ships' radar capabilities.

The Expeditionary Strike Group

Marine Expeditionary Units (MEUs) can be traced back to the mid-1960s as an answer to the navy's requirement for "Flexible Response" during the Cold War and the need for improved strategic and tactical mobility. The concept gathered steam, expanded, and began changing the navy from a fleet focused on fast attack aircraft carriers to one centered on the flexibility and readiness of a combined expeditionary unit and an amphibious ready group of marine fast responders. The still evolving Expeditionary Strike Group (ESG) provides operational freedom and expanded warfighting capabilities, not only by land with embarked marines, but at sea as well. The make-up of the ESG is constantly changing, and some senior officers believe that over time it will supersede the need for expensive attack carriers, but not for the present. The ESG already contains many of the same ships as the Carrier Strike Group, such as *Ticonderoga*-class cruisers, *Arleigh Burke*-class destroyers, and *Los Angeles*-class submarines, but the differences lay in the amphibious ships that make up the overall group.

Amphibious Assault Ships (LHA/LHD)

Although slightly different in configuration, both *Tarawa*-class LHAs and *Wasp*-class LHDs look more like small aircraft carriers than amphibious assault ships. The *Tarawa* (LHA-1) was first deployed on May 29, 1976, and the *Wasp* (LHD-1) made its deployment debut on July 29, 1989. There have been no more LHAs built since the *Peleliu* (LHA-5), but the new *Makin Island* (LHD-8) was scheduled to go into commission in July 2007. After that, LHDs will begin to give way to the new LHAR class, scheduled for 2013 when the new F-35B Joint Strike Harrier Fighters become available.

LHA/LHD amphibious assault ships currently carry six AV-8B Harrier attack aircraft; four CH-53E Sea Stallion helicopters; twelve CH-46 Sea Knight helicopters; three UH-1N Huey helicopters; and four AH-1W Super Cobra helicopters, some of which will be replaced by MV-22 Osprey tilt-rotor aircraft. The LHDs are armed with two RAM launchers; two Sea Sparrow launchers; two to three 20mm Phalanx mounts; four .50-caliber machine guns; and three to four 25mm Mk 38 machine guns. LHAs carry all but the Sea Sparrows. The ships' crews range from 104 officers and 1,004 enlisted personnel on LHDs to 82 officers and 882 enlisted on LHAs. Both amphibious ships carry a detachment of about 1,900 marines. The mission and purpose of amphibious assault ships is to get to trouble spots swiftly and put marines ashore in areas where they can accomplish the greatest tactical impact. Amphibious assault ships played a role in Desert Shield/Desert Storm, Somalia, Bosnia, Kosovo, Afghanistan, and Operation Iraqi Freedom. From all indications, they will continue to play a major role in the war against terrorism and in actions against rogue nations.

ABOVE: The Amphibious Assault Ship USS Kearsarge (LHD-3) leads a formation followed by Landing Craft, Air Cushions (LCAC), September 17, 2005. The guided missile cruiser USS Normandy (CG-60) follows on the left flank and the guided missile frigate USS Kaufman (FFG-59) on the right flank.

dictionary Fighting Vehicles. The ships are well armed with two Bushmaster II 30mm Close-in Guns and two Rolling Airframe Missile launchers, one of each fore and aft. Manned by 28 officers and 332 enlisted, LPDs carry an embarked landing force of 699 marines (66 officers and 633 enlisted).

Dock Landing Ship (LSD)

Although LSDs are currently part of the Expeditionary Strike Force, they are also scheduled for replacement by *San Antonio*-class LPDs. The 16,708-ton ships were originally designed to support amphibious operations with two to four Landing Craft Air Cushion vessels capable of transporting an embarked detachment of more than four hundred marines. Only twelve ships were ever built, the first being the *Whidbey Island* (LSD-41) in 1985 and the *Harpers Ferry* (LSD-49) in 1995. The ships were armed with machine guns and two 20mm Phalanx CIWS mounts but did not carry a helicopter air wing.

Amphibious Transport Dock (LPD)

LPDs are actually warships that embark, transport, and put ashore elements of a marine force for a variety of expeditionary warfare missions. The 17,000-ton *Austin*-class LPDs, first deployed during the Vietnam War, have given way to the 24,900-ton *San Antonio*-class, which will become a key element in the navy's sea-based transformation. The *San Antonio* (LPD-17) design, commissioned on January 14, 2006, will replace more than forty-one ships currently used in amphibious operations. Eight more modern LPDs are already in the building schedule, with the *New Orleans* (LPD-18), the *Mesa Verde* (LPD-19), the *Green Bay* (LPD-20), and the *New York* (LPD-21) scheduled for commissioning in 2007 and beyond.

Unlike the amphibious transports of the past, the new 684-foot, 22+-knot LPDs will carry two CH-53E Super Stallion helicopters or two MV-22 Ospreys and up to four CH-46 Sea Knight helicopters; two Landing Craft Air Cushion (LCAC) vessels; and fourteen Expe-

Frigates (FFG)

Because the Expeditionary Strike Group is much larger than a Carrier Strike Group and moves at a slower pace, the navy commissioned frigates primarily for antisubmarine warfare (ASW) and anti-air warfare. On December 17, 1977, the *Oliver Hazard Perry* (FFG-7), the first of the class still in service, went into commission. Sixty-one frigates have been commissioned, the most recent being the *Ingraham* (FFG-61). The frigates displace only 4,100 tons and require a crew of only 17 officers and 198 enlisted personnel. They are 445 feet long and can generate more than twenty-nine knots. They carry two SH-60 Seahawk helicopters for ASW and are armed with Standard and Harpoon missiles; six MK-46 torpedoes; one 76mm (3-inch)/.62-caliber MK 75 rapid-fire gun; and one Phalanx close-in-weapons system. Currently, there are no new frigates in the navy's five-year shipbuilding plan.

AV-8B Harrier II

The $24 million AV-8B McDonnell Douglas V/STOL Harrier, which is powered by one Rolls Royce turbofan engine, found a home on the amphibious assault ships of the Expeditionary Strike Group. Every LHA/LHD/LHA(R) carries a squadron of six Harriers piloted by marines. The planes are designed for close air support using conventional and high-tech weapons day or night. The armament capability is considerable, including MK 82 series 500-pound bombs; MK 83 series 1,000-pound bombs; GBU-12 500-pound and GBU-16 1,000-pound laser guided bombs; AGM-65F Maverick missiles; AGM-65E laser Maverick CBU-99 cluster bombs; AIM-9M Sidewinders; and a Lightning targeting pod to deliver GBU-1 bombs with pinpoint accuracy. Unlike *Nimitz*-class carriers, LHDs can bring Harriers much closer to action in shallow littoral waters like the Persian Sea, where during the ground war in Kuwait AV-8Bs operated as close as thirty-five nautical miles from shore. Harriers cannot match the speed of navy Super Hornets or Tomcats, but they can deliver much of the same weaponry.

Expeditionary Strike Group Helicopters

Amphibious assault ships also carry a mix of helicopters, each designed for a special purpose. Every LHD carries four Sikorsky CH-53E Super Stallions to transport heavy equipment and supplies during ship-to-shore amphibious assaults and during subsequent operations ashore. The big helicopter can generate 150 knots and can carry an internal load of 69,750 pounds or an external load of 73,500 pounds. It has a crew of three, a range of 540 nautical miles, and can carry 55 passengers. The Super Stallion can move and deliver more equipment over rugged terrain in bad weather faster than any other aircraft.

The Boeing CH-46E Sea Knight (a squadron of twelve on LHDs and a squadron of four on LPDs) is a medium-lift assault helicopter with twin rotors. The original Sea Knight has been around since 1964, where it met medium-lift requirements for marines in Vietnam. In combat, the helicopter carries a pilot, co-pilot, crew chief, two aerial gunners, and fourteen troops. For medical evacuation, Sea Knights are rigged with fifteen litters and carry two corpsmen. The helicopter flies at 145 knots and has a range of 132 nautical miles. The Sea Knight has proven so valuable and reliable that the navy has no plans to replace it.

Four Bell Textron AH-1W Super Cobra attack helicopters form part of the air wing on every LHA/LHD. They have a range of 256 nautical miles and a speed of 147 knots. They are armed with one 20mm turreted cannon of 750 rounds; four external wing stations that fire rockets; and a wide variety of precision-guided weapons, which include TOW/Hellfire, Sidewinder, and Sidearm missiles. The crew consists of two officers,

BELOW: While the pilot of a Marine Corps AV-8B Harrier II prepares to dock on the deck of the USS Peleliu *(LHA-5), the pilot of another Harrier in the foreground waits for a launching signal from the crewman on deck, April 6, 2005.*

Navy Enlisted Rates

For enlisted personnel, the proper word is "rate," not "rank." The rating badge is a combination of rate (pay grade, as indicated by chevrons) and rating (occupational specialty, as indicated by the symbol just above the chevrons for E-4 classifications and above.

Pay Grade	Rate	Abbreviation	Upper Sleeve	Collar & Cap
E-1	Seaman Recruit	SR	None	None
E-1	Seaman Apprentice	SA	▨	None
E-2	Seaman	SN	▨	None
E-3	Petty Officer Third Class	PO3	▨	▨
E-4	Petty Officer Second Class	PO2	▨	▨
E-5	Petty Officer First Class	PO1	▨	▨
E-6	Chief Petty Officer	CPO	▨	▨
E-7	Senior Chief Petty Officer	SCPO	▨	▨
E-8	Master Chief Petty Officer	MCPO	▨	▨
E-9	Master Chief Petty Officer of the Navy	MCPON	▨	▨

both of whom can fly and direct targeting. Although MV-22 Ospreys may displace some of the helicopters now in the Expeditionary Strike Group, the AH-1W is currently being outfitted with a Night Targeting System/Forward Looking Infrared laser range-finding and targeting system with camera capabilities.

The Future Fleet

The Carrier Strike Group, the Carrier Air Wing, and the Expeditionary Strike Group, augmented by the submarine fleet, fulfill Admiral Mullen's commitment "to sustain combat readiness." The CNO also acknowl-

edged the importance of building "a Navy capable of meeting the most demanding future threats." Iran, North Korea, the Middle East, and other areas continue to be perpetual threats. Mullen's program for the future is much like former CNO Vern Clark's concept of a navy based on technology with three guiding principles: Sea Strike, Sea Shield, and Sea Basing, all connected through a concept called Force Net. Every year finds another snip taken from the navy budget, so funds available for planning sea power for the next decade have to be spent judiciously.

In 2002 Admiral Clark envisioned a fleet of 375 ships. By 2006, the deployable battle force had already shrunk to 281 ships, raising the question whether a navy this size can supply deterrence in four possible theaters of war, fight and defeat two enemies at the same time, and still provide homeland defense.

Concepts of the Future Fleet

Ships, submarines, aircraft, and weaponry are all in a perpetual state of reconfiguration to meet the requirements of the future fleet. Every step invites new critics, especially because of soaring construction and weaponry costs. How this plays out over the next decade may depend upon the integration of land forces with naval forces and renewed interest in the development of a missile defense system, which back in the Cold War years was colloquially referred to as "Star Wars."

The CVNX Aircraft Carrier

The next generation aircraft carrier, currently named the CVNX-1, was scheduled to begin construction in 2006 and will have an operational life of fifty years. Because of the $10 billion cost, the future of the class is still unclear, but a carrier is needed to incorporate all the advanced technology for the next generation of fighter planes.

CVNX will have an Electromagnetic Aircraft Launch System and an Electromagnetic Aircraft Recov-

ery System, designed to work with new and existing aircraft, all of which will have electromagnetic pulse protection. A new, less labor-intensive nuclear propulsion system is designed to generate more electric power for future electromagnetic and energy weapons systems and provide automatic weapons-reloading systems for aircraft. While a carrier cannot be shielded like stealth aircraft, the CVNX-1 will have a decreased signal for enemy radars to detect but an increased detection range for identifying enemy threats. Although former CIA director and retired Admiral Stansfield Turner recently referred to expensive attack carriers as "superfluous"

The primary purpose of forward-deployed naval forces is to project American power from the sea to influence events ashore in the littoral regions of the world across the operational spectrum of peace, crisis, and war. This is what we do.
Admiral Jay L. Johnson, CNO, 1996-2000.

ABOVE: The CVN-78 is still in the navy's construction schedule but may not be built. Although the navy plans to retain a fleet of twelve large-deck carriers, the cost to build another could exceed $10 billion.

OPPOSITE TOP: On February 19, 2006, two Marine Corps CH-53Es begin takeoff from the flight deck of the USS Essex (LHD-2) to survey damage caused by the February 17 landslide on Leyte in the Philippines.

OPPOSITE BOTTOM: During exercises off North Carolina in 2005, a U.S. Marine Corps AH-1W Super Cobra circles the USS Carter Hall (LSD-50), which is a Harper's Ferry-class dock landing ship that serves as part of the navy's Expeditionary Strike Group.

ABOVE: Warships made of lighter-weight composite stealth materials, as in Northrop Grumman's DD(X) destroyer (also known as the DDG 1000 Zumwalt-calss destroyer), will become the navy of the future. Like the DD(X) with its arsenal of technology, cruisers and frigates are also currently on the design board.

RIGHT: On May 27, 2004, the navy released contracts to General Dynamics for the construction of a concept "Flight 0" Littoral Combat Ship (LCS), an entirely new breed of fast, agile, and networked warships with special warfighting capabilities.

and suggested that the navy "spread its striking power over as many ships as possible," meaning cruisers, destroyers, submarines, and amphibious ships, there will always be a need for airfields where they are not accessible, and fast carriers perform that function better than any ship in the world.

Because of the experimental nature of the CVNX, the carrier may be in production for as long as ten years. In the meantime, the future carrier battle group is likely to include two Aegis cruisers and four Aegis destroyers. Aegis cruisers are slated to carry 122 vertical missile launch cells, four antisubmarine rockets, eighty-two defense interceptor missiles, and a mix of Tomahawk and SM-2 Block IVA missiles. Destroyers will carry ninety vertical missile launch cells, four antisubmarine rockets, sixty defense interceptor missiles, and a mix of Tomahawk land attack missiles and SM-2s.

The DD(X) Destroyer

Like the CVNX carrier, the next generation destroyer has been on the table, off the table, and back on the table as the navy refocused on emerging technologies that could be integrated with land-based and sea-based platforms. Everything on a 14,000-ton DD(X) destroyer had to be incorporated with other future navy ships, and in particular the Littoral Combat Ship (LCS) designed for coastal warfare and the CG(X) air domi-

nance cruiser. The DD(X) will integrate improved dual-band radar for better target acquisition in adverse weather with improved fire control and armament on a new hull design. The ship will have a bow-mounted undersea warfare system with high-frequency sonar for antisubmarine and mine detection with an automatic tracking system. A Total Ship Computing Environment (TSCE) will enable all ship-controlled systems to be managed from the bridge. The DD(X) will have less vulnerability to enemy radar detection because of its Tumblehome radar-resistant hull and new split keel. Two unmanned Advanced Gun Systems (AGS) on the deck form part of the precision-guided weapon platform that provides pinpoint targeting and fires existing weapons along with Tomahawk missiles and the new Long Range Attack Projectile (LRLAP), which uses Global Positioning for guidance. Every shipboard system, including a Peripheral Vertical Launch System that provides back up protection if the ship is hit, has electromagnetic pulse protection.

As Captain C. H. Goddard recently declared, "DD(X) is the vanguard of the future." The new

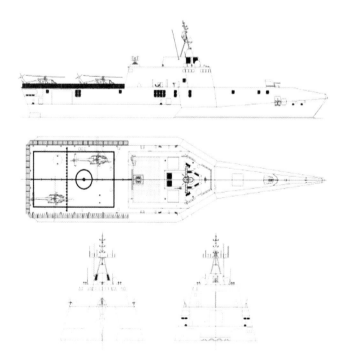

destroyer is still in the prototype mode and is not expected to debut until 2010 or later.

The Littoral Combat Ship (LCS)

In April 2006 the navy announced that the first four littoral combat ships would be based in San Diego, where the navy's Undersea Warfare Command and the future home of the Fleet Anti-Submarine and Mine Warfare Command are located. The *Freedom* (LCS-1) and the *Independence* (LCS-2) are currently under construction, but the navy is still debating whether the ship type truly delivers a littoral punch or is actually a new version of the frigate and in reality a blue-water FFG(X). Originally planned to displace 1,500 tons, the LCS has grown to 3,500 tons (frigates displace 4,100 tons). Part of the problem emanates from the navy's efforts to make the LCS multi-mission and super-survivable; hence, more FFG-like. The navy has also expressed concern over the vulnerability of LCS ships to stand-off air-launched missiles. Either way, two of the four authorized LCS ships will soon be in commission, and if the ships prove too valuable to risk

operating in littorals, the navy can always temporarily fall back on the *Cyclone* (PC-1)-class coastal patrol ships and provide the frigate fleet with a new state-of-the-art antisubmarine and missile ship.

Virginia-class Submarines

The navy's submarine capability suffered a setback when the *Seawolf*-class program was scrapped at the end of the Cold War and only three of the class were built. The new *Virginia*-class superseded the *Seawolf-*

ABOVE: Although Lockheed Martin received the contract for the first two Littoral Combat Ships (LCS), the Bath Iron Works of General Dynamics also proposed the pictured concept ship, which may well become the LCS of the future.

LEFT: The coastal patrol ship USS Cyclone (PC-1) adds another dimension to the navy, which in addition to fighting wars abroad also provides patrol capabilities wherever threats exist.

class with six submarines now in commission. The *Virginias* cost less and perform the same functions as the *Seawolfs*. In addition to providing support for the Carrier Strike Force and the Amphibious Strike Force, they attack inland targets with Tomahawk cruise missiles; destroy enemy submarines and surface ships; gather intelligence; and provide for the insertion and recovery of Special Forces.

No technology change occurs in the navy's surface fleet without impacting and upgrading submarines. Sensors have been improved to detect the stealthiest of submarines. Periscopes have been modified with "photonic masts" that transmit images to onboard display screens. Newer reactor cores will never have to be replaced. In addition to a fully interactive fleet system of Underwater Unmanned Vehicles (UUVs) used for reconnaissance and mine detection, the *Virginia* (SSN-774) carries a complement of thirty-eight weapons. The Mk 48 Advanced Capability (ADCAP) torpedo has a maximum range of twenty-seven nautical miles and runs at sixty knots. The new "supercavitating" torpedo streaks through the sea at fifty-six miles a minute. It is powered by a rocket motor that incorpo-

rates a chemical reaction in the nose cone that creates a sheath of air bubbles or water vapor around the fuselage. The chemical reaction reduces the drag of water and allows the torpedo to run at hundreds of miles an hour. *Virginia*-class submarines also carry a fifty-five-ton minisub for SEAL team missions.

Stealth Aircraft

While the F/A-18E/F Super Hornet fills the navy's need for a multi-role attack plane, the Joint Strike Fighter (JSF) program will provide the navy with its next generation of jet fighters. Instead of a host of different fighter planes for the air force, marines, and navy, the three services have attempted to agree on a base-model fighter plane that can be adapted to the requirements of each service, thereby minimizing costs and maximizing service integration. The navy's model began as the X-35C and developed into Lockheed Martin's F-35 Joint Strike Fighter, which will be deployed in 2008-2009. The F-35 is built on an all-aspect stealth platform and boasts all-weather precision strike capability with the next generation fused avionics/mission systems. It is designed as a *Nimitz*-class carrier plane with a reinforced internal structure for coping with punishing carrier landings. It has larger

wing and control surfaces and carries twice as much fuel as the standard F-18 Super Hornet. The F-35 carrier variant will work with the navy's future systems and carry both standard and emerging weaponry.

Unmanned Aircraft

To keep a persistent eye in the sky, Northrop Grumman is producing the MQ-8B Fire Scout, a Vertical Takeoff and Landing Unmanned Aerial Vehicle (VTUAV) that can be remotely controlled from a cruiser, destroyer, or amphibious assault ship. The rotary wing vehicle will provide unprecedented situational awareness and precision targeting support for warfighters at sea and marines on the ground. Fire Scout's fully autonomous ship landing and takeoff system will provide the navy with superior tactical intelligence, surveillance, reconnaissance, and targeting information, enabling missiles to do the work in place of manned aircraft.

Ballistic Missile Defense

Since the mid-1990s, the navy has been developing a two-tiered structure around the Theater Ballistic Missile Defense (TBMD) system. The TBMD consists of "lower tier" missiles for limited air defense and

"upper tier" missiles for a theater-wide defense capable of engaging supersonic long-range missile attacks, such as those recently threatened by Iran and North Korea. The Strategic Defense Initiative (SDI) program conceived during the Reagan administration faltered during the Clinton administration and went back on an implementation schedule for initial phasing in 2006.

The Navy Area Defense (NAD) system for the "lower tier" is designed to perform "goalkeeping." It is centered on the SM-2 Block IVA area defense interceptor missile, which has boosted, high mach, long-range, solid fuel, "dual mode" (infrared and semi-active radio frequency) homing using a blast-fragmentation warhead. The weapon is specially enhanced to intercept and destroy Scud-like missiles. Being proximity fused, it does not suffer the drawback of kinetic-energy hit-to-kill systems. Similar to the next generation Patriot PAC-3 missile, the SM-2 Block IVA is multi-mission capable and lethal against cruise missiles or manned aircraft. The weapon will be among the navy's active defense systems capable of engaging low-apogee, short-range missiles.

LEFT: Northrop Grumman's RQ-8A Fire Scout Vertical Takeoff and Landing Tactical Unmanned Vehicle (VTUAV) test fires the second of two MK 66 2.75-inch unguided rockets during trials at the Yuma Proving Grounds in Arizona, July 25, 2005.

BELOW: The F-35B STOVL Joint Strike Fighter (JSF) will be the next generation takeoff and vertical landing aircraft. Three variants will be produced, including one for the Marine Corps and one for the USAF.

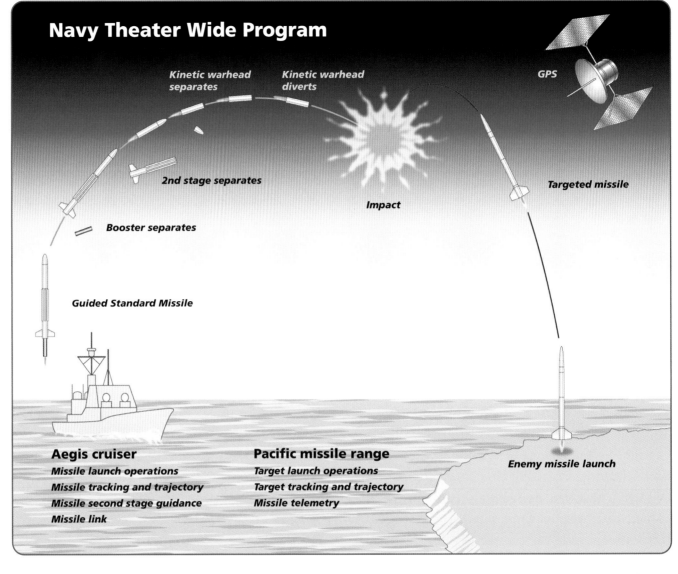

Navy Theater Wide Program

Kinetic warhead separates

Kinetic warhead diverts

GPS

2nd stage separates

Impact

Targeted missile

Booster separates

Guided Standard Missile

Enemy missile launch

Aegis cruiser
Missile launch operations
Missile tracking and trajectory
Missile second stage guidance
Missile link

Pacific missile range
Target launch operations
Target tracking and trajectory
Missile telemetry

The "upper tier" interceptor missile functions only outside the atmosphere, above forty-four miles, and is designed to defend against long-range, multi-stage ballistic missiles. Instead of "goalkeeping," the SM-3/LEAP KKV (Kinetic Kill Vehicle) performs "gatekeeping." The interceptor measures 21.5 feet in length, is a four-stage system with a Mark 72 booster and a Mark 104 solid rocket engine that it shares with the interceptor. It is scheduled for deployment in 2007, but prototypes are already in the works.

LEAP-carrying Aegis cruisers, destroyers, and frigates depend more upon being in the defended area than being near the defended target. The "area of negation" is the area of water over which Aegis ships can intercept ballistic missiles en route from a hostile launch area to an assortment of targets. A single Aegis

Although near-term requirements such as littoral operations may be the current rage, the Navy must keep its eyes on the prize—the Fleet of 2025.
Rear Admiral W. J. Holland, Jr.

cruiser in the Sea of Japan could protect South Korea as well as Japan. By being forward deployed near a launch site that can fire ballistic missiles at many targets in a great arc, the navy Theater-Wide (upper tier) system has the capability of defending an area covering tens of thousands of square miles.

Guidance systems used for such a long-range system rely upon a missile command uplink, an inertial Global Positioning System, and imaging infrared terminal homing. The interceptor warhead is the LEAP itself, which is a small, forty-pound projectile containing no explosive charge. Maneuvering autonomously with thrusters, the projectile homes on the infrared signature of the hot ballistic missile, and closes for the kill at 2.8 miles per second, which is three times greater than the velocity of the fastest bullet. If the hostile missile is carrying a chemical, biological, or nuclear payload, the components will be shattered and dispersed outside the atmosphere. The existing SM-2/LEAP missiles will be extremely effective against medium-range ballistic missiles, and work continues on developing a missile with the speed to overtake intercontinental ballistic missiles (ICBMs), which run at 3.75-4.38 miles per second.

Weapon systems have become immensely complex, which is the reason that Aegis ships carry so many different missiles. Every Aegis ship is armed with Tomahawks for attack and SM-2 Block IVA and SM-2/LEAP missiles for lower and upper tier defense. Such missiles are too heavy to be transferred at sea and offloaded into a ship's vertical launching stations. The Aegis ship will also carry four-missile packs of the "Evolved Sea Sparrow"; vertical-launch antisubmarine submarine rockets; several different types of Tomahawk land attack missiles and perhaps anti-armor Tomahawk (TSTARS); and a navalized version of the Army Tactical Missile System. Only the SM-2 Block IVA is a true multi-mission missile with capability against aircraft, cruise missiles, and theater ballistic missiles.

Future Naval Force Structure—2020

Aircraft Carriers	11
Surface Combatants	88
Littoral Combat Ships	55
Attack Submarines	48
Cruise Missile Submarines	4
Ballistic Missile Submarines	14
Expeditionary Warfare Ships	31
Combat Logistics Force	30
Maritime Prepositioning Force (Future)	12
Support Ships	20
Total Naval Force	313

The Fleet of 2025

The fleet of 2025 is the navy's biggest puzzle. It cannot be resolved in a constantly evolving and muddled environment where terrorism, which has no boundaries or nationality, and rogue nations, which have powerful weapons but no navies, continue to threaten the world. Former CNO Clark and current CNO Mullen envision a future naval force of 313 ships.

In all probability, today's deployable battle force of 281 ships is not likely to change much, and the navy that exists today will probably serve, with a few new innovative ships, for the next ten years. During defense budgeting through September 2006, Congress provided funds for only four new ships, half as many as requested. If extended over time, a four-ship-per-year rate would support a fleet of 120 ships, as opposed to the ships the current and former CNOs have projected for the future fleet.

A new puzzling era for the navy has dawned, mainly because of the difficulty of designing a strategy to contend with the variety of today's existing threats. The current administration, Congress, and the Department of Defense do not hold the answers, and until someone does come up with the answers for "Sea Strike, Sea Shield, and Sea Basing," the armed services will remain in a state of partial limbo.

BIBLIOGRAPHY

Abbazia, Patrick. *Mr. Roosevelt's Navy*. Annapolis: U.S. Naval Institute, 1975.

Abel, Elie. *The Missile Crisis.* Philadelphia: J. B. Lippincott Company, 1966.

Alden, John D. *The American Steel Navy*. Annapolis: Naval Institute Press, 1972.

Allen, Gardner W. *Our Navy and the Barbary Corsairs.* Boston: Houghton, Mifflin Company, 1905.

_____. *Our Naval War with France*. Boston: Houghton Mifflin Company, 1909.

Allen, Thomas B., and Polmar, Norman, et al. *War in the Gulf.* Atlanta: Turner Publishing, Inc. 1991.

Barlow, Jeffrey G. *Revolt of the Admirals.* Washington: Brassey's, 1998.

Bauer, K. Jack. *The Mexican War, 1846-1848.* New York: Macmillan Publishing, 1974.

Baxter, James P. *The Introduction of the Ironclad Warship*. Cambridge, Mass.: Harvard University Press, 1933.

Bennett, Frank M. *The Steam Navy of the United States*. Pittsburgh: Warren Publishing, 1896.

Buell, T. B. *Master of Sea Power: A Biography of Fleet Admiral E. J. King*. Boston: Little, Brown and Company, 1980.

Cagle, Malcolm W. "Task Force 77 in Action off Vietnam." U. S. Naval Institute *Proceedings*, vol. 98, no. 831 (May 1972), 66-109.

Cagle, Malcolm W. and Manson, Frank A. *The Sea War in Korea*. Annapolis: U. S. Naval Institute, 1957.

Clark, William Bell. *Lambert Wilkes: Sea Raider and Diplomat*. New Haven: Yale University Press, 1932.

_____. *Ben Franklin's Privateers: A Naval Epic of the American Revolution.* Baton Rouge: Louisiana State University Press, 1956.

Coletta, Paolo. *American Secretaries of the Navy*. 2 vols. Annapolis: Naval Institute Press, 1980.

Davis, Burke. *The Billy Mitchell Affair*. New York: Random House, 1967.

Davis, George T. *A Navy Second to None*. Westport, Conn.: Greenwood Publishers, 1971.

Davis, William C. *Duel Between the First Ironclads*. New York: Doubleday & Company, 1975.

Dolan, Edward F. *America in the Korean War.* Brookfield, Conn.: The Millbrook Press, 1998.

Dorr, Robert F. *Desert Shield; The Build-Up: The Complete Story*. Motorbooks International, 1991.

Dutton, Charles J. *Oliver Hazard Perry*. New York: Longmans, Green and Co., 1935.

Field, James A. *History of United States Naval Operations Korea*. Washington: Government Printing Office, 1962.

Fiske, Bradley A. *From Midshipman to Rear Admiral*. New York: The Century Co., 1919.

Fowler, William M., Jr. *Rebels Under Sail: The American Navy during the Revolution*. New York: Charles Scribner's Sons, 1976.

Friedman, Norman. *Seapower and Space: From the Dawn of the Missile Age to Net-Centric Warfare*. Annapolis: Naval Institute Press, 2000.

_____. *The Naval Institute Guide to World Naval Weapons Systems, 1991-1992*. Annapolis: Naval Institute Press, 1991.

_____. *Desert Victory: The War for Kuwait*. Annapolis: Naval Institute Press, 1991.

Gimpel, Herbert J. *The United States Nuclear Navy*. New York: Frederick Watts, Inc., 1965.

Goddard, C.H., and C.B. Marks, "DD(X) Navigates Uncharted Waters." U.S. Naval Institute *Proceedings*, 131, no. 1 (January 2005), 30-33.

Gregory, Barry. *The Vietnam War*. Vols. 5, 6, 9. Freeport, N.Y.: Marshall Cavendish Ltd., 1988.

Grider, John M. *War Birds*. E. W. Springs, ed. Fort Mill, S.C.: privately printed, 1951.

Halsey, William F. and Joseph Bryan III, *Admiral Halsey's Story*. New York: Whittlesey House, 1947.

Hart, Robert A. *The Great White Fleet.* Boston: Little, Brown & Company, 1965.

Haarts, Justin. The LCS: Built to Fight, U.S. Naval Institute *Proceedings*, 132, no. 7 (July 2006), 26-29.

Hearn, Chester G. *Admiral David Glasgow Farragut: The Civil War Years*. Annapolis: Naval Institute Press, 1997.

_____. *Admiral David Dixon Porter: The Civil War Years*. Annapolis: Naval Institute Press, 1996.

_____. *An Illustrated History of the United States Navy*. London: Salamander Books Ltd, 2002.

_____. *The Capture of New Orleans, 1862*. Baton Rouge: Louisiana State University Press, 1995.

_____. *Carriers in Combat: The Air War at Sea*. Westport, Conn.: Praeger International, 2005.

_____. *George Washington's Schooners: The First American Navy*. Annapolis: Naval Institute Press, 1995.

Heinl, Robert D., Jr. *Soldiers of the Sea*. Annapolis: U. S. Naval Institute, 1962.

_____. *Victory at High Tide*. Philadelphia: J. B. Lippincott Company, 1968.

Holland, W.J. "The Fleet: Low Profile Today, Vital Tomorrow." U.S. Naval Institute *Proceedings*, 132, No. 5 (May 2006), 52-57.

Hooper, Edward Bickford, and Oscar P. Fitzgerald, et al. *The United States Navy and the Viet Nam Conflict*. 2 vols. Washington: Naval Historical Center, 1976, 1986.

Hough, Richard. *Dreadnought: A History of the Modern Battleship*. London: Michael Joseph, 1965.

Howarth, Stephen. *To Shining Sea: A History of the United States Navy, 1775-*

1991. New York: Random House, 1991.

Isaacs, Jeremy, and Downing, Taylor. *Cold War, 1945-1991*. Boston: Little, Brown and Company, 1998,

Knox, Dudley W. *A History of the United States Navy*. New York. G. P. Putnam's Sons, 1948.

Kosnick, Mark E. "The Military Response to Terrorism," *Naval War College Press Review* (Spring, 2000), 1-30.

Layman, R. D. *Before the Aircraft Carrier: The Development of Aviation Vessels 1849-1922*. Annapolis: Naval Institute Press, 1989.

Lloyd, Christopher. *The Navy and the Slave Trade*. London: Frank Cass & Co., 1968.

Long, David F. *Nothing Too Daring: A Biography of Commodore David Porter, 1780-1843*. Annapolis: Naval Institute Press, 1970.

Lord, Clifford L. *History of United States Naval Aviation*. New York: Arno Press, 1972.

Lundstrom, John B. *The First South Pacific Campaign*. Annapolis: U. S. Naval Institute, 1976.

Maclay, Edgar S. *History of the U.S. Navy*. 2 vols. New York: D. Appleton, 1894.

Mahan, Alfred Thayer. *Sea Power in its Relations to the War of 1812*. 2 vols. New York: Haskell House Publishers Ltd., 1969.

_____. *The Influence of Sea Power upon History, 1660-1783*. Boston: Little, Brown and Company, 1918.

_____. *The Influence of Sea Power in its Relation to the War of 1812*. 2 vols. Boston: Little, Brown & Company, 1905.

_____. *From Sail to Steam*. New York: Harper Brothers, 1907.

Marolda, Edward J., and Fitzgerald, Oscar P., *The United States Navy and the Vietnam Conflict*. 2 vols. Washington, D.C.: Naval Historical Center, 1986.

Milholland, Ray. *The Splinter Fleet*. Indianapolis: Bobbs-Merrill Co., 1936.

Miller, Nathan. *Sea of Glory: The Continental Navy Fights for Independence, 1775-1783*. New York: David McKay Company, Inc., 1974.

_____. *The U. S. Navy, an Illustrated History*. New York: American Heritage Publishing Company, 1977.

Mitchell, Donald W. *History of the Modern American Navy*. New York: Alfred A. Knopf, 1946.

Morison, Elting E. *Admiral Sims and the Modern American Navy*. New York: Russell and Russell, 1968.

Morison, Samuel Eliot. *John Paul Jones: A Sailor's Biography*. Boston: Little, Brown & Company, 1959.

_____. *History of U.S. Naval Operations in World War II*. 15 vols. Edison, N.J.: Castle Books, 2001.

_____. *"Old Bruin": Matthew Calbraith Perry*. Boston: Little, Brown & Co., 1967.

Morris, Richard K. *John P. Holland*. Annapolis: U. S. Naval Institute, 1966.

Naval Documents Related to the United States Wars with the Barbary Powers. Dudley W. Knox, ed. 4 vols. Washington: Government Printing Office, 1939.

Naval Documents Related to the Quasi-War Between the United States and France. 7 vols. Washington: Government Printing Office, 1935.

Naval History Division. *Civil War Naval Chronology, 1861-1865*. Washington, D.C.: Government Printing Office, 1971.

Naval Theater Ballistic Missile Defense (TBMD) Operational Requirements Document. Washington, D.C.: U.S. Navy, 1995.

Niven, John. *Gideon Welles, Lincoln's Secretary of the Navy*. New York: Oxford University Press, 1976.

Nordhoff, Charles. *In Yankee Wind Jammers*. New York: Dodd, Mead and Co., 1940.

O'Gara, Gordon C. *Theodore Roosevelt and the Rise of the Modern Navy*. Princeton: Princeton University Press, 1943

Paullin, Charles Oscar. *Diplomatic Negotiations of American Naval Officers, 1778-1883*. Baltimore: The Johns Hopkins Press, 1912.

_____. *Paullin's History of Naval Administration, 1776-1911*. Princeton: Princeton University Press, 1966.

Polmar, Norman. *The Naval Institute Guide to the Ships and Aircraft of the U.S. Fleet*. Annapolis: Naval Institute Press, 2000.

Potter, E. B. *Nimitz*. Annapolis: U. S. Naval Institute, 1976.

"Role of Women in the Theater of Operations," *Conduct of the Persian Gulf War: Final Report to Congress."* vol. 2. Washington: Department of Defense, 1992, Appendix R.

Rees, David, ed. *The Korean War: History and Tactics*. New York: Crescent Books, 1984.

Sandler, Stanley, ed. *The Korean War: An Encyclopedia*. New York: Garland Publishing, 1995.

Scharf, J. Thomas. *History of the Confederate States Navy*. New York: Rogers and Sherwood, 1887.

Schwartz, Richard A. *Encyclopedia of the Persian Gulf War*. Jefferson, N.C.: McFarland & Company, 1998, 15.

Simmons, Dean, and Gould, Phillip, et al, "Air Operations over Bosnia," U.S. Naval Institute *Proceedings*, 123 (May, 1997) No. 5, 58-63.

Sims, William S. *The Victory at Sea*. Garden City, NY: Doubleday, Page & Co., 1920.

Smelser, Marshall. *The Congress Founds the Navy*. South Bend, Ind.: University of Notre Dame Press, 1959.

Smith, S. E. *The United States Navy in World War II*. New York: William Morrow and Company, 1966.

Soley, James Russell. *Historical Sketch of the United States Naval Academy*. Washington: Government Printing Office, 1876.

Sprout, Harold and Margaret. *The Rise of American Naval Power, 1776-1918*. Princeton: Princeton University Press, 1966.

Stout, Jay. *Hornets Over Kuwait*. Annapolis: Naval Institute Press, 1997.

Sweetman, Jack. *American Naval History: An Illustrated Chronology*. Annapolis: Naval Institute Press, 2002.

Turner, Stansfield. "Aircraft Carriers are on their way Out," U.S. Naval Institute *Proceedings*, 132, no. 7 (July 2006), 16-18.

Vego, Milan. "What Can We Learn from Enduring Freedom," U.S. Naval Institute *Proceedings*, 128, no. 7 (July 2002), 1-8.

Watson, H. W. *Battleships in Action*. Boston: Little, Brown & Company, 1926.

Wescott, Allan, ed. *American Sea Power Since 1775*. Philadelphia: J. B. Lippincott Company, 1947.

Wheeler, Richard. *In Pirate Waters*. New York: Thomas Y. Crowell Company, 1969.

Wimmel, Kenneth. *Theodore Roosevelt and the Great White Fleet*. Washington: Brassey's Inc., 1998.

Wohlstetter, Roberta. *Pearl Harbor: Warning and Decision*. Stanford, Cal.: Stanford University Press, 1962.

Zumwalt, Elmo R. Jr. *On Watch*. New York: Triangle Books, 1976.

INDEX